SAILING SMALL

SAILING SMALL

Inspiration and Instruction
for the Pocket Cruiser

EDITED BY
STAN GRAYSON

DEVEREUX BOOKS
Marblehead, Massachusetts

Copyright © 2004 by Devereux Books

Published by Devereux Books
PO Box 503
Marblehead, MA 01945

Internet address: www.devereuxbooks.com

Library of Congress Cataloging in Publication Data

Sailing Small, inspiration and instruction for the pocket cruiser / edited by Stan Grayson
    p. cm.
  ISBN: 1-928862-08-X
    1. Sailing I. Grayson, Stan, 1945-

GV811.S2553 2004
797.124—dc22   2004047757

Cover Photograph: the 22-foot cutter *Surprise* designed and built by Paul Gartside.
(Courtesy of Paul Gartside)
Back cover: a Precision 21 tied up in a rockbound harbor on Cape Ann, Massachusetts
(Photograph by Stan Grayson)

Book design by Fish Tank Media
Printed in Singapore

TABLE OF CONTENTS

ACKNOWLEDGMENTS

Thanks to the following individuals for their assistance in the preparation of this book: Todd Broadlick, John and Tally Garfield at Marshall Marine, Ron Hoddinott, Jim Johnson, Joe Keogh at Edey & Duff, Jim Leet at Marine Concepts, Precision Boatworks, Stan Shulman, Jim Taylor Yacht Design, Ron Walton, Ed Zeiser, and Rick Just of the Idaho Department of Parks and Recreation. In England to Philip Watts and to Ted Jones of the Dinghy Cruising Association, Summit House, 67 Thorley Hill, Bishop's Stortford, Herts CM23 3NF, England

Introduction

The design, selection, and use of small cruising sailboats have been topics of ongoing fascination for sailors of all sorts for many years. While the definition of "small" will always remain open to debate, the authors included here, have concluded that a small sailboat — a "pocket cruiser" — is a boat that may range from 17 to 23 feet in length. Today, with mooring waiting lists that can easily stretch 10 years or more, with expensive marina slip space at a premium, with overall expenses a key consideration for many, boats of this general size continue to exert an understandable appeal. In fact, the appeal of the small sailing yacht is a timeless one.

A word is in order regarding just how this particular group of authors was selected. There has been no attempt to search out those whose aim was to perform headline-grabbing stunts in overly tiny boats. Those represented here bought boats appropriate to their needs. None succumbed to the temptation to acquire more boat than necessary or more boat than they could comfortably afford. Nor, for the most part, have they felt impelled to seek adventure by ocean crossings in search of "paradise." None would argue against the broadening experience of the world cruiser about which a number of excellent books have been written. But this book is not about that sort of lifestyle. It is primarily about the sort of weekend/vacation sailing or extended coastwise cruising in which people from all walks of life — working people with jobs, families, and diverse shore-side interests — engage.

A variety of geographic locations was desired and, to a great extent, achieved. Most important in selection, however, was finding sailors who *really* use their boats. The overall result is a distillation of rich experience in small cruising sailboats that extends from the Thames Estuary to British Columbia, and a variety of places in between. This group of authors is an independent-minded bunch. They've gone to great lengths in their search for just the right boat, and each has been rigorous in evaluating, in an open-minded way, what really constitutes a practical, small cruising yacht. The result is a fascinating mix of wooden and fiberglass boats, some Bermudan rigged, others gaff rigged.

"Although money can be a limiting factor, the sort of boat you own is more likely to be a reflection of the sort of person you are," wrote Denny Desoutter, founder of that uniquely varied, independent, consumer-oriented British magazine, *Practical Boat Owner*. "Some people feel impelled to have all the latest gadgets. . . Others are content with a simpler life. . . . "

Sailing Small is the book for those who would live a simpler life. Whether you are newcomer to sailing, currently cruising in a small boat, or a longtime owner of a larger boat thinking of moving down in size, *Sailing Small* is intended to offer practical advice. May it also inspire you to consider how much can be accomplished aboard a small but able cruising sailboat that is selected and equipped specifically to meet your needs.

Stan Grayson
Publisher
DEVEREUX BOOKS

⚓

CHAPTER 1

Sailing Small

BY STAN GRAYSON

"It is my experience that it is rather more difficult to recapture directness and simplicity than to advance in the direction of ever more sophistication and complexity." — *E.F. Schumacher,* Small is Beautiful

WHAT COULD BE MORE SATISFYING than owning a small cruising sailboat that provides the simple necessities of life afloat in an affordable, seaworthy package that maximizes one's chance to be self-sufficient? The answer for many, including many who could readily afford a larger boat, is "not much"! The inherent fascination in living small, whether afloat or ashore, would be as familiar to many sailors and would-be sailors as it is to anyone who has pondered Henry Thoreau's brave experiment. Why move to a 10' x 15' cabin in the woods when he had a perfectly comfortable family home in Concord? Why indeed!

A variety of terms have been applied to the sort of boats that we consider here: pocket cruiser, pocket yacht, weekender, gunkholer, tabloid cruiser, micro cruiser, mini cruiser, trailer-sailer and, doubtless, others as well. But attempting to define the size of such boats has always been, and will always remain, open to discussion and individual interpretation. Most would agree that to spend even a weekend aboard in some comfort, one is hard-pressed to do so in anything less than 19–20 feet. Even that size boat may be a tight squeeze for all but the most physically and emotionally flexible. Couples seem to find that something around 22 feet is the minimum that offers the necessary overall combination of comfort, performance and, if necessary, trailerability. Advancing age or the demands of a spouse and growing family typically nudge even the more dedicated small boat enthusiast to the larger end of the spectrum, or often to a "big boat" which, in our terms, means 25 feet and larger.

Other than size, the general criteria for a pocket cruiser as defined here include simplicity, handling ease, ease of maintenance, potential trailerability, and — not to be forgotten — affordability. As we'll see, long-term contentment can be found on comparatively small vessels, and the creativity and resourcefulness of the small boat cruiser is displayed in all its glory in subsequent chapters. Whatever boat one selects, however, there are some common requirements that need to be met, and several of these were well-defined many years ago by British sailor and author J.D. Sleightholme in his *Pocket Cruisers, a New Approach*. "The essentials are proper sitting headroom (when leaning back), light and air, dryness and a carefully thought out system of stowage. Ideally one might add: a place where one may stand upright to dress and stretch. This latter requirement becomes more and more essential as one grows older."

It is surprising how few boats actually meet these requirements. Simply finding a boat that has a trunk cabin and offers adequate support when leaning back is a challenge. So, often, is adequate ventilation. One could add quite a few other requirements to the list, as well. These might include a reliable engine, with good access if it's an inboard, space to use the head in some privacy, berths that are both long enough and wide enough (not restricted by shelves or cupboards), and enough stowage capacity to meet anticipated needs without rearranging the whole boat every time something must be accessed. A rig that is easily handled from the cockpit by a single person is also key. So is a rig, for those who trailer regularly, that is simple to set up and a hull whose draft minimizes the drama of launch and retrieval.

In the end, of course, the decision to sail small is all about trade-offs, and those trade-offs have always been a key dynamic in sailing no matter what the boat's size. Consider the problem as expressed by Eugene Connett III in his *The Small Boat Skipper and His Problems*, published in 1951. "Each year before the season opens, I plan to buy a boat with full headroom, comfortable berths, self-bailing cockpit, and all those things that would add to my pleasure and comfort on my annual cruise. Then I sober up and wonder what I would do with my dream boat for the rest of the summer. . ."

Although he annually cruised Long Island Sound during his vacation, Connett spent the majority of his season in the shallow waters of Great South Bay. That is why he elected to steadily improve his 24' centerboard sloop with its 2 1/2' draft and sitting headroom rather than buy a deeper-draft boat with room to stand up. By sticking with his boat, Connett also adhered to the most basic rule of boat selection — get the boat best adapted to your home waters.

Living Small

Achieving a measure of comfort aboard any sailboat, and especially a small one, is an acquired skill. The awkwardness displayed by the inexperienced or the visitor gradually gives way to a seeming ability to adapt and shrink oneself to the scale of the boat. Movements become precise, bumping one's head becomes rare, and a place is found for each necessary item so that it can be reached with minimum effort.

Although living small may not be quite the same as living simply, the two generally go hand in hand. Experience teaches that complex equipment and technology sooner or later fail, and that failure will necessitate new parts or, depending on the nature of the equipment, a potentially time-consuming professional repair. Most people today are far removed from the approach to sailing espoused over a half-century ago by L. Francis Herreshoff whose articles on cruising skills were published in book form as *The Compleat Cruiser*. Although the book appeared in 1956, what Herreshoff was really describing — "teaching" is a more apt verb — was a 19th century approach to cruising. The boats were built and finished simply to reduce initial costs. Gear and equipment was limited to only that deemed necessary for comfort by a generation now far removed in expectation from our own.

"In my youth," wrote Herreshoff, "the small sailboat or cruiser had no engine, no toilet, or electrical devices so that (short of a collision or stranding) repairs through the summer season were almost unheard of, while we could cruise in most any direction without thought of expense or fuel consumption."

In the world of *The Compleat Cruiser*, the many skills involved in spending a self-sufficient summer afloat were practiced in a timeless manner that can only be described as art. Self-sufficiency was the goal and, to that end, the book's characters owned simple boats equipped with nothing more sophisticated than a gasoline engine, and sometimes no engine at all. One had a stove for cooking and to provide warmth, a leadline to check depth, a compass and the simplest of navigational tools, and such other items deemed needful for simple enjoyment. One always watched the barometer, noted the color of the sky and the shapes of clouds, and kept a weather eye. Herreshoff's spirit is alive and well in those who've written the following chapters.

Today, the question arises, as it did in Herreshoff's time — how much is too much? When is enough enough? What size boat is right for me? The answers to such questions must come from the individual. Herreshoff's skippers take pride in making do with less "stuff." So do the individuals who appear in this book. All own boats smaller than those of *The Compleat Cruiser* and the size of these sailboats imposes its own demand to dispense with excess. Most dedicated pocket cruisers have learned that the more items they rid themselves of, the easier life becomes. One thinks of Carruthers, the protaganist of Erskine Childers's *Riddle of the Sands* who never lost an opportunity to chuck something overboard.

Choosing Small

While a majority of pocket cruisers select their boats based on what they can afford, there are others who could readily buy a larger boat but choose not to do so. Many of the latter enthusiastically downsize. They're more than happy to sacrifice the comfort and performance of a 30' or larger boat to acquire one that demands less maintenance, less muscle, and less crew while also incurring lower yard bills, and, often, the chance to store the boat at home. Thus does the skipper of a heavy displacement ocean-ready 31-footer who no longer needs its capability find that the 15' West Wight Potter now stored by the garage fills the needs of his occasional weekend night aboard. Thus does the former owner of 35'-and-larger boats find contentment with a 23' catboat. There are also those on a tight budget who sell their 23- or 24-footer and replace it with a 17-footer (with cockpit tent) that not only reduces expense but opens the possibility for trailer-sailing with an economical tow vehicle rather than a fuel-hungry SUV or pickup truck.

Given the virtues of the small sailing cruiser, one could be forgiven for wondering why there aren't more of them being built. The answer is largely one of economics. Boatbuilders learned long ago that it is easier to create a viable business by making fewer larger boats than more smaller ones, especially really high quality smaller boats. Bigger boats are bought by those who generally have a more consistently high level of income than those who purchase smaller vessels. Bigger boats generate higher revenues and that permits the advertising budgets that spread the word. That, in turn, supports most boating magazines which, quite naturally, focus primarily on the introduction of the very latest 35–50 foot (or larger) models. It's easy to find the few ads for small sailboats. They're the ones toward the back of the magazine, and they seldom ever change.

Neither is it a simple matter for builders to juggle the sort of boat they might *like* to build with the sort of money most consumers are willing to spend to buy their product. The cost of building a small, high quality fiberglass cruising sailboat is typically more than the broader market will accept. Consider the 20' Flicka, the 23' Edey & Stuff Stone Horse, and the 23' Marine Concepts Rob Roy. These are but three examples of small sailing cruisers that eventually were priced out of the market by the availability of less expensive used models and the escalating costs of new construction. Said Marine Concept's Jim Leet of the Rob Roy, "we tended to overbuild and that drove the price up. In a market with a glut of used boats, it's difficult to keep something like the Rob Roy in production. The heart of the market for new boats is at the cheaper end of the scale."

Regarding the price-quality-value equation, one need only think of the Catalina 22 which, in several variants, has sold close to 16,000 boats since its introduction in 1970, and that with the most modest of advertising. Would the Catalina 22 have been so successful if it displaced half again as much, was built for off-shore cruising, was heavily trimmed in wood, and priced at three or four times its modest price? Not likely. Instead, it has always been built to a certain level that met the expectations and budgets of an audience that includes casual weekenders, those who actively race the boats in one-design fleets, and those who use them like waterborne (and trailerborne) RVs. Unlike the Catalina, pocket cruisers at the higher end of the market tend to all be limited production models built to order.

Each of the following chapters is based on the experience of a specific owner with a specific boat. As it happens, the vessels discussed include all the key basic types that one is likely to consider when shopping for a pocket cruiser or, for that matter, a larger boat. As will be evident, each of the boats proved generally well suited — in some cases, ideally suited — to its owner's needs. What's more, the authors have arguably demonstrated that, given enough time, energy, and thought, one can adapt to almost any sort of boat as long as its basic design and construction features have been well-executed. Following is a brief synopsis of the variety of small boat types discussed together with general comments on their pros and cons.

Sloop

Pros: certainly the most universal of rigs, the Bermudan sloop combines good performance and reasonably sized sails in a rig that will be familiar to the great majority of sailors. One of the subsequent chapters involves a production fiberglass sloop. Whether for daysailing or cruising, the rig has much to recommend it. Sails, running rigging, and hardware can all be improved or adapted according to individual desire and budget. Centerboard or keel/centerboard models are much more practical to trailer and launch than those with full, fin, or even wing keels. Let's admit, however, that a keel offers an added measure of simplicity and, in some cases, improved performance. There's an enormous variety of older 22–26 foot sloops to choose from, Pearson, Bristol, Columbia, Catalina, Ranger, Westerly, and O'Day among them. Although all of these boats (with the exception of the Catalinas) are long since out of production, refurbished examples are staples of the pocket cruiser. Likewise, the variety of new, sloop-rigged boats far exceeds that involving other rigs.

Cons: The winches, vangs, and other controls typical of the sloop rig that do so much to enhance performance also add complexity and maintenance tasks that not all sailors appreciate. That said, new boats may actually lack such refinements as a way to reduce prices. Many older boats require significant restoration but this may be a plus for those who wish to apply their own skills and creativity to their new boat.

Cutter

Pros: Three reasonably small sails are a comfort when one needs to reduce sail in the face of changing weather conditions. Three of the boats in this book are cutter-rigged. Two are gaff-rigged, and both include in their inventory that most romantic of all sails, the topsail. These days, the gaff rig has long since been forgotten by most, and with it the advantages of a shorter mast, easily accessed hardware, flexibility of sailplan, and the ability to readily control sail shape by adjusting halyards, topping lift, and outhauls. All that has been lost because of the insistence that a jib-headed mainsail is ultimately more efficient to windward! Whatever the shape of a cutter's mainsail, however, for maximum handling ease and safety, all lines should be led aft to the cockpit. The cutter rig is an excellent choice, whether one singlehands or not, for alongshore and offshore cruising.

Cons: With two sets of headsail sheets and a minimum of three halyards, there are lots of strings to pull — and that's not counting lines for furling mechanisms or the added rigging associated with a gaff rigger. Frequent tacking can be problematical given the tendency of the headsail to hang up on the staysail. Sometimes, those who don't need the cutter's flexibility dispense with the staysail and use only a larger genoa. At that point, a sloop might have made the most sense.

Catboat

Pros: Appealing, traditional looks, shallow draft, and extreme roominess for their overall length are all catboat strong points. So is the fact that these wide-beamed boats generally sail at a small angle of heel and this, combined with their wide, roomy cockpits, makes them especially comfortable. With running rigging limited to a mainsheet, and with winches not being required, the cat rig offers an inherent simplicity. The most popular models retain their value well. Impressive coastwise passages have been made in wooden or fiberglass catboats as small as 18 feet, and one of the longest cruises described in this book was made in a catboat.

Cons: All is not as simple as it may first appear with the traditional, gaff-rigged catboat. For one thing, there are two halyards — peak and throat — instead of one, and a much-needed topping lift. Learning to adjust these for best performance will be a new skill for most. The gaff rig, while a key attraction, also demands development of new skills in terms of both trimming and reefing, and the sail must be reefed in a timely fashion to maintain proper steering and safe handling. (Remember that an 18' catboat has as much sail area as most 22' sloops, but it's all in a single sail.) Limited headroom is the bane of most shoal-draft boats, but increasing topsides and cabin height to improve things adds windage, and generally detracts from appearance.

Yawl / Ketch

Pros: Tough to beat for a small (or large) cruising boat, these rigs — whether Bermudan or gaff — offer outstanding flexibility when it comes to shortening sail, plus the mizzen is a wonderful tool for balancing the boat and keeping it head to wind when on a mooring, heaving to, and so forth. This rig is a top choice for cruisers, and one of this book's chapters is based on the adventures of a 23' centerboard yawl.

Cons: A second mast adds expense and some complexity. The ketch's mizzen may get in the way. Neither rig is common, and their benefits are seldom considered worthwhile on the size boats considered here.

Sharpie

Pros: These ultra-shoal draft boats have an undeniable appeal. Skimming along a few inches above a rippled sand bottom and anchoring where few other sailboats can approach can be great fun. Trailerability is a plus given the shallow draft hull and a sharpie's comparatively light weight. The sprit rigs often found on these boats are easy to control, and sharpies can be quite fast off the wind and are surprisingly seaworthy.

Cons: At their worst in light air and the chop kicked up by powerboats, flat-bottom models are also more than annoyingly noisy when anchored in anything but perfectly calm water. Tacking can also be a problem in some conditions but this depends on the particular boat and one's own experience with it. The often narrow hulls and low topsides limit both headroom and overall interior accommodations. There also exists greater potential for a capsize than one would expect on other types, although this matter should not be overstated and proper design (and handling) does much to reduce the risk. Overall, these highly specialized boats make sense primarily for those who truly need their shoal water capabilities. Resale value is generally low.

Fiberglass Pocket Cruisers

Not only is a wide variety of fiberglass pocket cruisers available, but the various models come at a wide variety of price points. Boats include mass-production models that can take advantage of economies of scale, limited-production boats, and what are essentially custom yachts. The latter prove that being small does not necessarily mean a boat is inexpensive! As always, whether buying new or used, expect to pay more as displacement increases. What's more — expect to get what you pay for. Boats marketed with the idea of offering "the most boat for the money" must, of necessity, be built more quickly and with less attention to detail — thinner layups, comparatively weak deck-to-hull joints, undersized hardware, and so forth — than more expensive models. The accompanying charts are intended primarily as food for thought and compare a variety of different-size boats.

THREE WEEKENDERS

Model/ Manufacturer	West Wight Potter 15/International Marine	Precision 18/ Precision Boat Works	Sanderling/ Marshall Marine
Length Overall	15' 0"	17' 5"	18' 2"
Waterline Length	12' 0"	15' 5"	17' 6"
Beam	5' 6"	7' 5"	8' 6"
Draft	6"/3' 0"	1' 6"/4' 3"	1' 9"/4' 2"
Displacement	495 lbs.	1,100 lbs.	2,200 lbs.
Rig	Sloop	Sloop	Gaff cat
Sail Area (Main and jib)	87 sq. ft.	145 sq. ft.	253 sq. ft.
Auxiliary	2 hp Outboard	Outboard	Outboard or Opt. Yanmar 1GM10 9 hp diesel
Designer	Stanley Smith (et al.)	Jim Taylor	Breck Marshall
Price	$8,195	$12,495	$27,500

As this is written, all of these boats are in production and each will meet the needs of a variety of sailors, depending on specific tastes and budgets.

West Wight Potter 15: With its hard chine hull and low rig (the mast is only six inches longer than the hull), the P15 is a stable boat that is easily trailered behind a small car. The Potter is quickly rigged by one person and is easy to launch and retrieve — all attractive points for owners. So is the fact that the boat is readily beachable, which, as designer Stanley Smith once found, can be a life-saving advantage. Smith's original design was 14 feet long, the minimum length in which a full-length berth could be fitted while still leaving room enough for a cockpit that would hold two in reasonable comfort. Even with an added foot of length, today's P15 is more daysailer/overnighter than pocket cruiser, and it's not bought by folks expecting to cover a lot of ground fast — except on their trailers.

Ed Zeiser, who now lives aboard his Catalina 25 for much of the year, started sailing aboard an old, gunter-rigged 14' West Wight Potter purchased over the Internet for a mere $1,200. Ed refinished the little boat and trailered it behind his Ford Escort from New England to the Chesapeake. "It was quite nice and I loved it," he said. "I lived aboard on weekends. The biggest issue was there was no room in the cabin for the Porta Potty."

Potter lore is replete with impressive voyages — California to Hawaii, Seattle to Alaska, Falmouth to Trinidad — but these exploits rather miss the point. With its perky,

Family fun aboard a Potter, this one on the Shenandoah River at Luray, Virginia.

reverse sheer and well-planned and executed features, the Potter is a unique boat that does lots of things well. It has been steadily improved by a company known for its customer support and it appeals to friendly folks who probably feel they have nothing to prove.

Precision 18: With its beamy hull, light weight, tall (27') mast, and fractional sloop rig, this thoroughly modern design is aimed at combining lively performance with surprisingly ample berths and a 6' 4" cockpit. The shallow keel, centerboard, and rudder have foil-shaped cross-sections and are part of the performance orientation of naval architect Jim Taylor. Similar traits are shared by the larger Precision models. These are thoroughly contemporary looking boats having sparse wood trim but a variety of features aimed at function, such as opening ports and ample lockers.

Sanderling: In continuous, if limited, production since 1962, the Marshall Sanderling was among the earliest fiberglass production sailboats. A lot of fiberglass sailboats have come and gone while the Sanderling still scoots merrily along, and almost 800 have been built. The boats appeal to independent-minded sailors with an eye for tradition and a desire for simplicity. This is a *big* 18-footer, with almost twice the displacement of most comparable-length sloops, and its big, gaff-rigged sail requires patience to master. The cabin offers sitting headroom, a reasonable berth on each side, and a little, swing-up table on the centerboard trunk. Ventilation needs some thought by owners but there is also room for a portable head located sensibly by the bulkhead. These are deceptively fast boats and are popular as daysailers, weekenders, and one-design racers. Nobody buys one because they're cheap or because they are easy to trailer, although the introduction of a tabernacle mast has done much to simplify trailering and rigging. One of the voyages described in this book involved a Marshall 18.

A DIVERSE TRIO

Model/ Manufacturer	West Wight Potter 19/International Marine	Flicka/Pacific Seacraft	Precision 21/ Precision Boat Works
Length Overall		24'	
Waterline Length	18' 9"	20'	20' 9"
Beam	16' 4"	18' 2"	17' 6"
Draft	7' 6"	8'	1' 9"/4' 8"
Displacement	1,225 lbs.	5,500 lbs.	1,875 lbs.
Rig	Sloop	Sloop	Sloop
Sail Area (Main and jib)	117 sq. ft.	250 sq. ft.	203 sq. ft.
Auxiliary	Outboard	Outboard or Inboard	Outboard
Designer	Herbert E. Stewart	Bruce Bingham	Jim Taylor
Price	Approx. $10,000–$14,000	$20,000–$30,000	$18,495 base

West Wight Potter 19
Like the smaller Potter, the 19 has a hard-chine hull that imparts stiff sailing

qualities that are favored by those who buy these boats, and it can be beached if desired. The boat's additional size (compared to the Potter 15) permits a small galley, head, four berths, and ample storage. Despite its added length and weight compared to the Potter 15, the 19 is readily trailerable and can be rigged in some 45 minutes. Although clearly intended for alongshore sailing, the Potter 19 has also made at least one significant blue water passage. Owner Bill Teplow made some small but important modifications to his boat, loaded it with 320 pounds of food and water, added extra flotation, and sailed from San Francisco to Hawaii in 24 days with little drama.

Flicka

With its full keel, outboard rudder, through-bolted hull/deck joint, and molded-in planking lines (why did builders ever bother?), the Flicka was a unique proposition when introduced in the 1970s and, although out of

production, remains so today. The boat was conceived as a relatively heavy-displacement pocket cruiser and her heft and sail plan suggest the Flicka will be more at home when winds exceed 12 knots or so than otherwise. The boat was initially intended for amateur construction but her appealing looks and a then-growing sailboat market resulted in series production by Pacific Seacraft in 1978.

Despite a deck-stepped mast and the absence of bridge deck on pre-1983 models — there was a 10 1/2" lip between the cockpit sole and the first drop board — some Flickas have made blue-water passages. The Flicka spawned a devoted following and earned a reputation as a sturdy boat that could take a pounding while offering about as much living space as one would ever find aboard a 20-footer. There's 5' 11" of headroom, and an enclosed head was added in 1983. That said, the boat, like others, would fall victim to escalating production costs and the reality of just how much even an enthusiastic market would bear.

Precision 21

A contemporary interpretation of the weekender intended for series production and sale through a dealer network, the Precision 21 combines an emphasis on performance — chainplates are inboard to improve sheeting angles and the centerboard has a foil section — with an open and practical interior layout. The science of ergonomics, so prevalent in the design of automobiles and other design disciplines, is evident in this boat. It has a seven-foot long cockpit with the coamings angled to provide comfortable seating, and there's also a pair of seats on the stern pulpit, that can be used to provide extra visibility when sailing. The forward part of the cabin is sloped downward to the deck and, while this does suggest one might be cautious about footing in this area, it permits the big fore hatch to funnel quite a bit

of air into the cabin. Down below, there's a built-in galley, a large cooler, and room for a head. In keeping with most production models today, wood trim is minimal. The traveler is conveniently out of the way at the aft end of the cockpit and a serviceable topping lift supports the boom. This is the sort of pocket cruiser that can be built at a price acceptable to the market, and it's a good performing boat that will appeal to many of today's sailors.

A TRIO OF 22-FOOTERS

Model/ Manufacturer	Catalina 22 Mk II/ Catalina Yachts	Marshall22/ Marshall Marine	Falmouth Cutter/ Sam L. Morse Co.
Length Overall			30' 6"
Length On Deck	21' 6"	22' 2"	22'
Waterline Length	19' 4"	21' 7"	20' 10"
Beam	8' 4"	10' 2"	8'
Draft	3' 6" Fin Keel 2' 6" Wing Keel 2'/5' Centerboard	2'/5'5"	3' 6"
Displacement	2,603 lbs., Fin Keel 2,546 lbs., Wing Keel 2,290 lbs., Centerboard	5,660 lbs.	7,400 lbs.
Rig Type	Masthead Sloop	Cat (opt. gaff sloop)	Cutter
Sail Area (Main and jib)	306 sq. ft.	388 sq. ft.	403 sq. ft.
Auxiliary	5-7 hp Outboard	Yanmar 2GM20 18 hp	Yanmar 1GM10 9 hp diesel
Designer	Frank Butler	Breck Marshall	Lyle Hess
Price	$14,694 centerboard	$58,000	$125,000

What is one to make of three such different boats at three such different prices? The only thing they have in common is their length and that they're all built of fiberglass. It might be said, first, that each is going to appeal to a very different buyer and that those buyers will likely get exactly what they expect.

Catalina 22

This boat, the first and only model offered by Catalina at the time of its founding in 1969, has always appealed to the mainstream sailing market. Owners either like or overlook the boat's generic looks in favor of its other qualities and, of course, its price. The current Mark II version was introduced

in 1995 and sports a hull that is eight inches wider at deck level than the previous models. This opened up the interior.

Although performance may not be particularly outstanding in any one regard, this is not an issue for those who race in one-design fleets. The real attraction here is the overall package – a combination of features and finish at an attractive price. The Catalina has demonstrated its suitability for bay and lake sailing and has also proven to be relatively comfortable for those who adapt to its layout.

"We picked it," said Bob Endicott, a Florida Catalina 22 owner, "because, with its pop top, it was the least claustrophobic of the boats we looked at. Plus, there are so many used boats out there that they're cheap. We've found it durable and predictable." The Endicotts have occasionally considered trading up to a Catalina 25 but the much easier trailering of the 22 has kept them from making the move. That's not to say that trailering the 22 is a cinch, and the tow vehicle should have at least a 3,000-pound capacity, but the 22 is probably half the weight of a cruise-ready 25 and trailer. With so many used boats to choose from, potential buyers should carefully check everything they can. The keel/centerboard is worth inspection, especially on boats used in salt water where dissimilar metals may have resulted in corrosion. Areas around hardware (including the outboard bracket) that may not have been mounted with a backing plate should be checked as well.

There's an active class association for the boat that can provide advice in many areas, and camaraderie, both important ingredients in the Catalina 22's success story.

Marshall 22

The Marshall 22's added ton of displacement is merely one of the differences between it and the Catalina 22. In fact, the Marshall 18 with its 2,200-pound displacement, 8' 6" beam and 253 sq. ft. sail, has more in common with the Catalina (and other 22' sloops) although its $27,500 base price is significantly higher. Like the 18, the Marshall 22, with its 388 sq. ft. sail, and gaff rig represent an entirely different conception than a contemporary sloop. The boats appeal to those interested in the traditions they represent and the advantages of their shoal draft.

That said, this is a miniature coastal cruiser in all regards. It has an inboard diesel engine, marine head with holding tank, and built-in galley. These boats have made passages from New England to Florida and at least one was sailed across the Gulf Stream from Florida to the Bahamas. Catboats probably represent something like one percent of the sailboat market, but it's a solid niche, and the resale value of Marshalls, in particular, has always been good.

With a single reef in its big sail, this Marshall 22 is moving well and steering easily. The dodger does much to keep the cockpit dry in heavier winds and swells and gives the boat the feel of a much larger vessel.

Falmouth Cutter

As a pocket offshore cruiser capable of crossing oceans, the Falmouth Cutter enjoys its own limited but unique market niche. There are few, if

any, boats this stout that can be trailered behind a powerful V-8 pick-up truck or SUV from one ocean to the other and then set off on a deep-sea passage. As with any boat this small, an extended voyage will mean careful stowage but, even so, one will probably be doing quite a bit of shifting of one thing to get to another. The boat reflects what would in times past be referred to as "heavy scantlings." That is, the fiberglass structure is comparatively heavy with the layup all done by hand, and the bulkheads within the boat securely bonded to the hull. Building a boat like this is time consuming and costly, but the result is very special. One of the following chapters involves a . Falmouth Cutter.

THREE 23-FOOTERS

Model/ Manufacturer	Com-Pac 23/3 The Hutchins Co.	Tempest/ O'Day	Stone Horse/ Edey & Duff
Length Overall	23' 11"	23' 2"	23'
Waterline Length	20' 2"	17'	18'4"
Beam	8' 0"	7' 8"	7' 1"
Draft	2' 3"	3' 9"	3' 6"
Displacement	3,000 lbs.	3,000 lbs.	4,490 lbs.
Rig Type	Sloop	Sloop	Cutter
Sail Area	250 sq. ft.	211 sq. ft.	339 sq. ft.
Auxiliary	Outboard	5-7 hp Outboard	Inboard
Designer	Clark Mills	Phillip Rhodes	Sam Crocker
Price	$14,694	Used: $500–$7,500	Used: $9,000–$45,000

Compac 23/3

This boat and a tandem-axle trailer, probably represents the limit that most people would feel practical for regular trailering. There's no keel/centerboard here but, rather, a long shallow keel that, at 2' 3" is again about the most draft that is practical for frequent launching and retrieving. Clearly, one will be watching the tide tables. Whatever trade-off exists between overall performance, launching ease, and interior accommodations is something for the individual to consider. This is a boat that leans toward traditional rather than contemporary topsides "style," and bronze hardware and wood trim above and below deck reinforces this. There's no mistaking the interior of a Catalina 22 and a Compac 23. One could wish the builder would offer a layout with head located elsewhere than between the v-berths, and that four-inch rather than three-inch cushions were made standard, but the boat still represents an attractive package to those searching for its unique combination of design and quality.

O'Day Tempest

While traditional-looking sloops like this one designed by Phil Rhodes were a market staple in the 1960s and 1970s, they and the companies that built them are now long gone. The Tempest, introduced in 1963 and built until 1970, is conservatively rigged — the standard sailplan has 18 percent less area than the Compac 23/3 although the boats have the same 3,000-pound displacement. This is a boat probably at her best in 10 -15 knots of wind and

she'll need a reef and probably be wet in anything heavier. Still, Tempests are known to provide good, safe, all-around sailing ability.

The Tempest is included here primarily to show the variety of pocket cruisers that may be found at quite reasonable prices, if one has the will and skill to do the needed restoration. Spongy decks or cockpit, a delaminating wooden rudder, chainplates that need checking, an iron fin keel that may well need to be removed, refinished, and reset — these are just some of the challenges that may await. They account for the wide range of prices asked for the boats, $1,000–$7,500 at the time of publication.

The Tempest is not an overly roomy boat — she's a daysailer with camp-cruiser accommodations — but those who buy them learn to cope. Some later model O'Day 23s were more contemporary and offered pop-top cabins that provided standing headroom. There were two different varieties and weather tightness is known to be a problem with one version. As with the Tempest, these later boats are available at a variety of comparatively low price points but care should be taken regarding the condition of all components and the soundness of the hull laminate so that one understands what may lie ahead.

Stone Horse

This little boat has it all: good looks, a convenient rig, an inboard engine, and enough room beneath its flush deck for two to cruise in acceptable comfort. The cutter rig involves lots of strings but, once learned, they make it easy to control the sails. There's lots of wood and rigging on the boat, and a Stone Horse will require more maintenance than more spartan vessels.

The Stone Horse was supported by what was, perhaps, the best ad copy ever written in the boat business. Its author was company co-founder Peter Duff, a delightful man of many gifts who wrote eloquently of this very traditional Crocker-designed boat that embodied much cruising wisdom. The last new Stone Horse was launched in 1995. By then, the costs of building this wood-trimmed, comparatively heavy-displacement pocket cruiser far exceeded what the market would bear, while used boats could be acquired, painted, and even re-powered for, perhaps, $30,000. A boat like this isn't a trailer-sailer, nor is it ideal for really shoal water exploration. Otherwise, in terms of a pocket cruiser, the Stone Horse is hard to best.

A TRIO OF 24-FOOTERS

Model/ Manufacturer	Bridges Point 24/Bridges Point Boatyard	Dana/ Pacific Seacraft	Bristol 24/ Bristol Yachts
Length Overall		27' 3"	
Length on Deck	24' 0"	24' 2"	24' 7"
Waterline Length	18' 8"	21' 5"	18' 1"
Beam	7' 9"	8' 7"	8' 0"
Draft	3' 5"	3' 10"	3' 5"
Displacement	3,944 lbs.	8,000 lbs.	5,930 lbs.
Rig	Sloop	Cutter	Sloop
Sail Area	278 sq. ft.	358 sq. ft.	296 sq. ft.
Auxiliary	Outboard Yanmar GM10	Inboard	Outboard
Designer	Joel White	W.I.B. Crealock	Paul Coble
Price	$39,000 (w/o engine); $60,000 is a more typical price.	$96,000 (fully equipped)	Used: $6,000–$15,000

Bridges Point 24

Boats like this one — a traditional-looking, wood-trimmed, full-keel, 24'

sloop — are rare these days, thanks largely to the cost of building them. That said, Bridges Point Boat Yard has turned out a few of these boats each year, on average, since it was introduced in 1985. Builder Wade Dow remembers taking a drawing of a Sea Sprite to designer Joel White as a thought-starter. "He knew what we were after," Wade remembers. "but he came up with something original, although I see a bit of L. Frances Herreshoff in the shapes." According to the builder, each boat is, in essence, a custom job created for customers who "want something they can stand the sight of on the mooring" as well as a boat that sails well. This is not a particularly "big" 24-footer and the builder reports that most owners use the boat as a daysailer and weekender. That said, it would not be hard to imagine a resourceful sailor equipping a Bridges Point 24 for more ambitious cruising.

Dana

The Dana is often described in advertising as "the ultimate pocket cruiser," and those who own one would probably agree. Like the Falmouth Cutter, this is essentially a miniature of an ocean-going cutter, albeit with a deck-stepped mast to gain space below. The boat has just enough size to permit an enclosed but workable head together with a galley with stove and oven. The open design of the

interior, its standing headroom, and easily accessed v-berth make the Dana a surprisingly comfortable little boat (assuming one isn't seeking a real sea berth). So does the design of the cockpit seats, which have angled backs. This, combined with the transom-mounted traveler and a hinged tiller that can be tilted up when anchored, result in a cockpit that offers a higher degree of comfort than some larger boats. Unusually good engine access is afforded by a hatch in the cockpit sole. This is a small boat with all the systems of a larger one and, as pocket cruisers go, probably represents the most comfort one is likely to find — at a commensurate price.

Bristol 24

Simple, reasonably solid, and attractive (qualities also shared by the Bristol 22), the Bristol 24 is a good example of the "classic plastic" pocket cruiser of the 1970s and early 1980s. The boat's comparatively heavy displacement is an indication of her accommodations, which included a door between the main and forward cabins, an enclosed head, and six-foot headroom. Boats like this are generally used as weekenders but some dedicated owners have made coastal and even bluewater cruises.

"I suppose that, in a way, you can tell how much someone uses their boat based on how many holes are in the bulkheads," agreed Jim and Sue Johnson, who bought their Bristol 24 new in 1973. The couple has, during that period, revised the boat from, literally, top (non-skid decks, dorade boxes, anchoring bowsprit and windlass) to bottom (epoxied beneath the waterline). The majority of work was done in the cabin. The galley was completely revised with a deeper sink, gimballed two-burner kerosene stove and dish rack. Book racks, shelves, handholds, and a chart holder were added. Structurally, the hull/deck joint — a weak point on many production boats then as now — was redone. The original stainless steel staples were replaced by thru-bolts, and the rubber rub rail was replaced by a heavier-duty teak rail. A small diesel inboard was installed beneath a hatch newly made in the cockpit sole, and the outboard well was sealed and converted to storage space.

Modifications like these are what the ideal pocket cruiser is really all about — a boat adapted by patient, caring owners within their own time constraints and budget until it exactly meets their needs. The usual cautions are also at work here. Is the basic boat structurally sound — glasswork, chainplates, hull/deck joint, mast step or whatever structure is in place to support a deck-stepped mast — and worth this level of work? If the answer is "yes," a patient search will probably turn up an older boat that, over time, can become exactly what you want it to be.

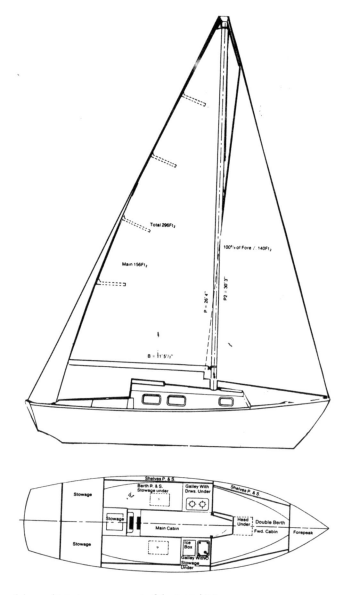

The sailplan and interior arrangement of the Bristol 24.

Farther Afield

The boats discussed thus far are merely a few of the most readily available fiberglass models on today's new or used boat market. The fact is, however, that there is an entire world of wooden boats and boat plans that offer intriguing alternatives for those so inclined. A great many designers have given intense thought to the small cruising sailboat, and one of them, Paul Gartside, shares his approach in Chapter Nine.

Unlike fiberglass boats intended for commercial production, those designed for wooden construction seldom suffer from the perceived market-driven need to create an interior that sleeps more than is either practical or desirable. Cabin arrangements on small wooden yachts typically reflect real-world needs. Most have just two berths and they may well be positioned aft of the forepeak so as to be usable when the boat is under way. The head can usually be found either forward of the berths in the forepeak or aft of the berths (often with a curtain arrangement for some privacy) — anywhere but *between* the berths where one's head would normally rest. What's more, wooden boats are more easily customized or improved than fiberglass boats, which often continue in production with known deficiencies because builders generally find it uneconomical to spend money on retooling a mold.

The wonderful variety of wooden pocket cruisers draws its diversity from the unique experience and skill of many different designers. Most have revisited the challenge time and again, either out of their own curiosity or for a changing clientele. There's plenty of food for thought in the resultant plans. A good place to start is *WoodenBoat* magazine and its plan catalogs. Libraries often offer a variety of books on the subject and the Internet is a rich source of ideas, photos, and drawings. (At the time of publication, *sailingabout.com* was an excellent portal to many different plans sources.)

It should come as no surprise that small sailing cruisers have long been popular in England where disposable income has typically been less than in the United States. In contrast to most American designs, these boats often possess a reverse sheer to gain additional headroom in the cabin, and cockpits that are proportionally smaller than on most American boats. While these sorts of craft may at first look quite foreign to the casual observer, they offer significant functional advantages not to be dismissed.

In the 1950s and 1960s, British designer Robert Tucker turned out a whole series of little sailboats from the Potter-like 14' Midshipman to the 21' Debutante (see Chapter Four). Of plywood, hard-chine construction, these remain just the sort of boats that a homebuilder would find of interest. One of them, the 17' 2" Silhouette, production built in fiberglass, is still supported by an active owners' association in the U.K. What's more, the largely British-developed sport of dinghy cruising includes boats like the 17' 1" Rebell pictured here. Designed for coastal and estuary waters, this is a boat that could be built of quality material at a modest cost. With a weight of about 1,000 pounds, this boat can be towed by a small, front-drive automobile, yet its tiny cabin combined with tented-in cockpit (the tent designed to be set up on hoops) provides a pair of 6' 3" berths and room for a head beneath the hatch. This is an extremely well-thought-out boat and,

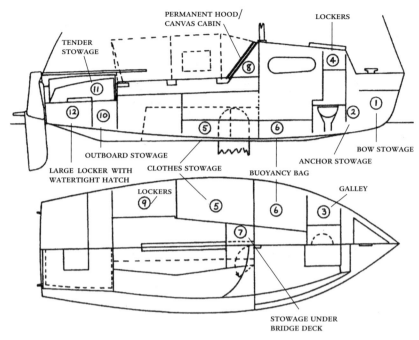

A real British cruising dinghy: the Rebell 17 was designed in the 1960s by Eric Coleman. A well-engineered boom tent enhances the tiny fixed cabin. Plans may be had from the Dinghy Cruising Association whose address is noted on the Credits page.

equipped with proper camp-cruising gear and a sail inventory that includes jib, storm jib, and spinnaker, would offer a quite exciting performance.

Whatever boat one ultimately selects, its transformation into a true pocket cruiser is always a highly individual process that generally plays out over a period of at least several seasons. In some cases, owners continue making refinements over a period of many years. Such is the nature of the cruising sailboat, whether large or small, and the following chapters provide ample examples, based on those who've lived with their boats, and modified them, over time.

Rebell
>   LOA: 17' 1"
>   Beam: 6' 5"
>   Draft: 10"/4' 4"
>   Displacement: 1,000 lbs.
>   Sail Area: Main 71 sq. ft., Genoa 80 sq. ft., jib 48 sq. ft.,
>   storm jib 21 sq. ft., spinnaker 189 sq. ft.
>   Construction: Marine plywood over internal framework

CHAPTER 2

⛵

40 years and 70,000 Miles Aboard
a Small Sailboat

BY CHARLES STOCK

Born in Essex, England in 1927, Charles Stock became interested in sailing in 1944 when he purchased a paperback book called Yachting on a Small Income *that had been written by yacht designer Maurice Griffiths. Mr. Stock served in the Royal Marines before beginning a career in farm management in 1949. Mr. Stock has found endless fascination in exploring his home waters and had, by the summer of 2003, covered over 70,000 miles. In 1990, he sailed his wooden 16 1/2-foot gaff cutter* Shoal Waters *across the English Channel to celebrate, with other boats, the 50ᵗʰ anniversary of the evacuation of Dunkirk. Skillfully using the tide, Shoal Waters made the trip averaging five knots while bigger boats, not paying so much attention, averaged a knot less. Mr. Stock is the author of* Sailing Just for Fun *(Seafarer Books), a book that details his many cruises and thoughts on small vs. larger boats. Among the considerations: larger boats need larger engines, larger sails, heavier anchoring gear, and the "avalanche of gadgets" that they often carry somewhat negates much of the maintenance advantage that fiberglass boats may have over wooden ones. As for Mr. Stock, he has happily cruised* Shoal Waters *without the need of an engine, using oars, a quant (push pole) and, on inland canals, a towrope.*

MY ORIGINAL AIM WAS TO SAIL AROUND THE WORLD. Three things prevented me from doing so. I never had the money; I never had the time, but I did have a wife and four children. Sailing the wide oceans, visiting the palm-fringed atolls and sweltering tropic ports where the jungle drops down the mountainside to kiss the warm seas remains a pastime for winter evenings in the comfort of an armchair with one of the endless books on the subject. Before retirement and thanks to an understanding wife, on some dozen weekends each year, I was free to sail as far round the world as I liked, provided that I was back in good time to go to work on Monday morning. Did this mean just puttering about in the river with all my season's hopes pinned on fine weather for the precious summer holiday or could I still find some real sailing year in and year out? Did I have to race to get some sort of interest, challenge, and excitement? Did my modest means compel me to crew on larger craft to enjoy offshore and night sailing?

Not at all.

Instead, I found wonderful adventure just a couple of hours from London's crowded railway stations. The maze of beautiful rivers that reach deep into the countryside bordering England's east coast, the Thames Estuary, and the sandbank-riddled waters adjacent to it might have been designed for the small, shoal-draft sailing cruiser. A trip around Whitaker Beacon at the northeasternmost edge of Foulness Sand may not have the glamour of a trip 'round Cape Horn, but careful research has shown that a man drowned in local waters is just as dead as one drowned off the tip of South America.

What a sailing world I found! Every bank, every creek has its name and legends. Men have traded in this area since the beginning of recorded history. The routes they used, their shortcuts, the tricks of working the winds and tides are still there for the modern yachtsman to test his skill and the ability of his craft. Despite its many challenges, the Thames Estuary is basically a safe area. You can make mistakes such as going aground on a sandbank for a few hours and merely get back to your mooring late. In contrast, on rockier parts of the coast, a similar mistake could mean almost certain loss of one's boat, or worse. Still, as I cast off the mooring on a Friday evening for 50 hours of freedom and adventure, I was always aware that I was on my own, much like those skippers of the thousands upon thousands of craft that have used these waters over the centuries.

This then, was the area that I would explore for over half a century. I learned that the sheer exhilaration of sailing back to your mooring after a successful trip, whether it be an Atlantic crossing or merely your first rounding of a buoy a few miles outside the river's mouth, has to be experienced to be believed. There, among the creeks and marshes, under the wide skies of the eternally restless tides of the outer Thames Estuary, I experienced the calm and healing effects of nature. Even after so much time has passed, it seems to me that in an increasingly cockeyed world, navigating

a small boat is about the only thing that continues to make sense. I have owned two such boats, and this is their story.

Learning to Cruise

"Of course, there is the *Zephyr*," said a voice in the twilight as I waited for a bus in the little coastal town of Maldon. "Her gear is all right but her hull is ripe as a pear."

My heart took a jump at those words and sank. They were not intended for me but I couldn't resist the temptation to listen in on a conversation about the postwar dearth of affordable small boats. It was April 1948 and I had just bought the 16-foot, half-decked, gunter-rigged sloop *Zephyr* that very evening. The purchase price of 75 pounds (including an outboard motor that I later sold for 10 pounds) represented a couple of years of steady saving during my spell in the Royal Marines just after the war. Saving this modest sum had earned me the title of "Baron Stock" on the mess deck of H.M.S. *Buchan Ness*, headquarters ship of 416 Flotilla, Royal Marine Landing Craft. It was at our base that I had learned to sail and where, on my birthday, August 3, 1947, I went out sailing in charge of a boat — a 14-foot dinghy — for the first time. Each week thereafter, I scrutinized the papers, learning that postwar prices had rocketed and that a cabin boat was then beyond my means. It was through one of those newspaper ads that I became *Zephyr*'s owner.

It was apparent that she had been built by an amateur, first as an open boat and then decked in. She had a short bowsprit and a steel dagger board, which weighed about 80 pounds. The planking was sound in most places but she leaked around the garboards. The stem had rotted through completely and had been covered with a brass overlay which, in fact, I failed to notice. There were also lead patches on the corners of the transom covering you can guess what. No mention was made by the boat's seller but I later discovered a 250-pound lead keel affixed to the boat's bottom. One slight snag was that the rudder was fixed and reached a few inches below the keel, which meant that when the dagger board was up, the rudder was the first thing to touch the mud (or hard sand).

The first task on *Zephyr* was to remove the stem and use it as a pattern to make another. Unfortunately, when I removed it, the rotten wood fell to pieces. To shape the new wood, I painted inside the stempost and plank ends and repeatedly offered up my piece of stock, rasping wood away wherever paint adhered. Three 7" x 1/4" mild steel bolts, the longest that I could buy, were used to fasten the stem, but I never quite managed to fix the lower one properly. Over the years I often wondered how much strength they had left in them but when the boat was broken up in 1963, the bolts were still in fine order.

Then I burned off all the paint in the manner of all new owners of wooden boats and started from scratch, a thing that I have never done since nor expect to do again. I have long since realized that if paint will not fall off, it is best left on. New paint put on damp wood in spring often comes off again within the year, but this time I was lucky, for Easter 1949 was the warmest of the century, and by Monday evening, she began to look very smart. My thoughts turned to cruising and I decided to try a trip to the Isle of Wight.

Immediately after Easter, I gave notice at work for the end of April and began to sort out the details. Over the winter, I had made a host of plans and sketches of lifting cabin tops and ingenious tents, but they all cost far too much money so I eventually sent off for a sheet of barrage balloon material 30 x 12 feet. After the war, this material was advertised widely and it proved very watertight and durable. Keeping clothes dry was the next problem. This was solved by the purchase of a couple of war surplus ammunition boxes 20" x 36" x 11". These proved to be among the most important pieces of my equipment. For cooking, I bought a primus stove and a book on cookery for men only. Things were looking up. A galvanized two-gallon water can was an expensive but necessary purchase as I made final preparations to embark on Saturday the 7th of May.

That afternoon, I put my gear aboard while the tide was out. Almost by chance, I took along my knee-length water boots, and these turned out to be essential for the type of cruising I was to do, for then as now, as I take no dinghy. Just how valuable they were was brought home later in the cruise when, one evening, I left the boots in the mud by the side of the boat and forgot them when I bedded down for the night. The tide floated them off and the high cost of replacements ensured that I never afterward forgot to tie the boots to the boat. That evening brought a light breeze from the northeast that gradually freshened and veered east. The sun sank behind me in a crimson glow as *Zephyr* dropped down the river while the moon rose bold and clear on the starboard bow. My plan was to moor somewhere downriver and wait for the ebb tide the following morning. But I was not particularly tired and I sailed in the brilliant moonlight until after midnight and then anchored. In fact, I toyed with the idea of a night passage but my nerve failed when I pointed the bowsprit into the blackness. It was a grand night so I laid the tent on the floorboards and gazed up at the stars until sleep overtook me.

The first signs of dawn were visible in the eastern sky when I woke a few hours later. My back ached and the cold of the night had got into my bones. I put the tent up and made a cup of tea. This was the first time I had ever used a primus stove. It looked very bright and shiny as I read the instructions by the light of my torch but it was not to stay that way long in the salt air. Tea was made by sprinkling tea leaves onto the water in an ex-army mess tin as it came to the boil. After standing for a few minutes, the leaves sink to the bottom and the liquid could be poured off into a pint mug.

While drinking my first brew, it suddenly occurred to me to lash the oars on the foredeck from the bowsprit to the shrouds in which fashion I carried them for many years. When I came to get the anchor, I coiled the 10 fathoms of rope on the foredeck, hooked the anchor 'round the samson post with the shank across the foredeck and the stock vertical on the rubbing strake. At first, I put a lashing round the warp but later gave up the practice for it never moved even during the foulest weather. Then, while twisting and turning among my belongings, I discovered that one of the steel clothing boxes could be fitted on the boat's starboard side against the center thwart. The gap left between the box and the stern seat could be filled with the bucket covered by the hatch cover from the transom locker. This gave a reasonably flat area over six feet long and at least 2 1/2 feet wide on which I slept for the next few weeks. It was hard but a shirt folded under my hip bone helped a lot. After another spell of dozing rather than actual sleep, I found a lovely morning with the promise of a breeze from the northwest. At 0745, I got under way as the ebb started and the trip was on.

Essex has many detractors, but few of them can ever have been in the Blackwater Estuary on a fine summer morning as the mist is swallowed up by the first warm rays of the sun. The next several days of the cruise found *Zephyr* exploring the channels and creeks of the region and found me getting to know my boat. This was before the days of cam cleats and other such devices but, over the winter, I had devised a "clever" fitting for holding the mainsheet that would enable me to release it instantly in a sudden squall. Off Potton Point I gave it a test and found that it didn't work! The boat heeled over wildly as she lumbered 'round into the wind with water pouring over the coamings, giving me the first real scare of my sailing career. Water was well over the floorboards by the time she righted herself but this was the first sign that *Zephyr* was the type of boat that suffered fools gladly. She was to suffer many times at the hands of this fool over the years ahead.

The business of getting ashore without a dinghy would turn out to be the main problem with the sort of cruising I wanted to do. I soon learned to beach the boat on the mud against a wall of saltings, which are usually about two feet high. It is then convenient to step ashore in shoes. There is, of course, the danger that the boat could topple outward as the tide falls and, to counter this, I took a line from the masthead to the anchor, which I planted out in the field. I soon learned, however, that this had its dangers. On one early occasion, I had secured the boat and settled down to sleep only to wake and find the boat heeling over. I clambered out to find that the tide was well away and the boat had shifted, for I hadn't troubled about fore and aft lines. Her stern was well aground but the bow was high over the saltings and as she settled, the weight was taken by the bowsprit. Already the bobstay was as tight as a fiddle string as it cut through the rough grass into the firm mud. Suddenly, my eye alighted on the dagger board, a fine piece of armored plate that a previous owner had put it to improve her windward qualities for racing. It did noble work that night as a gigantic spade. I soon cut a slot into the saltings for the bowsprit to drop into, and the panic was over for another 12 hours. That is the only advantage I have ever discovered for a dagger board over a centerboard! I climbed back aboard and went to sleep again.

I found a nice easterly when I awoke and sailed at the turn of the tide. I had a long trip ahead of me to reach my destination on the river Roach and I had to make it before the tide turned against me. With a falling wind, I just reached my planned anchorage, gliding in on the last of the tide. Magic is the only word to describe that evening. The light was fading and the moon quietly introduced herself above the sea wall. Even the sea birds seemed to have lost their normal fears and just stood there in the silent gloom as I glided past. The only sound was the occasional ripple of the water over some irregularity in the shiny mudbanks.

I spent the next morning shaping the tent to the coamings so that I could walk on tip-toe along the side decks when it was erected. Brass hooks were screwed in every six inches. The edge of the balloon material was cut to shape and the lower edge doubled back. Holes were made every three inches and a line threaded through, which gave alternate three-inch lengths outside and inside. The outer ones clipped over the brass hooks. At the bow and the stern I fitted double flaps so that the outer one kept the wind out whichever way the boat lay.

Later, I was given a galvanized pipe cot and a piece of canvas of the sort used to make a stretcher. The canvas fitted the cot frame, which I set up between the center thwart and the stern seat resulting in a berth that was sheer paradise after three weeks sleeping on a hard steel box. The only snag was that I couldn't reach down and push the legs of my pajamas right down to my ankles because the foredeck was in the way at the foot of my new berth. I solved this by changing the central upright supports for the tent from being joined together to being separate. That meant I could reach up and remove one for a moment and use it to push my pajama legs down to my ankles. All the boat's spare gear could be stowed on the bunk and, when the tent was folded, I still left it fixed to the coamings from the mast around the starboard side as far as the center thwart. That meant I merely had to lift it over the boom to set it up at night. Life began to get organized, which is the real secret of all small boat cruising.

Today, looking back on that first cruise over 50 years after it ended, I realize that it was the most important sailing experience of my life. Sailing day in and day out, one gets the feel of the boat and the problems of winds and tides and learns far more than can ever be absorbed in years of day and weekend sailing. I sailed well over 300 miles in 5 1/2 weeks, which is not much by my standards today but it had given me a working knowledge of the whole estuary on which to build for the future. As for *Zephyr*, I improved her with a larger jib with reef points, feeling they would be useful when running without the mainsail in heavy weather.

Early in 1952, I secured a job as a farm manager in the little Essex village of High Easter and *Zephyr* then languished at her mooring. I eventually fitted out very hurriedly in late May and spent a few weeks on the river. In September, I set out with a friend one Saturday evening at high water to make a 24-hour round trip from Maldon to Havengore, returning on Sunday evening, a trip of 60 miles. It was a portent of things to come but it would be a long, long time before I could follow it up. For one thing, I got married.

Joy and I had been friends for several years, ever since I found her crewing a Snipe racing at the Maldon Yacht Club. She came on her first cruise with me in *Zephyr* in June that year and we had an idyllic trip, sleeping ashore when possible. Unfortunately, she suffered from seasickness in open water but it never seemed to affect her within the rivers, however wide they might be. The following summer of 1954 found Joy still sleeping on the boat three weeks before the arrival of our daughter Priscilla. By now, we had a car, which made our trips to the boat very much easier. Still, with the family and work demands, I got less and less sailing each year. In the summer of 1956, *Zephyr* sat on a stake near her mooring and we floated her onto the saltings. The time had come to give up sailing. I varnished the anchor and hung it on the wall of our sitting room as a reminder of some gloriously happy times.

Yet, *Zephyr* still had some life in her. In 1957, we decided to fit her out again. The dagger board would have to go as the case leaked so badly when it was used, but I knew she sailed tolerably well without it. But a new mainsail was essential. Joy bought me some unbleached calico as a birthday present and we set about making it up. I decided to convert from the gunter to gaff rig at this time, one of the most important decisions of my sailing life. A friend gave me a mast from an 18-foot National dinghy, which I cut down to size. I used a part of *Zephyr*'s old mast to fashion a fine new bowsprit and the remainder to make a gaff.

In view of the limited time that I had for sailing, the sail was made loose-footed with toggles to the mast so that I could take it home each time that I left the boat. Her windward performance would be poor now and make it even more difficult to get back to Maldon Yacht Club once the ebb set it with the prevailing westerly winds, so I reluctantly left Maldon and joined the Blackwater Sailing Club. It was a mile down the river in open marshland that I found much to my liking. The location enabled me to return to my mooring in clear sailing water untroubled by buildings and high ground.

Over the next five years, I spent a few hours afloat when possible but old *Zephyr* was deserted for weeks on end and often sank at her moorings. I moved her close inshore near the club jetty where she dried for longer than she floated to give the water that leaked in time to leak out again. The surprising thing was that although she leaked like a sieve when afloat, water refused to run out of her when hauled ashore, and we had to bail out the water that we hosed in to wash her out. A complete refit including a lot of hot tar inside and out didn't solve the problems and, by 1962, after many glorious adventures, I knew it was time to salvage as much of *Zephyr*'s rig and gear as possible and use them in a new hull.

Shoal Waters

Once I had stripped *Zephyr*'s hull of all things useful, I spent the remainder of 1962 studying other hulls on the market that would be appropriate for Zephyr's gear. The Tucker-designed Silhouette was selling like mad at that time, with kits costing roughly 300 dollars, the equivalent of 12-15 week's wages for many at that time. Another vessel available as a kit was the Firecrest design and we examined it and others besides. At that time, there were at least two firms completing Fairey Falcon hulls with tiny cabins and I liked the looks of these boats, the *Bristol Venturer* and the *Sea Hawk*. All things considered, I decided on the Falcon and the bare hull complete with transom and centerboard case and board was ordered at the 1963 London Boat Show. The cost including delivery to the farm was 137 pounds, and she arrived in February.

The great advantage of the Falcon hull was that it was made of four layers of agba veneer laid diagonally and hot-molded with no concern for weight savings. In 40 years and over 70,000 miles of cruising, I have never fitted a bilge pump, simply removing with a sponge any water that comes aboard. Although I tried my hand at sketching cabin and deck arrangements, I am no draftsman and it was clear she would have to be to built on the basis that what looks right is right. Fortunately, I had a fine workshop in a brick shed. I ordered two four by eight sheets of marine plywood, one 1/4" thick, the other 3/8ths, and 100 feet of one-inch square mahogany.

After that, it was a matter of deciding what I needed, ordering it, and waiting for delivery. Gripfast nails, brass screws, and waterproof glue were used with caulking compound to fill the gaps left by my lack of carpentry skills. I had recently attended a dinghy-building class and remembered the admonition that the days of the tongue-and-groove joint were over. Instead, just butt two pieces of wood together and nail a piece of ply across the angle and you have a strong joint. Clodhopper carpentry had arrived just in time!

Fitting a shallow keel to protect the hull when grounding or hauled ashore for the winter was the first challenge. Shaping a solid piece of wood was beyond my skill so I used two 1/2" x 3" strips laid on each side of the keel ridge, gluing them to the hull and then fixing them with alternate nails and screws every three inches. The gunwale came next. I sandwiched the hull laminate between a one-inch square inner wale and 1 1/2" x 1/2" outer wale. The decks laid over this gave an end seal to the hull veneers. Finally, the rubbing strake was later screwed to the outer wale rather than into the hull so that the strip could be renewed if damaged without interfering with the precious molded hull.

An examination of the plywood soon convinced me that I should use the 3/8" material throughout and keep the thinner 1/4" sheet for the cabin top. Starting the task of cabin building was daunting but a start had to be made somewhere and the support for the centerboard case seemed to be a natural spot to begin. When the Fairey hull was used for a half-decked boat, the center thwart provided support for the case. In my case, I made a bulkhead on each side of the case just in front of the pivot bolt and the same height as the case itself. The bulkheads were joined to the hull with adhesive compound so that, again, no screws or nails went through the skin of the hull. I located the forward bulkhead to give six-foot-long bunks in the bow. I next added a one-foot-wide bridge deck.

At first, I expected to sleep two adults in quarter berths and two children forward. The bridge deck was set three inches higher than the cockpit seats to give a little more knee room and supported aft by a 1" x 3" frame to strengthen the assembly. Additional support to the after end of the case was made with 2 1/4" x 1 1/4" mahogany boards contributed by a man I had met in the midst of chopping up a billiard table for firewood.

As I was using 3/8" ply, no framing had to be built. The one-inch square mahogany merely served to join adjacent sheets of plywood. The foredeck and side decks were next glued to the gunwale. Then the side decks were trimmed off nine inches wide, and one-inch square mahogany was fitted along the inner edge to take the cabin sides. The cabin sides were carried six inches into the cabin to make a sort of box girder around the cabin and provide some useful lockers for small items. Cabin beams were a problem, for even beams of modest curvature had to be cut from a deep, expensive piece of wood. I solved this by using wood one inch deeper than the finished beam, cutting the curve and then gluing the offcuts from the top back on the bottom. With a backing of plywood, this solved my problem in an economical fashion. A piece of oak from a barn provided the samson post, and that completed the work on the cabin since no money was available for floorboards.

A deep, comfortable cockpit was made along the lines of *Zephyr*'s, with the coamings the same height above the seats as the arms of my favorite armchair at home for maximum comfort at the helm and a clear view forward over the cabin top for safety while underway. Perhaps the most comfortable seat on the boat, however, is that for the crew when facing forward sitting on the bridge deck with feet in the cabin and elbows resting on the cabin top while using binoculars. At the stern, a nine-inch-wide afterdeck was made to give a locker underneath and to provide the helmsman with a feeling of security from the sea astern, so lacking in those craft with just a bare transom.

A toe rail 1 1/2-inches high runs around the edge of, and at right angles to, the deck. The deck itself had sand sprinkled on the wet undercoat before the topcoat to give a superb non-slip effect. I bought two packets of International deck sand that lasted for over 25 years and this must be the cheapest form of safety on the market. The 17 1/2-pound fisherman anchor stows neatly on the foredeck with the crown over the bow, and the 90 feet of chain is collected in a plastic bucket jammed forward of the samson post.

For the first season, I used the rudder off *Zephyr* but the next season was able to make a drop rudder to the design that came with the hull. For the first year, I painted the whole hull green and left it so that the weed would grow on the bottom to give me a waterline. It took less paint for the hull than I expected but pint after pint of varnish vanished into the woodwork. Finally, in the spring of 1963, all was ready and the great moment came. The rigging made for me at the local chandler fitted perfectly and within a few minutes, I realized that I had a winner on my hands. Soon after launching, I did a rudimentary stability test at the mooring by standing in the water and pulling down on the peak halyard until the boat was horizontal. I let go and she came upright instantly.

By August, I had recast the lead ballast from *Zephyr* and put it inside my new boat, christened *Shoal Waters*. Without anti-fouling paint, the weed and barnacles grew quickly. In order to scrub the bottom, I anchored the boat in three feet of water and asked my wife to heave down on the halyard to careen the hull. She was unable to get the boat over far enough for my liking so I handed her the brush and took the halyard myself. To my delight, when the boat came over at 45 degrees, my feet came off the bottom and I swung toward the ship. Stability was not going to be a problem! People are so concerned for buoyancy that they have forgotten the stabilizing effect of ballast to prevent a capsize. I have since tried some stiff tests under sail in shallow water where the boat could be recovered easily if necessary, but she doesn't go over enough to get water over the coamings. Of course, she could capsize on the face of a large, steep wave, if I ever went out in such conditions, but the fact is that I do not.

At first, foam cushions for the bunks were out of the question but a feather bed failed to get a bid at a village sale and I got it cheaply. The feathers were restowed in plastic bags and served well for several years. Nowadays we have two cushioned bunks forward in the cabin, a galley aft on the port side and a seat that lifts to provide a third bunk on the starboard quarter. It will never be a roomy boat but it is warm, dry, and very comfortable.

The subject of rig was one to which I gave much thought. The one thing that I came to dread about *Zephyr*'s gunter rig was lowering her long yard in a following wind and sea in order to run under headsail only. The sail invariably went into the water and had to be hauled back on board dripping wet. Of course, I didn't then know about the age-old solution of double lifts or lazy jacks that both support the boom and provide a guide for the yard (or gaff) and sail when lowered. When I designed *Zephyr*'s new gaff rig in 1957, I eliminated my problems with the previous rig's yard, found that the gaff rig performed well and that, above all, I just liked the look of it. So, when *Shoal Waters* set out on her maiden voyage, it was with the rig from *Zephyr* but also with the hope that funds would soon be available to buy a new suit of sails at the end of the first season.

At this time there were few gaff-rigged boats about and those one did see were not very inspiring examples of the breed. Unknown to me as I built *Shoal Waters* during the long, cold winter of 1963, a small group of enthusiasts were then organizing the first East Coast Old Gaffers race for July of that year. They hoped for 12 entries and got 30, including the month-old *Shoal Waters*. If I had any doubts about choosing gaff rig versus Bermudan, two things resolved them. On the day after the Old Gaffers race, as I ran back to my mooring, I met a dreary stream of Bermudan boats that, in contrast to the vessels I had just sailed with, seemed to be nonentities. Then, on a short cruise in August, *Shoal Waters* beat easily up the coast to the River Ore against a northeast wind and, when the wind shifted southwest the next day, she beat her way home without any problem at all. That was all the performance I needed.

Now, 40 years later, I no longer have to apologize for my old-fashioned rig. New gaff vessels are advertised in the yachting press and are on view at the boat shows. The Old Gaffers Race on the Blackwater each July is now a festival of the sailmaker's art with over half the craft sporting topsails. I have made rather extensive studies of the comparative windward performance of Bermudan and gaff-rigged boats and learned that the former does generally enjoy an advantage in windward sailing, generally of 14 to 19 percent. But a glance at the compass and the wind direction will show that nearly three-quarters of the time you spend sailing will be off the wind. If we think of the case of the gaffer beating with a fair tide with a performance 20 percent less than the Bermudan boat, the gaffer has got to be at least 10 percent better on all other points of sailing. I have demonstrated to my satisfaction that she will be.

Few people have experience of both types of rig on the same boat, but I have met one. He lost his gaff rig and topsail after a rigging failure and took the opportunity to go Bermudan. In spite of cutting 100 square feet from the mainsail, he was surprised to find that he had to add another 350 pounds of ballast to the keel to restore her original stiffness, which seems to answer the criticism that the gaff rig has too much weight aloft. I suspect that the explanation has much to do with the tendency of the gaff to sag to leeward. This is normally quoted as a deficiency of the rig, usually by people who have never used it. In practice, this is actually a major safety factor for, as the boat heels to a squall, the sagging gaff lets much of the force of the wind escape harmlessly over the top. In the same situation, a Bermudan-rigged boat with the boom vanged down can only relieve the pressure of the wind by heeling over even farther.

The point that I have tried to make is that if you are going to spend a lot of time beating against a head tide, go Bermudan. But if you can order your affairs as to normally work a fair tide to windward, gaff rig will serve you better. Of course, the cruising man will take a fair tide as naturally as he selects the up or down escalator depending on whether he wants to go up or down.

At the end of the 1963 season, I took *Shoal Waters* round to the local sail loft where we "measured the hole." Then, the sailmaker drew out the existing sail plan, which we adjusted to give a bigger sail area that "looked right." After 40 years and almost 70,000 miles, I would have no hesitation in ordering the same thing again, although I would make each of the two mainsail reefs six inches deeper. The main was made loose-footed, which enables one to easily adjust the draft to suit the wind, flattening the sail when it blows hard and curving it more deeply for light airs.

At first, the boat was sloop-rigged with a very short bowsprit, but I changed it to a cutter rig. Apart from the advantages of the extra foresail, the change involved a picturesque longer bowsprit with a bobstay to support it. I feel this brings more safety than many of the more expensive gimmicks pumped into the market these days under the title of safety enhancers, for the bobstay presents a ready route back on board for a person in the water. When I speak with people about safety, I urge them to imagine they are in the water with their chin level with the waterline of any boat they are thinking about buying.

"How will you get back on board?" "Is there anything you can reach to hang on to?"

In fact, our bobstay once served as a lifesaver when a man from a troubled motor cruiser was in danger of drowning and could not get back aboard the boat with its high topsides, a design feature now common to many new boats, whether sail or power.

Both of *Shoal Water*'s headsails are set on old-fashioned but simple and reliable Whykham Martin furling gear, invented at the turn of the last century. The fittings revolve on bicycle ball bearings packed with grease. The lower one picks up salt water and needs repacking every two or three years, but the top fitting seems to go on forever. I have three staysails – the smallest a spitfire jib just under 12 square feet in area. This and the other head sails were also made by my local loft. Sails are so important that the slight extra cost of personal service is money well spent, as opposed to chasing discounts.

The Whykham Martin gear is only for furling, not reefing, although with the cutter rig, the furling of one sail halves the area forward of the mast. These days there are many roller-reefing gears on the market for headsails and owners seem satisfied with them. I don't like them, for the strain on the drum and line when a sail is used half-rolled must be considerable. One flaw in any part of the fitting or the breaking of the line and the lot could suddenly unroll in a gale. Changing my furled headsails is easy. No flogging mass of stiff, wet sailcloth to fight on a heaving foredeck, just one docile sausage to change for a smaller one while the boat looks after herself under the mainsail only. Of course, the headsail roller reefing gear may suit the chap who sticks to sheltered water.

The topsail came late, the first one made from the jib of an Albacore given to me by a friend. Initially intended only as a bit of fun, the topsail soon proved to earn its keep, for there is more wind the higher up you go. A year later, I had a proper topsail made up. At first, we lashed it to a bamboo yard each time we wanted to use it but now it is a working sail, which is used much of the time and stays lashed on the yard all season. It stows in the cabin portside above the bunk. I rigged it in a traditional style with a bowline to the peak as a sheet and a downhaul, but I have since become lazy and now merely tie the tack and clew to the boom so that I only have the halyard to contend with. This can be let fly in a squall or for low bridges, but of course the whole mainsail must be lowered to take in the topsail when it pipes up.

A word of warning for anyone thinking of fitting a topsail for the first time. It is difficult to get the sail to set well at first but I recalled the best comment on topsails, which was made by the great yachting writer Francis

B. Cooke, who sailed our east coast from the 1890s until after World War II. He wrote: "Men cursed them and swore that they would have done with them. Then they went to their sailmakers and ordered larger ones. Topsails, the glory of gaff rig."

My new rig soon proved flexible over all the conditions that I have faced. There are two rows of reef points on the mainsail and the reef pendants and tack lashings are in place at all times. The first reef reduces the mainsail by 20 percent and, used with the staysail, gives a well-balanced rig once the wind gets too much for full working sail. In crowded harbors and anchorages, I furl the staysail and use the jib instead, as it gives better visibility. The second reef reduces sail area another 20 percent and makes life comfortable when things begin to get really lively. A double-reefed main can be used with either the staysail or the tiny spitfire jib.

It will be apparent from the above details that I stick firmly to the good old-fashioned tradition of keeping the balance of the sail plan when reducing sail. Not for me this modern fad of headsail only, mainsail only or, worse still, reefing the main and retaining a large headsail. A tiny headsail has two great virtues. First, it can used aback to knock the boat's head around when tacking into the sort of short fussy waves one meets when beating with the tide. Second, in a sudden squall, the main can be eased a little and the headsail sheeted in hard so that it drives the wind off the leach into the luff of the main, causing it to lift and, in effect, reducing the working area of that sail until the squall has passed.

Reefing procedure is as follows: 1) Harden up the topping lift, which is led to the after end of the starboard cabintop. 2) On starboard tack, release the tiller and mainsheet. 3) Move to the mast and lower throat and peak halyards to have the mainsail's area. 4) Tie the appropriate luff reef cringle to the tack; go aft and heave in reef pennant and make it fast. 5) Return to the mast and hoist the reefed sail. 6) Return to the tiller, and trim the mainsheet. 7) Unroll the headsail.

If windspeed increases past Force 5, my trysail comes out from its hiding place right forward under the foredeck where it is always bent onto its own small gaff and is therefore ready at all times. It is strongly made, five feet at the head, six at the hoist, and seven in the foot to give about 45 square feet or 30 when reefed. To set it, the mainsail is lowered and firmly lashed into the scissors-type boom crutch. The main sheet and topping lift are stowed out of the way and the trysail is laid along the boom. The gaff jaws are lashed in place around the mast and the peak and throat halyards transferred from the mainsail to the trysail. The tack is made fast to the gooseneck using a lashing permanently in place on the trysail, and the gaff is then hoisted.

All of *Shoal Water*'s sails must be controlled from the cockpit, so sheet layouts are crucial. The main sheet leads from the traveler on the afterdeck up through two blocks along the boom and down to a cam cleat in the center of the bridge deck. That puts the sheet right beside my knee and ready for instant release. Essentially, this is a single-purchase arrangement that minimizes the length (and expense) of the sheet. When released, the sheet runs out much more quickly than a multiple-purchase arrangement. It is harder to trim the sail in but I can always luff up a little or reach up and get a purchase by "swigging" down (tugging) on the sheet between the blocks.

The jib and staysail sheets lead in through the coamings just behind the cabin to a pair of clam cleats. When tacking, they can be handled together with a final adjustment to each sheet as the boat gathers way on the new tack.

The hoist for the centerboard is a fourfold purchase with the tail in a clam cleat beneath the mainsheet cleat. Again, it is handy to the helmsman and ready for instant attention as soon as the board whispers to me that it's scraping the bottom.

This, then, is *Shoal Waters*, my 16-foot sailing cruiser. Since her launching well over 40 years ago, the boats I've met around the coast seem to have gotten bigger each season. There is no doubt that larger boats give better accommodation, in particular, sufficient room to invite guests for a cruise. But do they give more and better sailing? I think not. I have always sought some sort of challenge when going afloat. I find that a 60-or-70 mile weekend trip is a satisfying achievement. The same trip in a 40-footer would just be a milk run. Remember that the sheer joy of using the wind to travel in delightful maritime surroundings is the main object of the exercise.

Living Comfortably on a Small Boat

The roughly triangular area of sea, mud, and sand known as the Thames Estuary starts some 40 miles downstream from London Bridge where the River Thames suddenly opens out to over a mile wide. To the south, the Kentish shore continues for another 40 miles with high land in the background that eventually merges with the sea along the white chalk cliffs of North Foreland with its famous lighthouse that warns of dangerous, off-lying ledges. On the northern Essex shore, a seawall soon vanishes from view as the off-lying sands widen and the main channel heads out in a maze of waterways known as deeps, gats, swatchways, and channels. All of these features edge a wide area of sand and mudbanks exposed at low water. Twelve navigable rivers flow into this area giving over 120 miles of sheltered water. There are also two small local canals and access to England's network

Here is Shoal Waters *doing what she was designed to do — comfortably grounded out on a soft, muddy bottom and awaiting the return of the tide.*

of inland waterways.

I built *Shoal Waters* to enable her to savor the best of this world, from its open water to the old wharves, jetties, and tidemills deep in the heart of the river-laced countryside. Over the years, she has proved her ability to reach the head of every navigation and is much admired everywhere she goes, but I am constantly asked: "How do you manage to live on so small a boat?" In spite of our assurances, few people seem to believe that we live, eat, and sleep comfortably.

Rule Number One is to keep the inside of the cabin dry. I never cease to read with amazement of the leaking decks of some craft including many new expensive yachts. It's a long-standing tradition in boating that there is no such thing as a waterproof fore hatch, and some small boats are designed without one. But we have one and it does not leak. Let's face it, life inevitably gets a bit crummy even with only one person cooking and sleeping in such a small space, so we take every opportunity to open up the forehatch and let a draft through to freshen things up. There is also an opening porthole on each side of the cabin side,

Problems adhering to Rule One obviously can arise in wet weather. So, Rule Number Two is to never go into the cabin in wet foul weather gear. This means having all essential gear such as charts, tide tables, and snacks ready within reach of a person in the cockpit. When mooring after a wet day, our system is a tent over the boom enclosing the cockpit in which wet gear can be sponged down, carefully removed and hung to dry. Any crew has a clear choice: stay dry inside or bundle up and keep outside! We never wear shoes inside the cabin, preferring our bare or stocking feet on the carpet, got for a pittance from the small samples sold off by the stores.

Space inside is the main problem. *Shoal Waters* is 16 1/2-feet long with a six-foot beam. There is 38 inches of headroom in a cabin area six feet long and nearly four feet wide. The centerboard trunk cuts this area in half and extends for a foot into the cockpit and about a foot under the foredeck. A four-foot bench on the starboard side gives just enough room to sit upright with space for our bare feet on the cabin sole. (I am 5' 8" tall, my wife, Joy, a little less.)

All the space forward into the bow is taken up with a vee-berth with four-inch cushions. In practice, Joy likes more foot room and, recently, I made a board extension to extend my berth aft and to give her more room. During the day, this stows neatly in the starboard quarter berth which, these days, is used as stowage now that our four children are long gone. The port quarterberth has long been blocked off to make a cockpit locker. That part inside the cabin as far as the port bunk is now the galley. It is equipped with a Gaz stove set in the middle and lockers either side of the centerboard trunk under the bridge deck. To port, also, is the car battery that is charged from

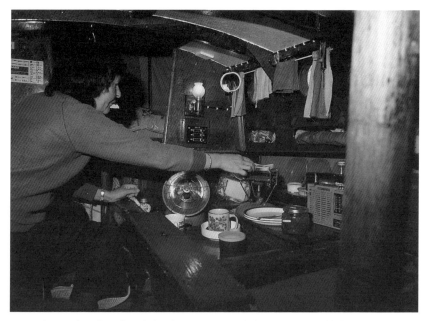

Joy Stock at work in the galley of Shoal Waters. *A single-burner stove quickly brews the tea.*

Shoal Waters' *boom tent is supported by a sturdy but easily set-up framework.*

a five-watt solar panel on the port side of the cabin top.

The space between the centerboard and the galley holds a radiant gas heater and a plastic milk crate that holds our supply of canned food. It has a plywood top that serves as a working surface and brace for Joy as she climbs into her berth. The starboard berth is easier to enter but I am the one who gets out quickly during the night should the need arise. The cabin sides extend six inches below the deck level to make a sort of box girder along each side of the boat, which is divided into three small lockers. Below the lockers, at the head of each bunk, is a bookcase of sorts. On my side, it serves to hold charts and radio while, on Joy's side, the medical gear and assorted other bits are kept.

As for the centerboard trunk, a flat insert acts as a tiny table. It is normally stowed under the port side of the cockpit in the same area as the scissors boom crutch. A different top, curved to accept the board as it is raised, is used when underway to keep the cabin dry.

We have developed a set routine over the more than 40 years aboard *Shoal Waters*. On waking, my first task is to reach over and light the stove under the kettle, which is always filled before we turn in. The lighter is kept in a wooden fitting on the cabin bulkhead. I assemble the teapot and cups from the rack

behind the cooker, warm the pot, and put in a teabag from the caddy, which is kept in the rack next to the lighter. The milk is in the milk crate. (We have no icebox or cooler.) After lingering over the tea and, if possible, listening to the forecast on the radio, I wash

Thanks to its tapered forward section, Shoal Waters' *boom tent minimizes windage and can be left in place even in gale conditions.*

and shave in a small plastic bowl kept in the cockpit locker complete with soap and sponge. There is a small adjustable mirror at the junction of the cabin bulkhead and cabin side.

Our washing gear hangs on the curtain rail of the aft, portside porthole, the towels on the starboard side in similar fashion. Once dressed, I move out into the cockpit and drop in the washboards to give Joy 20 or 30 minutes of privacy. If moored alongside or dry on firm mud or sand, I go for a walk and stretch my legs. If afloat, there are always a few jobs to do and plenty to watch, including other craft and wild life galore. When Joy has finished, she pushes the sleeping bags, and so forth right up into the bows out of the way and I pass in the gear that we chucked out into the cockpit before we turned in.

Ready food is kept in two rectangular plastic buckets stowed on the port bunk leaving the starboard bunk clear for use during the day by reclining with feet aft and head resting on the bedding. (We've found that, even in warm weather, one seems to cool down rapidly when lying down to rest, and so appreciate the warmth of the sleeping bag.)

One aspect of life aboard a small boat that is vitally important but rarely written about is using the toilet facilities. Sea toilets with overboard discharge are still the rule here but more articles are appearing in the magazines about holding tanks. To date, however, there are few facilities on shore to pump out or empty such tanks. What's more, most public facilities have prominent notices banning the emptying of chemical toilets as the chemicals inhibit the sewage works. In England, the inland waterways already ban discharge and do have reasonable pump-out facilities, some in boatyards, and others available to licensed craft with a special key.

In practice, we use public toilets wherever possible. Afloat, I use a plastic bailer for water and the other is the traditional "bucket and chuck it." In sheltered areas, we use chemical fluid until we are in open water or near the river mouth with an ebb tide. Our bucket stows under the helmsman's seat and is used in the cockpit when the tent is up or when we are in a very isolated area. But when necessary, the bucket can be used inside the cabin with the wash boards in for privacy. As a last point on this subject, don't use the last quarter roll of the toilet paper on board. Instead, save it to take ashore in your pocket when visiting a public facility, just in case!

Our procedure for getting under way is for Joy to take the helm until we get moving and then for her to sit on the bridge deck with her feet in the cabin. This seat, together with other features in the cockpit, was designed for comfort as the occupant can rest the elbows on the cabin top when using binoculars. In fact, Joy is better qualified than I as she completed her formal Royal Yachting Association Day Skippers Certificate, but arthritis prevents her spending long periods at the tiller these days. She takes the helm when mooring or going alongside, leaving me to handle the sails, lower the anchor, or take the mooring lines ashore.

We also have a set routine for anchoring or mooring. The first step is to harden up the topping lift, go forward to cast off the peak and throat halyard, and let the gaff come down on top of the boom. This rarely takes over 10 seconds. During this time, Joy has set up the boom crutch in its slots on the afterdeck. I then ease the topping lift to let the boom into the crutch and use the main sheet to make it fast to the traveler. Now, the boom becomes a firm hand hold which we stow the sail with four ties. Joy then takes over as she likes a neat harbor furl, and I get the tent ready to fling over the boom. Then we are ready to get the kettle going.

An ongoing challenge for the skipper of a small sailing craft (and for many larger ones!) is the problem, of towing a sturdy dinghy. All manner of inflatable or folding craft have been devised but the cold statistics show that while few people drown from yachts, a number do so each year while using dinghies. While one can sometimes tie up alongside, getting ashore without a dinghy remains a major problem if you cannot afford marina prices. With no refrigerator on board and carrying only four gallons of fresh water, getting ashore every day or two is essential. This is where *Shoal Waters'* ability to sit upright on the shore like a fat, contented duck comes in, for we just beach and walk ashore. It does take an understanding of the tides but mistakes make good tutors.

The air of freedom and space aboard a small boat beached out on the sands or near the head of some rural creek contrasts favorably with a marina berth overshadowed by bigger boats, which probably have no alternative berth. But, of course, they will have an easier time fetching supplies. Like so much else in the world of sailing, you pay your money and take your choice. Life will be easier on a larger craft, but I console myself with the old adage "the smaller the boat, the better the sport"!

Christmas Aboard

Yachting writer Francis B. Cooke did it before World War I. Designer and writer Maurice Griffiths did it between the wars. The idea of spending Christmas aboard had always fascinated me, too, but my family was not interested. Finally, in December 1993, in my fifth year of retirement, I decided it was now or never. I would spend the Christmas holiday aboard *Shoal Waters*.

Preparation was everything. She is too small for a solid fuel stove but I have a radiant heater and Gaz cooker. The underside of the deck is lined with insulating polystyrene tiles and the inside of the hull with sheets of closed cell foam sheet material like that used to make cups. I have two sleeping bags, which are kept warm continuously with two hot water bottles. I decided to stock up on a supply of the best steaks and mince pies and made no plans for an ambitious cruise but planned to stay within my beloved River Blackwater.

There was a gale warning for the Thames at 1400 hours on Christmas Eve and I spent the day anchored off Ray Island, alone with a few wading birds as the wind screamed out of the northwest and the rain lashed down. High water was at 2030 hours. With one reef and guided by a fitful moon, I tore across the wild mouth of the river and sounded with my cane (sounding pole) into the lee of the St. Peters Flats. The red lights on the nearby power station breakwater vanished behind the seawall and the massive building itself moved south to come in line with the little church, which has stood since the year 675 AD, crouching behind the sea wall. I swung the bowsprit west toward the little creek leading to St. Peters and suddenly, the water smoothed out; the dim shapes of the saltings appeared on either hand, and I furled the staysail and rushed forward to drop the anchor into two or three feet of water.

There is only water in the creek for two or three hours and so by midnight, *Shoal Waters* was perched on the firm mud. After a nap, I opened the tent at midnight to be greeted by the vivid shadows of the mast and rigging thrown onto the mud by the brilliant moonlight, for the sky had cleared and the wind had dropped. Out to sea, I could pick out the flashes of well-known buoys under the great constellation of Orion, which dominated the eastern sky. Midnight mass came over the radio with "Silent Night."

Next morning brought high water and the marshes were alive with vast flocks of hungry waders and geese waiting to feed on the exposed mud as soon as the tide retreated. After lunch, the sun burst through as I tramped the miles of lonely shore, studying the ravages of the sea. A stake that I had driven on the inner edge of a cockleshell bank in early August was now fully 12 yards into the gleaming shells, which seem to kill off the vegetation and leave the mud bare and a soft target for the waves to attack. No wonder the farms in the region are a mile or more inland. Clouds of gulls and geese wheeled and turned over the endless mud and marsh outside the 10-mile-long sea wall between the Rivers Blackwater and Crouch.

As night closed in after a perfect marshland sunset, I bedded down until the night tide when I sailed across the river to a new anchorage at the entrance to the Besum Fleet for the rest of the night. The sun rose clean out of the sea the next morning and I made sail and moved past the gently moving withies (saplings used to mark channels) on the oyster beds up to an ancient causeway, which is covered at spring tides. Halfway back, I anchored in the lee of Ray Island to chuck a steak and a couple of eggs into the frying pan as a fleet of sailing dinghies flowed out on the river, their gleaming white sails contrasting with the sparkling blue water. That afternoon, I reached up the river over the ebb to anchor for the night off the old pier at Osea Island, ready to pick up my mooring on Monday.

Another minor ambition achieved!

Shoal Waters Key Specifications
Hull Builder: Fairey Marine, Hamble, U.K.
Length Overall: 21' 4" (bowsprit is retractable)
Length on Deck: 16 1/2 feet
Length of Waterline: 15 feet
Beam: 6 feet
Draft (board up/down) 12"/48"
Ballast: 28 lead pigs totaling 280 pounds
Total Sail Area (including topsail): 170 sq. ft.
Whykham Martin furling on both headsails
Tabernacle Mast
Construction Material: Hot molded agba hull, mahogany marine plywood cabin, mahogany framing and trim. Wood came from such diverse sources as a billiard table, the top of a baby grand piano, and part of the counter from a Lloyds bank!

Shoal Waters — Key Equipment
Electrical System: 12-volt car battery for navigation and cabin lights. Five-watt solar panel.
Cook Stove: 6 lb. Gaz brand
Four-inch mattresses
8 x 50 Zeiss binoculars
Two fenders
Oil anchor light
Auxiliary power: two paddles and quant
17 1/2-lb. Fisherman anchor
Clam cleats for centerboard hoist and headsail sheets

CHAPTER 3

⚲

A Sharpie, a Catboat, and a Sloop

BY LANCE GUNDERSON

Sailor Lance Gunderson is a professional musician and teacher who has been featured on more than 30 recordings. He has appeared on numerous radio and TV programs in addition to performing extensively in the U.S., Canada, and Europe. His specialty is the guitar with a focus on classical, jazz, and flamenco. His Ramirez flamenco guitar accompanies him on all his sailing adventures, the most notable of which was a voyage from Maine to Florida and back aboard a Marshall 18-foot catboat. He lives in Maine.

ALTHOUGH I GREW UP AROUND THE WATERFRONT AND BOATS, the boat bug didn't really bite me until the summer of 1972. That's when my good friend Maitland Edey of Martha's Vineyard invited me to crew on his L. Francis Herreshoff Meadowlark leeboard sharpie gaff ketch in the annual Vineyard Gaff Riggers Race. We won. Even though I knew nothing about what was happening and served mainly as human ballast I had an exciting time. I remember Mait was rather fussy about how things were done on the boat — no shoes below decks, and no sand in the dinghy from soles of shoes, which had been ashore, for example.

Shortly after that exciting and memorable race, Mait invited me to join him on a round-trip cruise from Vineyard Haven to Bassett's Island on the Buzzard's Bay side of Cape Cod. This event revealed to me another aspect of sailing — cruising in the L. Francis Herreshoff spartan tradition. The sail to Bassett's Island was idyllic, but on the return leg the next day it blew a fresh breeze and in the infamous Buzzard's Bay chop *Shoal Waters* developed a leak, which turned out to be a broken through hull fitting. I stayed below with a big bucket, bailing all the way back to Vineyard Haven. I was very seasick, but when we finally arrived safely in Vineyard Haven harbor I felt exhilarated. I'd had a great time and, since then, my passion for sailing and cruising has only increased. I feel very fortunate to have been introduced to the sport by such an experienced sailor as Mait. I began at the top, so to speak, sailing a wholesome traditional boat and cruising in the most rewarding way. Soon I wanted a boat of my own that I could mess around in on my own time, and make my own mistakes. Mait recommended a Gloucester Gull dory, designed by Phil Bolger and built by Harold H. "Dynamite" Payson of South Thomaston, Maine. I called Dynamite, bought the one dory he happened to have for sale, car-topped it home to Kittery Point atop my 1968 Volvo, and commenced learning to row, trying to recall what my father had taught me about proper rowing. His father had been a professional yacht captain and in his youth my father had crewed for him and learned basic seamanship skills. Although my father actually disliked the sea and boats, I found that I loved rowing, and still do. I learned quickly. The Gloucester Gull dory is a very easy boat to row, and is very seaworthy, although tippy and tender, like most good rowing craft naturally must be.

I read voraciously about the sea, and bought or borrowed just about every nautical book I could get my hands on. Mait recommended several books and kindly loaned them to me. I recall Jan Adkins's *Craft of Sail* was especially captivating and useful, as was L. Francis Herreshoff's *The Compleat Cruiser*.

I also took my first cruises in the little dory, with back-packing gear aboard. Over the summer I explored all the tributaries of the Piscataqua River and Great Bay, and the waters around my home town of Kittery Point, Maine, especially Brave Boat Harbor, a Rachel Carson wildlife refuge where I tented ashore often. I car-topped the dory to Vinalhaven and circumnavigated the island under oars over a three-day period. I entered Bill Gribell's "Short Ships" race from Rockport to North Haven and back and was the only single oarsman. In September I entered the first Great 'Round Gerrish Island Race in Kittery Point and was the first single oarsman to finish. I loved that little light dory and highly recommend her type to anyone wanting to learn as I did, in style, with a salty boat.

In 1977 I visited with Dynamite Payson, who had by then become a dear friend. While sitting on his front step relaxing, the subject of a book he was working on came up, and before I'd left Dynamite that day he'd talked me into building a boat. It was to be one of his stock plans, the 15 ½ -foot Surf, a flat-bottomed Chesapeake Bay crab skiff with a single leg o' mutton sprit sail and a leeboard. The boat was also designed by Bolger and was supposedly very easy, simple, and quick to build, which suited me as I had no carpentry skills beyond high school shop classes. In fact, I had never really built anything before and knew almost nothing about boat building. I didn't even know what a bevel was. My assignment was to chronicle my progress and Dynamite would include it in his forthcoming book, *Instant Boats*, which he did.

I built the little skiff in my parents' garage, with hand tools and no workbench. Fiberglassing the plywood was the only aspect I didn't enjoy. Otherwise the project went well and was completed in a few months of part-time labor and at minimal cost. I bought the spritsail, a tanbark one, from Bohndell of Rockport, but otherwise made everything myself. I liked my little sailing skiff and enjoyed the experience of building her, with occasional advice and guidance from Dynamite, who is a fine teacher.

Meanwhile I took a basic sailing course at Community Boating on the Charles River in Boston and got my "helmsman's ticket." At home with my little crab skiff I now explored my nautical environment under sail, and had my share of adventures, and made my share of mistakes as well.

The *Surf* is forgiving and very safe, with positive flotation and an easily handled, simple sprit rig. She was painfully slow to windward, but a paragon of all the virtues on all other points of sail, especially downwind. If I needed to stop, I could simply let go of the sheet, and the clew would blow forward — no shrouds to crash against. She was fast on a reach and even faster if I removed her one lee board. Of course, she'd slip sideways a little without the board, but in 10 knots of wind or more, I could get her going fast enough so that she would tack if I put the helm down smartly. I had great fun with her reaching back and forth between Newcastle and Fort Foster at the mouth of the Piscataqua River, where in a southerly on the ebb a substantial sea develops. The Surf could also be made to steer herself with some patient tinkering of sail trim, crew weight, and tied-off tiller. I once sailed her from Whaleback to Gosport Harbor (Isles of Shoals), without touching the tiller. I camp-cruised in her often, and after a few years sold her to someone on the Vineyard, where I believe she still resides.

My next boat was a giant step up, a 17' L. Francis Herreshoff centerboard knockabout, design #39, created in 1929 as the Suicide Class. She was masterfully built in Camden, Maine, by Bill Cannell and his crew. I've owned her since 1982 and would hate to part with her. She is very fast and a first class ghoster. Her four-inch draft allows marsh crawling and easy trailering. She weighs around 600 lbs. without her rig and can be moved around relatively easily on shore. She sails wonderfully on all points but wants a reef early. I don't hesitate to tuck in a reef with her because she sails fine reefed, even in light air. Her 125-square-foot sail area is about perfect for her size. I like her self-tending club jib, great for single-handing, even though she would no doubt sail even better with a loose-footed jib. She is built exactly according to Herreshoff's plans and I've had no desire to change anything. I've camp-cruised (Mait Edey calls it "damp cruising.") in her to Brave Boat Harbor and the Isles of Shoals, and have had countless pleasurable day sails around Pepperell Cove. Her only vice is rather extreme tenderness. She has no ballast, which is one reason she is so fast in light air, and I've capsized four times in her. I have blocks of Styrofoam strapped in fore and aft, which allows her to be bailed out with me aboard in the event of a hard chance. She is perhaps the most beautiful boat I have ever seen. Her lines have the magic of the Francis Herreshoff classic *Rozinante*, and the simplicity of his *Quiet Tune*. Like both of them, she is miniature — she looks bigger than she actually is, and you realize that when you go aboard. She's most comfortable when I sit sideways, butt on the narrow deck, facing to leeward. I have a hiking stick on the tiller, and I hike out frequently. With two aboard she is more stable and seems just as fast, but she can be cramped. The crew must be lively.

There is another Design #39 in Pepperell Cove now, a cold-molded, super-light version built by Brad Story. She capsized on her mooring last year. I've always worried about mine doing that (it was a common occurrence for my *Surf*), but she never has yet. My boat is carvel-planked, cedar on oak and is much heavier than Brad Story's version, especially her mast, which is actually the mizzen taken from an old *Rozinante*. Cannell built her right. After all these years she still doesn't leak, and looks as new except for black stains on her oak rub rails. I love her dearly.

But I had the urge to do some serious cruising and my little knockabout just wasn't big enough. I studied plans, hobnobbed with other boaters, and watched the classified ads. Mait urged me to consider shoal draft as a requisite. I'd fallen in love with Phil Bolger's Black Skimmer design when I first laid eyes on her plans in the book, *The Folding Schooner*, which also had been where the *Surf* had caught my eye. Black Skimmer was like a larger version of my *Surf*. She had two leeboards and a one-foot draft. She had plenty of sprawl space below, a big double berth, floatation, and a simple cat yawl rig. Outboard power was plenty enough to move her in a calm. I thought perhaps she could be rowed or sculled. I took imaginary cruises in her in my easy chair, plans in hand. Then I heard that Walter Barron of Wellfleet was building a Black Skimmer for a client. Mait and I went to Walter's shop to inspect it. She looked big to me, and Mait approved of her, but she was too expensive! Out of my league then and now. But good things come to those who wait patiently, and in 1984, *Tashtego*, the very same Black

Skimmer Walter had built, came up for sale. With a bit of luck I managed to buy her. She was stored uncovered at a boatyard in Orleans, Massachusetts, and needed some TLC, which I gave her between February and her launch in late April. I installed a Lunenberg Foundry "Gift" cast iron solid fuel stove in her and slept aboard her in the boatyard several cold weekends so I could get more work done. Painting her topsides took longer than expected; I'd finish too late in the day. That night there was a frost on the Cape, and when I returned to my boat her topsides were no longer clean, bright Interlux Sea Green, but were an ugly mass of ice crystal patterns. I had to sand it all off and begin again. Don't paint late in the day!

I had *Tashtego* more or less ready for her late April launch date at Meetinghouse Pond. All went as planned, except the Chrysler outboard motor wouldn't start. It would be a thorn in my side as long as I owned the boat. We stepped the mast easily with a front-end loader. Once out on the mooring I commenced bending on sail. I'd oiled the spruce spars as directed, but the oil had not dried sufficiently, and I couldn't raise the Dutch-laced mainsail until it had thoroughly dried, which took several days, but eventually the big main went up and especially down slick as a whistle. I became fond of Dutch lacing. I slept aboard *Tashtego* weekends during May with the stove glowing. I was getting used to her gradually. Our relationship deepened when I had my first sail in her one brisk afternoon in early May. She proved to be quite different from what I'd expected and hoped. She wouldn't tack! She'd look up into the eye of the wind and stop, then fall back on the previous tack. I almost lost her on a lee shore, but for once the motor started, and I was able to power her around at the last moment. Bolger recommended sailing her to windward with both leeboards down when short-handed, but I found that despite the fresh breeze she had far too much drag with both boards down. Her leeboards were unworkably heavy, and I had to haul one of them every tack, which proved vexing and exhausting. Even with diligent leeboard tending, *Tashtego* still wouldn't tack. Eventually I learned to smartly back the main or mizzen; it didn't seem to matter which, and she would briefly sail backward and then usually manage to fall off on the desired tack.

A wide, flat bottom with eddying outside chines, coupled with big leeboards and a high-windage rig do not for good windward performance make. I eventually made it safely to a designated mooring in Pleasant Bay, got things squared away, and collapsed below exhausted and rather disappointed with my new boat's maiden voyage. In fact, I was downright depressed. What had looked like my dream boat on paper had proved something of a nightmare in reality. *Tashtego* hated to tack, and for an inveterate single-hander who rather enjoys sailing to windward, that was anathema. I'd learned she could be unreliable in stays, and difficult to control in a breeze

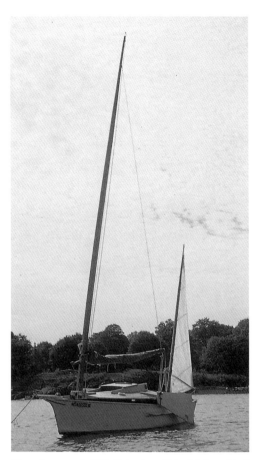

Here is one of Phil Bolger's rakish 25-foot Black Skimmers, a flat-bottom, leeboard sharpie with a cat yawl rig.

in shoal waters when her leeboards had to be up. She could, in fact, be a dangerous boat in some circumstances. I wondered if I would be able to single-hand her and realize my cruising dreams. I called Mait on the Vineyard and asked his advice. He'd chartered a Black Skimmer from Key Largo Shoal Water Cruises in Florida and had experience sailing the type. He kindly offered to come to Pleasant Bay and sail with me to the Vineyard to see what could be done to improve *Tashtego*'s performance.

Mait and I had an exciting and varied sail from Chatham to Hyannis, then on to Vineyard Haven. We tucked in reefs and shook them out. For a while we were double- reefed. Mait decided *Tashtego* needed a topping lift and block and tackle on the leeboards to make them less of an ordeal to tend. These improvements were promptly made once we arrived in Vineyard Haven, and they indeed made *Tashtego* easier to single-hand. We also found that with a crew of two she could sometimes be made to tack if the leeboard was tended smartly and the main quickly and radically backed. But when single-handed, I was never able to get her through the eye of the wind, not even once!

During the course of that pleasant summer season, I did eventually become better acquainted with *Tashtego*'s many vices and virtues. I sailed her all around Vineyard Sound, taking advantage of her extreme shoal draft. We put into Cuttyhunk, Quick's Hole, Robinson's Hole, Tarpaulin Cove, Menemsha, Lake Tashmoo, Edgartown, Cape Pogue, Nantucket, Wauwinet, Polpis Harbor, back to Vineyard Haven and eventually home to Maine via Red Brook Harbor, Scituate, Gloucester, and Kittery Point. Later I sailed her Down East as far as Somes Sound, putting in at Kennebunkport, Jewell Island, Harpswell, Cape Newagen, Boothbay Harbor, Round Pond, Harbor Island, Allen Island, Carver's Harbor, Seal Bay, Perry Creek, Pulpit Harbor, Brooklin, Bass Harbor, and no doubt a few other places now forgotten. I learned to sail her on her side when possible, as is recommended for sharpie types when attempting to go to windward. I learned to take advantage of her self-steering capabilities and sailed her from Mark Island Light in Deer Isle Thoroughfare to Winter Harbor in Vinalhaven without touching the tiller; ditto from Nubble Light in York to Kittery Point. *Tashtego* was fine downwind; wing and wing with lee boards up, she flew. But to windward and in light air she was far too slow for me. I put her on the market and she quickly sold by October. I subsequently sailed her in Florida Bay where her new owners kept her. She was really in her element there and is ideally suited for those shoal waters.

Today, many years later, I sometimes miss the Black Skimmer, and all the things that only a extremely shoal draft boat like her can do. I suspect Bolger's Skillegallee design would be an improvement on Black Skimmer. Skillegallee's lengthened water line should make her faster to windward, and her off-centerboard would make her much easier to tack while preserving most of the desirable sprawl space below. In fact, I almost bought the original Skillegallee; I really wanted her and the price was right, but she was on the West Coast and to get her east would have cost too much, so I had to let her go. But I still dream of her. I very much like the cat yawl rig and sprit booms for cruising, and the wet wells fore and aft prove handy and workable. The simplicity of sharpies makes them easy to maintain and keep clean. Just don't expect head room. In a chop, nights aboard can be like trying to sleep inside Gene Krupa's bass drum. Bolger admits it is best to hunt up some shoal creek for a quiet night. That said, a sharpie may be the most boat for the money. For running and reaching they perform exceptionally well and can often be made to self-steer with a patient adjustment of board and sail trim, and in the *Surf's* case, crew weight.

On that memorable, vexing maiden voyage with *Tashtego*, after I finally made my assigned mooring in Pleasant Bay, I was standing in the companionway looking aft, feeling glad to be secure in the gusty northwest wind, when I spied a small sail on the horizon to the southeast. As the boat tacked closer and closer, I recognized it as a double-reefed Marshall Sanderling, an 18-foot fiberglass catboat, beating in from Chatham and seeming to be having an easy time of it. Eventually she sailed up to a mooring near to mine. Her experienced skipper picked up the pennant smartly, quickly and easily doused the gaff main, and had things squared away and was ashore in no time. I thought to myself: "That's the boat I should have bought."

With *Tashtego* gone, I again found myself without a cruising boat. Again I networked and scanned the ads. I looked at a few Alberg Sea Sprites, a Cape Dory 25, a Tartan 27, a Sparkman and Stephens Yankee Dolphin, a Herreshoff Marlin, a Mason Ostkust, a Folkboat, and others unmemorable. All were either too expensive or too far gone. But in early summer I noticed an ad for a Marshall 18-foot catboat located in Plymouth. I went down to inspect her and found her neglected, but a price was agreed upon and I had myself another cruising boat, one I liked and knew would sail well. However, in the days it took to finalize the transaction and get the catboat registered and shipshape, a hurricane slid up the East Coast, headed straight for Plymouth. Mait had invited me to join him on a short cruise from Vineyard Haven to Nantucket aboard his new 36-foot Bolger-designed tandem centerboard sharpie cat yawl *Dakini*, and I found myself anchored with him in Nantucket Harbor as the menacing storm steadily drew closer. I suspected Mait could manage well without me, so I took the last ferry from Nantucket and just made Plymouth before the storm. I didn't want to have my new purchase sitting there unattended. The storm proved to be an anticlimax, but my first night aboard my new catboat was spent riding out the remnants of a hurricane, an auspicious beginning. After the storm was well past, I sailed the little Sanderling home to Kittery Point via Gloucester. She proved delightful to sail, just as I hoped she would be. She wanted a reef early, but once that was done she handled well in all reasonable conditions. Double-reefed she could take a really fresh breeze in stride. I never missed stays in her, unlike with *Tashtego*. The Marshall sailed well with very little centerboard down, which made her a better gunkholer than *Tashtego* had been. Her obvious vices were the small cabin, cramped by the centerboard trunk, and the inevitable catboat weather helm, but both had been anticipated and were acceptable to me at that time.

I renamed her *Rum Tum*, after T. S. Eliot's *The Book of Practical Cats*. The dinghy was *Tugger*. I found no reason to alter the standard Marshall Sanderling configuration; everything worked and seemed to work well. Mait had already taught me how to raise and lower gaff rig, and how to reef smartly. The topping lift kept the long boom out of the waves when broad off and out of the cockpit when raising and lowering sail. The Mercury outboard even worked after a fashion. *Rum Tum* would even steer herself when going to windward, though never running and reaching like the sharpies would do. *Rum Tum* proved to be surprisingly seaworthy; only a short, steep chop could stop her. She was dry in a seaway and quite comfortable by my spartan standards. When I let go of the main sheet, she would round up to about 50-60 degrees to the wind and sit there like a duck, happy as could be while

I went about doing what needed to be done; when I was ready to get under way again, a tug on the mainsheet got her moving easily. Jibing was a bit of an adventure, but I'd read a fair amount of how to handle catboats, and *Rum Tum* did everything as expected. I don't recall ever having an accidental jibe in her. She did take a knockdown once, in Lake Tashmoo on the Vineyard, when we were close-hauled and the gusty northwest suddenly shifted aft, but she recovered without damage except to some stores and my ego. The ballast didn't shift. We bailed out and continued on. In subsequent years we went through some nasty weather together. She never let me down.

I worried about the centerboard scuppers being a potential hazard and kept them plugged with large thermos corks when underway. Once in a while one of those corks would pop out and water would sometimes rush in through the inch-and-a-half holes. Then I'd retrieve the errant cork, plug the spouting scupper, and bail out when I found time. This didn't happen very often and wasn't much of a problem, though it was a source of worry. The mast proved to be the boat's Achilles heel, but more on that later.

Anchoring a catboat that doesn't have a bowsprit can be challenging. I usually carried my anchors (a Danforth and a 25-pound Herreshoff) in the cockpit, secured under the seats. If I anticipated anchoring, I would round up, let go the main sheet and heave to. Then I'd go forward carefully and cleat the anchor rode, run it back through the bow chock and leave enough loose scope for something like a 5:1 ratio, in the usual relatively shoal water I normally preferred to anchor in. Then I'd haul in the main sheet and get under way again to my chosen anchoring spot. Once it was selected I'd head up into the wind, sheet uncleated, let her lose way, and slowly and carefully lower the chosen anchor overboard from the cockpit. Once the anchor was on the bottom I'd quickly douse sail, which usually landed neatly in its lazy jacks; the topping lift held the boom up until I found time to rig its crutch. If the anchor needed further setting (it usually didn't) I'd go forward after everything was secure, pay out more scope and snub it. I like big heavy anchors. I used about eight feet of chain on both of them, though now, like the late Joel White, I dispense with the chain on the Herreshoff, which makes it less of a mess to clean. It still holds the same, I think.

Hoisting anchor was more of an ordeal; I'd have to go forward on that tiny forepeak, sail luffing, and hope I could break the anchor out with my own strength; if I couldn't, I'd attempt to sail around on short scope to break it out. If that failed, I'd resort to the motor and head in the opposite direction from which the anchor had been set. Once the anchor was free, it was hasty work to clean it and get it stowed. Hopefully I would have enough sea room. In close quarters, I'd let the anchor dangle off the bow while I sailed or motored clear, then I'd finish dealing with it when we had sufficient sea room. A little bowsprit, like *Tashtego* had, would have been nice on *Rum Tum*. Sometimes I'd set the anchor when sailing downwind; I'd smartly lower it over the side from the cockpit and let the weight and momentum of the vessel snub it. This would really dig it in, and if I managed to quickly douse sail just as she rounded up it could look really salty.

Rum Tum sailed well in light air, so I only used her motor as a last resort. She was quick to get under way and put to bed. I sailed her often, and later that first summer I took her up the Maine coast just as I'd done with *Tashtego* the year before. *Rum Tum* and I put into Hog Island, Maple Juice Cove, Crockett Cove, Winter Harbor on Vinalhaven, and Somes Sound in addition to those places I'd visited previously in *Tashtego*. *Rum Tum*'s 18-inch draft and short length were wonderful for gunkholing, and we did plenty of it. I began to seriously consider my long-held dream of sailing down the Intracoastal Waterway and duplicating the voyage of Henry Plummer, as described in his epic cruising story *The Boy, Me and the Cat*.

In September of 1987, I found my way clear to undertake that demanding voyage. *Rum Tum* seemed up to the task, and so did I. *The Boy, Me and the Cat* is one of my favorite cruising stories. I'd imagined duplicating the *Mascot*'s feat for many years; I'd read everything I could find regarding the ICW; I studied maps and charts, and tried to imagine what the trip might be like in a small, shoal draft cruising boat. I was, I think, relatively well prepared for the undertaking, but money would be a problem. I would have to live frugally and have good luck. I had some savings, and planned to rent my house and use some of that income to live on during the ICW cruise, which I estimated would take a year to complete. I estimated I'd need to spend about $80 per week to cruise, in 1987 dollars.

We were under way by early September, provisioned with more of everything that we needed except warm clothes. I was to be cold and shivering for much of the downward leg of the voyage. My goal was to average 30-40 miles per day, sometimes more when conditions were right, and to lay over in protected anchorages whenever nasty weather was predicted. I hoped to keep on schedule with Henry Plummer and the *Mascot*, and be in warm southern waters by Christmas. I asked a Southern friend of mine how far I should expect to go before warm weather would be routine. "Key West", he replied! I thought he was exaggerating, but he was proven correct.

Heading south from Maine is usually a windward trip. And the afternoon sun is glaring off the water in your face. In fall, warm clothing, sunglasses, and sunscreen are a must. The wind penetrates your clothing. I'd planned to sail as much as possible and resort to the motor only in calms and when negotiating bridges and locks. As it turned out, there would be plenty of windward work, more than I expected.

We departed Pepperrell Cove in Kittery Point on September 7th, 1987 and put into Lighthouse Cove in Gloucester, North River, Red Brook Harbor, Great Harbor at Woods Hole, and finally Lake Tashmoo on Martha's Vineyard, where we spent a very pleasant layover, provisioning and visiting the Edeys.

Henry Plummer and the *Mascot* departed New Bedford on September 15th, 1912 to begin their voyage south. *Rum Tum* and I departed Lake Tashmoo on September 15th, 1987. We were able to stay more or less on schedule with Plummer throughout the voyage. Plummer put into Annapolis on November 16th, 1912; we arrived there on November 8th, 1987. Plummer made Beaufort, North Carolina on December 5th; we were there on December 2nd. Plummer was in Fernandina Beach, Florida, on January 27th, 1913; we were there on December 26th, 1987. Plummer and his *Mascot* arrived in Miami on March 3rd, 1913; we made Miami on January 24th, 1988. Plummer turned around at Miami and began his homeward leg. *Rum Tum* and I continued on southward and made Key West on March 3rd, the same day Plummer turned around at Miami and headed for home. We continued on and explored the Gulf of Mexico, went up the Florida west coast, through the Caloosahatchee and across Lake Okeechobee to Stuart, and back home from there. We caught up with Plummer again, more or less, at Fernandina; he was there on March 5th, we returned to Fernandina on April 8th; Mascot made Cape Romain on April 16th, *Rum Tum* on April 21st. He was in Norfolk on April 30th, we were there on May 11th. He made the C&D Canal on May 18th, and we made it on June 19th after a layover in Solomons, Maryland. *Mascot* was in Oyster Bay, New York, on June 3rd, and we put in there on June 24th. Plummer and the *Mascot* completed their voyage on June 22nd; we arrived in Padanaram, near where the Mascot started, on June 29th. We were home in Kittery Point on July 13th, 10 months and five days from when we began. We spent 166 days underway versus 104 days for Plummer (remember we went much further, and no doubt sailed much faster than the *Mascot*). *Mascot's* voyage took eight months and eight days, and she put into 101 different anchorages. *Rum Tum* put her hook down in 168 different anchorages. So we sailed faster, went farther, visited more ports, and did it all single-handed in a smaller boat. Plummer suffered a serious grounding on deadly Frying Pan Shoals near Cape Fear, South Carolina, on December 10th, 1913, and nearly lost his boat. *Rum Tum* endured numerous motor failures and the necessary repairs delayed her several times on our downward leg, but our worst moment was a dismasting on October 29th, 1987, near the mouth of the Sassafras River in Chesapeake Bay. With a loud report the unstayed aluminum mast suddenly broke completely off at the partners, just as we came on a port tack in about a 15-knot southerly, much as we'd done thousands of times before. Fortunately we had sea room and sea conditions were moderate. With Herculean effort I was able to eventually get all the gear on board after a fashion and motor on up the Sassafras to a friendly boatyard for help. Corrosion caused by electrolysis at the stainless steel halyard collar had chosen just that moment to reveal its weakness and cause mast failure. There was no visible sign of this serious problem before the dismasting. I thought my mast was fine until it suddenly failed without warning. Mast failure like this is a not uncommon problem with older Marshall catboats. There is tremendous stress and strain at the partners on any mast without shrouds; it's surprising they last as long as they do. I was anxious about *Tashtego*'s totally unstayed spruce mast failing just as *Rum Tum*'s aluminum one had done, and though it gave no trouble when I owned her it subsequently did fail later when she was under new ownership. Keep an eye on your unstayed mast and expect to have to replace it someday. Some catboats do have shrouds but it's tricky to get enough spread to make them useful. Shrouds also create windage, added expense, and hassle. *Rum Tum* got a new aluminum extrusion from Marshall's, and we refitted and continued on our way without further mast problems.

Other than motor and mast failure *Rum Tum* proved to be a wonderful vessel for the ICW voyage, though *Tashtego* might have been even better, with her larger cuddy, storage space, handy anchor and motor wells, mizzen, and eight-inch draft. But alas, I'd already sold her. The Marshall Sanderling was very handy when poking up narrow creeks and channels; she could be turned around with relative ease, and was always responsive to her tiller (except when broad reaching in a stiff breeze, when her extreme weather helm could make her hard-mouthed). It's not exactly easy to live in such a small, cramped cuddy for 10 months and five days; my back began to bother me along toward the end of it. But many things in boating are a trade-off or compromise, and the bigger the boat, the bigger the problems.

With *Rum Tum* and *Tashtego* I could take off the motor and carry it ashore for repairs. Gas and oil could be kept out of the sleeping area. *Tashtego* had no through hull fittings to give trouble; *Rum Tum* had only one and I kept a close eye on it. Simplicity is golden in small boat cruising. Get rid of everything you don't need or use. Don't rely on motors or radios (neither boat had a VHF radio; I did carry a battery powered NOAA weather receiver to monitor weather forecasts). A small cruising boat should be handy under sail, and should be maneuverable under oars or towable from a dinghy. I always carried at least two stout anchors; you can't have too many in the event of a storm. The Bahama moor was my choice for the shifting currents of the ICW; it kept us more or less in place and where we intended to be, and helped promote sound sleep. I'm very fond of my Herreshoff/Luke anchor and would hate to cruise without it. For grass, weed, rock, or hard bottom, it is my first choice. A Danforth type, with its wide surface area, is a good choice for soft bottom such as mud or beach sand. All anchors like plenty of scope. If you don't have swinging room, consider the Bahama moor. Just watch out that no one else fouls one of your rodes.

I prefer a hard dinghy for cruising. I enjoy rowing and appreciate good rowing qualities in a tender. Positive flotation is highly desirable, as is lightness and relatively small size. I think Joel White's Nutshell pram makes an ideal tender. I used my Gloucester Gull dory as a tender for *Tashtego* and they made a handsome couple, but the light dory didn't tow especially well as she loved to surf down the face of following seas and attack the transom of the mother ship. She was a joy to row however, and after anchoring, I usually took a long leisurely row around the area to explore and scope things out. With an attractive rowing boat one is often hailed; a friendly gam ensues and you may be invited aboard for a drink or dinner. That is less likely to happen if you are racing around the anchorage in a noisy smelly inflatable. Alas, my beloved little dory was destroyed by a careless tree surgeon who dropped a 100-year-old pine tree right on top of her. I got restitution and purchased a 14' Lincoln Rangeley, a fiberglass replica of a 19th century Rangeley Lakes rowing boat, such as was popular before the advent of the outboard motor. I suspected the Lincoln Rangeley, with its modern low maintenance fiberglass construction and positive flotation, would be an overall improvement on the light dory. The Rangeley was my faithful tender on all my cruises in *Rum Tum*, including the entire ICW trip. Though rather heavy for her type, she proved an excellent choice for my intended purposes; she rows well in all conditions, has two rowing stations, can carry a load, and is very pretty. She is ruggedly constructed and has held up well after years of hard use. I still have her and row her often.

I realize that a long, lean pulling boat is not the ideal tender for everyone. Such types tend to be expensive, relatively fragile, and in some cases more boat than one needs for the purpose. There's much to be said for an inflatable on the rocky coast of Maine, for example, where landing can be hard on an expensive, fragile, light pulling boat. With the inflatable, you just charge right on in. But towing the inflatable is problematic. Perhaps the Nutshell pram or something similar is the best all-around choice for a cruising tender. She rows and even sails well, is pretty, and is small and relatively light in weight. Her type seems to tow about as well as any. Currently I'm using a similar type of small pram for my tender, an eight-foot plywood and fiberglass three-seater, easy to tow and small enough to squeeze into crowded floats. She's not so valuable that I would be heartbroken if I lost her. But I do miss rowing around the anchorages in style, so the Rangeley may be pressed into service again as my cruising tender.

I kept *Rum Tum* for a few years after completion of the ICW trip and found no serious fault with her. I always admired her looks and still do. But I'd never owned a keel sloop and was curious about owning one and cruising in it. *Rum Tum* and *Tashtego* had both been good safe cruising boats overall, but I'd sometimes been a bit anxious about the possibility of a capsize, and in *Rum Tum*'s case being pooped by a following sea. This never even came close to happening, but the sloop's ability to handle rough sea conditions, its good windward performance, and the possibility of full headroom seemed appealing, and I thought I wanted a bigger boat. The Marshall catboats hold their value well, and when I hesitantly put *Rum Tum* on the market she sold right away, just as *Tashtego* had done, and I suddenly found myself without a cruising boat again. I thought I'd be able to quickly replace *Rum Tum* with a 25-30-foot keel sloop. There were numerous attractive values on the market then if you could do your own work and didn't mind doing it. I'd seen Pearson Vanguards, Alberg 30's, Contessa 26's, Bristol 29's, Tartan 27's, and the like at bargain prices, though they would need considerable work and TLC. I scoured the want ads and prowled around boatyards in search of just the right cruising sloop that would touch my heart, but it would be more than 10 years before I found her. It seemed everything I wanted was either just sold, too expensive, or too far gone. At one point I even came perilously close to buying another Bolger Black Skimmer, but wisely backed out of the deal at the last minute when I discovered extensive hidden dry rot in her plywood hull. I consoled myself in the meantime with day sailing around Pepperrell Cove in my little Herreshoff knockabout, which is not exactly suffering, after all. In fact it's about as much fun as it's possible to have in a boat, but it's not cruising, and I yearned to go cruising once again.

I looked at countless boats and traveled far and wide to inspect them but without success. Then, thanks to a friend, I discovered the existence of a 28-foot Philip Rhodes Ranger sloop, which had been stored in a heated garage, unused, for more than 9 years. The boat was less than a mile from my house in Kittery Point. I'd long admired the Rhodes Ranger sloops, and could even vaguely recall seeing this very one at her mooring in Kittery Point many years before, and coveting her. I called her owner and made arrangements to inspect her that very day. I liked her even though she needed work. I made an offer and she was mine. By then it was the end of the season, so rather than launch her (she was fit enough to be commissioned even then) I had her hauled to my house and I commenced sanding and re-coring the decks following the West System manual to the letter, with good results. I finished the decks with Interlux Brightsides Off White, sprinkling sand in the paint where necessary to provide a non-skid surface.

By the following July I had her ready for launching. After several day sails and a short cruise to the Isles of Shoals I felt ready for an extended cruise and managed to pry out the time for it in August. *Cygnus*, the original name of my "new" 1962 Rhodes Ranger sloop, proved to be all I'd hoped she'd be. Despite her modest sail area (308 sq. ft.) she does surprisingly well in light air, which seems to be the norm on the coast of Maine in summer. Yet she can take quite a bit of wind before she demands a reef. She came with a roller-furling jib, something I'd always distrusted and would never have bought otherwise, but to my surprise I quickly became fond of it. I could roll it part way up and shorten sail quickly and easily, which I now do often. *Cygnus* sails well under the main alone, or under jib alone, which is very handy. I usually don't reef the main unless the wind is over 20 knots. She goes to windward well in all conditions anyone would want to be out in, and slices through a chop nicely. She is relatively dry, and has a nice motion most of the time, though downwind in light air and a beam sea she can "snap the buttons off your shirt" as they say. Her relatively narrow eight-foot beam and 3' 10" draft help keep her handy for her type, though she has a wide turning radius compared to my previous boats. It took me awhile to get used to that, just as it did sailing a boat with a deep draft. I have to pay closer attention to my navigation now. I've already run aground twice because of careless plotting, fortunately without serious damage. I now have a radio and an inboard engine, an Atomic Four, and yes, I can smell it in my sleeping quarter, which I dislike. *Cygnus* is more expensive to maintain, haul, and register than any of my previous boats, and I seem to be spending more time working on her than sailing her so far. She needed attention when I bought her, and her price reflected that. She's not yet quite up to my standards of appearance but I hope she will be close soon. I'm on my third summer with her now and plan to take her Down East in August, just as I've done the previous two summers.

Her draft prevents exploring the gunkholes like I've done with great pleasure in my previous sharpie and catboat, but her full headroom, solid construction, shiny varnished mahogany trim and exquisite lines are very pleasing. Phil Rhodes knew how to draw a pretty boat. I miss *Tashtego*'s little bowsprit and mizzen; I miss *Rum Tum*'s handiness and readiness to get under way and put away (I could be sailing in a matter of seconds with *Rum Tum*), and of course shoal draft allows access to what Phil Bolger refers to as "the cream of the sport." But all boats are somewhat of a compromise, I suppose. You can't have everything in any of them. I may well own another shoal draft boat someday, but for now the classic Rhodes sloop seems to be giving great satisfaction.

My sloop is a lot of boat for the money, just as all my boats have been.

I've been very fortunate in this respect, though most boat owners would probably not want to put as much hard labor into a project just to save money. But for anyone with a few tools, reasonable skills and patience and perseverance, there are still fine, suitable cruising boats waiting to be had at affordable prices. Ten thousand dollars could get you a whole lot of boat if you are patient and willing to do your own dirty work.

Old project boats are probably not cost effective if you are paying yard rates. The cheapest boat to buy may not be the cheapest boat to own, but if you can do your own work, and you worship simplicity, you definitely don't have to be rich to go cruising. You can even come out with a small profit in the end, provided you never figure in your own labor. But you'll have to constantly upgrade and do the required maintenance, the lack of which made your bargain price possible at the beginning. And don't forget the annual cost of boat ownership: hauling, storage, taxes, insurance, plus annual upkeep even under the best of circumstances, and the bigger the boat the quicker these costs multiply. Sometimes a kayak looks mighty attractive. But you can't sleep, cook, sprawl on the deck or even stand up in a kayak. You can't experience the marvel of wind power harnessed in your interest, and you can't take friends aboard, and you can't get it to steer itself while you relax and take in the view. Sailboat cruising is an acquired taste and it's perhaps not for everyone, but to those once smitten by its unique charms, it seems one of life's great pleasures. You don't have to be rich to do it. Your small, affordable boat will get you to all the places really worth visiting, and in your own unique style. Think about what you really want in a boat, and what really makes you happy and satisfied. Perhaps it's the boat itself, its seductive beauty and charm; you'll enjoy looking at her lovely lines and shape as you row away from her after a day sail. Maybe you enjoy boat work, and may even derive greater satisfaction from building than sailing, as the late Bud McIntosh claimed he did. Or, perhaps like me, it's using your boat that gives the greatest reward, going places only a boat can take you, living aboard, with a movable waterfront view. Perhaps you like to study wildlife and marine biology, or you are an artist, deriving inspiration from the nautical environment. Or maybe you cherish a quiet place to study, dream, and escape the rat race. Once you've been seduced by boating it seems really hard to be without it. I dread the day when I'm too old to sail. No time to lose . . . better get out there now and start sanding for that next coat of varnish, or else we'll never get to Brooklin by August.

Editor's Note: for specifications of the Marshall 18, see Chapter One.

CHAPTER 4

⚠

My Years with *Sea Dart*

BY RON REIL

*Ron Reil was born in 1946, the son of a highly decorated World War
II Air Force officer. He spent his formative years on Okinawa where
he leaned to sail and SCUBA dive. The China Sea soon became his
playground, and he was spending almost as much time on and in it as
attending school. Following his graduation from high school in a small
Oregon coast community, Ron attended Oregon State University for a
short time, and then opted to enter the Navy. After discharge, Ron took
off on a long dreamed-of exploration of the world by sailboat. This was
a direct result of having read Thor Heyerdahl's Kon Tiki. Years later,
aboard his first small yacht Vega, Ron met Thor who was then at sea on
the Ra II off Barbados. Following his sailing years, Ron returned to OSU
to obtain a degree in engineering. Presently he teaches science at the junior
high level in Boise, Idaho, and owns a small metal arts studio, Golden Age
Forge, where he produces custom decorative blacksmith and Repousse'
metalwork for clients as far away as Japan and New Zealand.*

M Y RELATIONSHIP WITH THE 21-FOOT YACHT *Sea Dart* began
when I was stationed at the U.S. Navy's facility in Barbados in the late
'60s. One day a Navy friend who was interested in owning a small yacht for
use with his family asked whether I would go with him to look at a boat that
had sailed in from England and was for sale. I already owned another small
English-built fiberglass yacht, *Vega*, so I was not particularly interested in
owning a second boat, but I was also preparing for an extended world cruise
that would begin when my enlistment in the Navy concluded in October of

1972, so other available yachts were always of interest to me.

We arranged to meet the owner and to go aboard *Sea Dart* one afternoon. The boat was anchored behind the Barbados Yacht Club. We arrived on schedule, only to find that the owner was nowhere in sight. We waited for a suitable period of time, and then had to decide whether we would leave, and have to make another appointment and drive the long drive down the island again, or go have a look on our own. We decided to swim out the quarter mile distance and look over the boat on our own even though we would not have access to the interior of the cabin.

As we approached the salty little yacht I was initially impressed by *Dart*'s bowsprit, which was a small spruce spar stayed with three heavy chains. This was a stout little craft, and the attention to important details was clearly evident, even from a distance. What really struck me was what came into view as I swam up under the bow. I looked up and saw two hand-carved blue dolphins that were attached on either side of the bow, just below the sprit. They were beautifully done, and they bespoke the attention to detail and loving care that had gone into the construction and fitting out of little *Sea Dart*. I was impressed. I also felt a touch of envy that my friend might become the owner of *Dart*. *Sea Dart* was a *lot* more boat than my *Vega*, even though, by comparison, *Vega* was a sports car and *Sea Dart* a long-haul freighter.

We climbed up into the cockpit where the beauty of the varnished wood of the cockpit and decorative Turks-heads adorning the tiller gave a seafaring flavor to the boat that I had never experienced in any other yacht, especially the sterile plastic boats like my *Vega*. It was apparent that the owner or builder of this boat loved it, and had spent an enormous amount of time in preparing *Sea Dart* for her destiny. I fell in love with *Dart* on the spot.

A few minutes later the owner arrived in a little inflatable dinghy. After the formalities were over, Captain Osborne opened the boat so we could go inside. Entering *Dart*'s cabin that first time evoked feelings that are hard to describe. I was in awe at what I saw. This was a boat fit for the ocean, and in fact she was built to transit the Northwest Passage. The cabin seemed permeated with seagoing tradition. There was more decorative ropework, and the rich hardwood interior was equipped with top quality, fully gimbaled, kerosene lights in every location that a light might be needed, and they were lights unlike any I had seen in the United States. They were of extraordinary quality.

Topside, and below deck, all of *Dart*'s hardware was unlike any I had seen before. I had been on many yachts over the years, but none had hardware like I saw on *Dart*. No cheap-looking chromed fittings were to be seen. All of the hardware was brass or bronze, and designed for a boat at least twice *Dart*'s size. The standing rigging was galvanized, high-strength cable, having traditional eye splices at the ends that had been turned and served in ancient seagoing tradition. Everything, including the cable itself, was heavily coated in linseed oil. The shrouds were sized for a boat much larger than *Dart*, even though they supported a mast that was only about two thirds the length expected for a boat of *Dart*'s length.

Dart had three shrouds on each side, two forestays to make running two jibs wing and wing very easy, and twin backstays. She also had two heavy eight-foot long spruce whisker poles that clipped to fittings at the base of the mast, and splayed out to clip on the outer shroud line on each side. A radar reflector was mounted between the two backstays. It was apparent that while *Dart* might not be rigged for speed, she was extremely well equipped, and she could probably weather a hurricane and survive.

Everything about *Dart* was "old school." The only modern piece of hardware I observed was a roller reefing main boom. The mainsail was also equipped with three rows of reefing points in case the roller system should pack up at sea. Probably the most telling feature I observed, and one that told me how knowledgeable the owner must be, was the lack of rigging inside the aluminum mast. All halyards went through blocks firmly shackled to the top of the mast, making them instantly accessible for repair should a failure occur at sea.

Dart was built of marine plywood. There was one vertical joint on each side of the boat that was heavily backed with an internal wood splice plate. I didn't like the fact that the splice was at the same location on each side, creating a possible "hinge point" at that location, but the boat was very well designed in other respects. The forepeak bulkhead, and the double walls that created a little storage area just forward of the galley, provided extreme stiffness to the boxy little boat. In addition, the deck had a reverse shear turtleback design that you could jump on with as much force as you could muster, and it was rock solid — no give whatsoever.

According to Osborne the hull was coated with 21 laminations of an impermeable rubberized silk fabric, and that may be why the interior of the bilges remained bone dry after so many years in the water. The hull coating had kept *Dart* dry, but when I later pulled *Dart* to work on her hull, I had to strip off a number of layers because they had delaminated. I didn't remove all of them, and I didn't remove any one layer completely, just in those locations were it was unsound. After I painted the bottom with several heavy coatings of antifouling paint, I had no further problems with the hull.

The portholes were also a step above the norm. There was an internal Lexan plate that was the watertight member. On the outside was a second heavy Lexan or Plexiglas plate that was a "pressure plate," to withstand whatever impacts the sea might deliver. This design was used for all the ports on *Dart*, in the hull as well as the doghouse. There was also a small hole drilled in the bottom of each pressure plate to connect the internal trapped air space to the outside to provide a moisture escape route. Everything was bedded in mastic to provide an absolute barrier to the water, including the plywood edges between the two Lexan plates. Because *Dart* always sailed with her lee rail under, the lee ports were almost always underwater when under sail, so we had an interesting view into the sea from the cabin interior. When sailing in shoal waters it was like being in a glass-bottomed boat.

Dart had a tall wind vane steering gear mounted on the stern. It was not one with a complex servo system, just a very simple design that derived the force to control its own little rudder totally from the wind...not very effective in light winds, but it made up for its limitations with its simplicity. As I would later learn, *Dart* could be trimmed to sail very well on most headings without the use of the wind vane at all. That ability to balance and trim *Sea Dart* to sail on a given heading made the use of such a simple and "weak" wind vane steering gear possible as well as effective.

Captain Osborne showed us the equipment and supplies that went with *Dart*, should one of us purchase her. All the various storage spaces, including the bilges, were packed with equipment and food. When he lifted the deck boards to access the bilge, I was astounded. The bilges were still totally dry; having never seen water since the boat first touched the brine. There was still sawdust in corners that had never been cleaned out since the time of her construction six or eight years earlier, and this boat had crossed an ocean! The bilge was full of little waterproof plastic containers holding everything from spare rigging to medicines. There were also cans of food, including cans of Lyle's Syrup, and a very large can containing an entire chicken. The cans were dry and unrusted, and still had their original paper labels glued on them, untouched by moisture. I had never seen a wooden boat that was so totally dry inside. The actual space in the bilges was very small, only a few inches deep. Most of the space for storage was under the four bunks. Removing the thin mattress pad and opening hatches accessed this space.

In one corner of the boat there was a very large wicker-covered hand-blown green glass jug, complete with a stout wicker handle. It must have held one-and-a-half or two gallons. That jug eventually became my rum jug, and was always kept filled with rum from the last island that I had spent time on. I still regret not keeping that jug when I later sold *Dart* to Tristan Jones.

One of the details that struck anyone entering the cabin was a series of numbers carved deeply into the deck beam, just inside its little dog-house. This was *Dart*'s documentation number. She was a registered British vessel, and wore her registry proudly for all to see. To enter the cabin you ducked under the sliding hatch cover. It was very heavily constructed of hardwood and cambered plywood, and was additionally reinforced against the power of the sea and storm with a very heavy canvas cover that was track mounted to the top of the doghouse. The hatch cover slid up under it, and it was longer than the hatch cover to allow full movement of the sliding hatch. When the sliding hatch cover was pushed aft and the removable companionway boards were in place, the canvas hatch cover could be cinched down with a heavy draw cord, so there was no possible avenue for water to enter the cabin, even in a full knock-down or rollover. This boat was built for the worst the sea could offer in every detail. The canvas cover was adorned in black and red marking pens with the names of the various places *Dart* had visited during her voyage from England to Barbados.

When we looked into the forepeak storage locker there was a 70-pound two-piece Fisherman anchor. It was *Dart*'s emergency storm anchor, and I would take it out of the locker for use only twice during the three years that I owned *Dart*. There was also about 35 feet of chain that led up through a small chain pipe to the heavy CQR pattern anchor that was tied down to fittings on *Dart*'s foredeck when *Dart* was under way. The forepeak hatch was decorated with a painting of a tall ship.

Also packed into the minimal forepeak locker space were two jibs, including a large genoa that was, however, anything but a light air sail. Because space was limited, limiting the number of sails, all the sails on *Dart* were built for heavy weather, not for ghosting along in light winds. All the sails on *Dart* were made of very heavy synthetic fabric that could stand the rigors of a North Sea gale, critical if she was to survive the storms during a voyage through the Northwest Passage. They were all handmade sails. In places where the stresses would be the greatest there were as many as 21 layers of heavy canvas sewn together. I know that because I once had to repair one of the sails the old-fashioned way, with palm and sail needle. I had to hand-sew all 21 layers of fabric. It took me over two days to complete the sewing! That was a job that I would not want to have to repeat.

Among the sails was a tiny triangular sail that was made of the heaviest canvas I had ever seen in a sail. It was massive in every regard except size. It was *Dart*'s storm-trysail. To have need for that sail it would indeed have to be the ultimate storm. Little did I know that I would one day skipper a boat not much larger than *Dart* through just such a storm in a five-day fight for survival.

The only item of equipment on *Dart* that was not top quality was the engine. The engine was a small outboard motor that was hidden in a well at the back of the cockpit. The outboard motor shaft stuck down through a small opening in the hull, which had two little doors with cutouts that exactly fit the shape of the outboard shaft they closed around. The problem with the arrangement was that the engine was air-cooled. Trapped inside the poorly ventilated engine compartment, the outboard would overheat after only 10-15 minutes of operation. Although that sounds like a big problem, it wasn't. *Dart* went almost everywhere under sail, so the only time the engine was ever used was to make short moves in an anchorage where it might be needed a few minutes at most. It was never used at sea. I wanted to get a good water-cooled engine to replace it, but I never did change it.

In the stern, *Dart* had a spacious lazarette that held just about anything that wouldn't fit elsewhere, including the deflated dinghy, another anchor, spare line, and many miscellaneous items, including a very fine taffrail-log used for measuring distance covered at sea. When mounted on its bracket on the stern, it towed a gray spinner or rotor that spun the trailing cord. The spinning cord registered the distance run in a given time on an ornate clock-like dial on the brass-housed instrument. It was a wonderfully precise device that I used extensively in the years I sailed her. Fortunately it had spare rotors because I soon learned why you don't trail them when near land...they are wonderful lures for sharks or other predator fish. They are painted gray to minimize the chance of attack, but they are still prone to be eaten when near land where there are high concentrations of fish.

Dart was a very stubby little boat. She had a reasonably broad seven-foot beam, hard chines, and exceptionally shallow 2' 3" draft. She had three keels. The main keel was massive, lead weighted, center mounted, and had a flat bottom about 10 inches wide. It stuck down below the hull only about a foot. On either side of the main ballast keel were steel bilge keels that were firmly attached at an outward angle, and were separated from the center keel by perhaps a foot of distance where they contacted the hull. They splayed outward toward Dart's hard chines. This arrangement of three keels had some distinct advantages, and some disadvantages. The main disadvantage was speed. *Dart* was slow, and rarely sailed over four knots, a little over five at most, and all that surface area added a lot of drag, especially if not kept clean.

The three keels provided some unique advantages, however. Of course the one obvious advantage is her ability to "take to the hard." The bottom was not something to be feared with *Dart*. She could be sailed into shallow water at high tide and allowed to ground as the tide went out. She would stand there solidly and securely on her three keels and stout rudder bracket with her mast standing vertical. Living on a boat that can take to the hard and remain vertical is a distinct advantage in places where there is a big tide range. However, the tropics have a minimal tide range, so this was not of great advantage where I sailed *Dart*.

What was of particular advantage in the tropical seas was *Dart*'s shoal draft. Considering that there are many places in the Caribbean and the West Indies that can be visited only by a shoal draft boat, this gave *Dart* access to a great many locations that other "normal" boats could not get into. This also gave *Dart* added security because she could sail into very shallow protected bays during stormy weather, besides having the ability to just explore where others couldn't go.

The fellow who asked me to go with him to look at *Dart* confided to me on our way home that *Dart* was way more boat than he wanted to get involved with, and that he would not be making an offer for her. That was music to my ears, and I immediately began planning to purchase *Dart* myself. I knew nothing about the boat's heritage other than it was one of a class of boats known generally as the Debutante class. More important was what I could see of the boat with my own eyes, and the impression the vessel gave me of her suitability for ocean cruising. In these regards, *Sea Dart* gave me every confidence.

Captain Osborne wanted $3,500 for the boat, and considering everything I had seen, I felt that was more than fair. There was just one problem. I couldn't buy *Dart* in U.S. currency, to which I had very limited access, so the purchase would have to be in Barbadian currency. I went to Barclay's Bank one morning and arranged to have the equivalent amount of local currency made available to me. That came out to $7,000 in cash. Thanks to a host of legal problems, I had to make the purchase in cash.

Because I didn't have a car, I arranged to have my house-mate and dear friend Jack drive me to the bank to pick up the cash and then drive me down to Bridgetown to make the transaction. In Barbados they had no bills larger than $20 at the time, and the bank didn't have all that many twenties, so I ended up with huge stacks of cash that covered the entire back seat of Jack's car some six inches deep! That was a memorable drive. If we had been stopped for any reason it would have been interesting to see the reaction of the local police when they saw the mass of cash piled on the seat. We were not stopped, and *Dart* became mine.

I suddenly found myself the proud owner of two yachts. Actually I owned half of *Vega*, Jack owned the other half, and I now additionally owned *Sea Dart*. It was an interesting period of my life, but was later reconciled when Jack bought out my half- ownership of *Vega*. What was also a bit surprising is that I had bought *Sea Dart* without ever having sailed her. However, I was very confident of her qualities and limitations, having sailed many different boats since the age of 12. I had become a very good judge of boats and their abilities and, in fact, I encountered no disappointments or major surprises with *Dart. Sea Dart* was everything I had expected, and much more.

The weekend following her purchase in early 1970, I sailed *Sea Dart* the 15 miles up to Gibb's Bay where my home on the beach was located, and brought her up to within 20 feet of the shore. A number of my friends from the Navy base were waiting there for me to welcome *Sea Dart* to her new home. When I sailed in they immediately swam or waded out and climbed aboard. I soon had so many people standing on *Dart*'s deck that she was becoming dangerously top heavy and threatening to roll over far enough to dump everyone into the sea. Soon *Dart* was safely anchored just off the beach, and the number of people on her dwindled to just a few. The only thing remaining to do was to provide *Dart* a permanent mooring a safe distance off shore alongside *Vega*. Several massive bronze rings, discarded by the Navy, soon found their place on the bottom of Gibb's Bay as *Dart*'s new mooring anchor.

Buying *Sea Dart* was a big gamble for me. I still had almost two years remaining in the Navy, and I was getting "short" in Barbados. As expected, I soon received orders that would take me away from the laid-back tropical life I had lived for the past four years. I was ordered to report for duty in Norfolk, Virginia. This was expected, but still hard to accept. I had to find someone to care for *Dart* while I was away, and there were a great many unknowns involved. The logical person was the same fellow who had originally asked me to go look at *Sea Dart* with him, so I asked him whether he would like to have Dart until I returned after my discharge from the Navy. It was a totally win-win situation for him and he quickly accepted.

My final year in the Navy passed agonizingly slowly, especially so while I followed the path of each Atlantic hurricane on its track north. However no hurricanes hit Barbados that year, and the magic day finally arrived. On October 22, 1972, I became a civilian, free to once again return to Barbados and *Sea Dart*. After a short visit with my parents in Oregon, and a stop in the Florida Keys to pick up my sailing companion, Brooks Fitzpatrick, I found myself flying south toward Barbados and whatever lay ahead. My plans were to sail *Sea Dart* around the world, but no one knows what events may alter their carefully crafted plans.

I had not been idle while in Norfolk. During that final year in the Navy I had become friends with a local yachting hardware supplier. Every few weeks I would make a large purchase of hardware or supplies and he would ship it down to a friend of mine on the Navy base in Barbados, saving me a tremendous amount in shipping costs. When I arrived in Barbados I discovered I had filled an entire room with crates and boxes of supplies. Among the pile were three 600-foot spools of 3/4-inch nylon line. Such a large amount of line may seem unreasonable for such a small boat, but soon that 1800 feet of line would make all the difference in a life-and-death struggle to save *Dart* from the largest seas to strike Barbados in over 30 years. Arriving in Barbados was not without its own trauma and problems. The local authorities didn't want to grant us entrance to the island because we didn't have return airline tickets. They were unimpressed with my story about owning a boat that was anchored in Barbados, or my plans to sail away on a world cruise. They finally accepted my story and Fitz and I began our great adventure.

My first trauma, following our arrival on Barbados, was the condition of *Dart* when I first saw her. My "friend" had not done very well in upholding his part of the bargain. He and his family had free use of *Dart* while I was gone in exchange for maintaining her in a reasonable condition. He had certainly sailed her, but maintain her he had not. I was horrified by what I saw when I opened the hatch and looked into the cabin. A strong musty smell greeted me as I looked in at piles of wet sails left as they had been dumped after a wet day of sailing. Not only were the sails in bad condition, but the dampness from the wet sails, together with the tropical heat, had warped the floor boards, and done other damage. I sat looking in disbelief at the mess that greeted me. I had a huge job ahead to restore *Dart* to what she had been when I last saw her.

I swallowed my anger and went to work to put things right onboard *Dart*, and to get Fitz and me on our way to explore the world. The first order of business was to remove everything that was removable from *Dart* and take it ashore. I was fortunate to have use of my old home on Gibb's Bay. Fitz and I soon had *Dart* emptied out and the house filled up with the hundreds of items that were aboard *Dart* when I bought her. At least *Dart*'s store of supplies and equipment had not been removed while I was gone.

Once *Dart* was empty of all the cargo she had carried across the Atlantic, I had a new worry. Looking at the pile of equipment and supplies removed from *Dart*, and all the stuff I had shipped down in the past year, it didn't seem possible to get it all loaded on such a tiny boat. And we still had to obtain and store our food! Where would it all go?

Three months later, after almost around-the-clock work by Fitz and me, *Dart* was a new boat. She had shiny new light blue and white paint on her sides, red antifouling paint on her bottom, white paint inside, and varnish on all varnished surfaces inside and out. We had sailed *Dart* down to Bridgetown and lifted her out onto the pier with the government crane. One of the discoveries I made when working on the hull was of critical importance. The fasteners that had been used for the rudder fittings were made of brass, and the action of electrolysis had reduced the brass to a copper sponge. I could break the screws and bolts between my fingers! Obtaining the right bronze or stainless hardware became a daily struggle. I was finally able to obtain the necessary hardware, and to get it all installed, but it was a very difficult and frustrating time for me.

It was at this point that I determined the layered canvas that was covering *Dart*'s turtle back foredeck had to come off. Water had gotten under it and had caused damage. Fortunately I had discovered it early, so the damage was minimal, but the outer protective covering needed to be replaced. What to do?

I finally gritted my teeth and started ripping the covering off. That was a tough day for me. I was not at all certain I would not find massive water damage, and possibly need to replace the decking too. The complex shape of the turtleback deck would not make replacement easy, especially with the limited facilities available in Barbados. I was lucky. The deck was sound. I finally decided that the simplest solution was to use multiple layers of high quality paint, and mix sand in the top layer to provide traction. What I didn't expect was the prolonged time the very thick sanded coating would require to fully dry. It was many days before we could walk on the deck. Apparently my solution to the deck problem was a good one. It never leaked, nor did the paint bubble or peel.

The day finally arrived when all of the equipment, spare parts, newly purchased food, and Fitz and I, were permanently moved aboard. *Dart* now had a new waterline that was *two inches* higher on her sides than the painted waterline. I corrected the waterline at a later time when the opportunity presented itself. In fact, *Dart* had settled into the water by almost six inches over her empty waterline! I was almost afraid to hoist anchor and try sailing the boat. So loaded down was she that I was not at all certain she would still be stable. I shouldn't have worried. *Dart* was most certainly not fast, but her weight gave her an inertia that allowed her to plow through chop that would have slowed lighter craft of her size. She was fit for the sea, even if she was the slowest boat out there. When your life depends on the craft you live aboard, speed becomes secondary to survivability, and there was almost certainly not another boat her size afloat in the world that was more survivable than *Dart*. She was in it for the long haul.

Once I was living aboard *Dart*, her special features showed the genius that the builder had demonstrated when including them in her structure. The first, and by far most significant, was her compass and its mounting location. To enter the cabin you had to descend several steps leading down the companionway. At the top, where the cockpit met the entrance to the cabin, there was a clear waterproof Lexan plate set into the wood, providing a view down into a little compartment that was built up under the cockpit deck, or top step. In this totally protected and waterproof location was mounted the fully gimbaled, six-inch diameter, flat-faced, grid steering compass. It was wonderfully stable, no matter how bad the sea conditions, moving smoothly in its back and forth while leaving the compass card totally readable.

The longer I lived on *Dart* the more I appreciated the compass design, both the gimbaled grid steering compass itself, and its unique protected below deck location. Grid steering compasses are the only sane kind of compass for a small cruising boat. The domed compasses that are in fashion in the United States are a sad toy by comparison. The grid steering compass allows adjustment of a big outer bezel ring to the heading you wish to sail, and the large degree-circle was graduated to a single degree, so setting the course could be very precise. This was easily done by reaching under the companionway top step into the protected space and adjusting the bezel while looking down from above. It sounds awkward, but it wasn't.

The grid steering compass had a big outline north arrow on the rotating bezel cover glass. The arrow glowed brightly in the dark also, so the compass needed no electric lights. On the face of the compass card there was an identical, but slightly smaller, arrow which also glowed in the dark. When I was sailing at night, I only had to occasionally glance down to see if the two arrows lined up, one inside the other, to know if I was on course. This could have been done from a distance of 20 feet, if it were possible to get that far away. I didn't have to try to read dancing degree numbers that were moving constantly because of the boat's movement. The degree numbers were also clearly visible around the compass card without additional lights. So, if you wanted to look at degree numbers for course setting, they were there also, and very easy to read without causing eye strain. The Brits know how to build a compass!

Dart had a second compass that was mounted on the bulkhead just above the bunk where I slept. When *Dart* was under way at night, and I wasn't needed on deck and could get some sleep, I would occasionally wake up long enough to glance at the little three-inch diameter gimbaled compass, and be reassured that we were still on course. It was of value when at anchor also. When the winds change during the night it may mean an approaching storm, so seeing that the boat was still lying in the same direction provided for good sleep. It became an automatic routine for me to lift my head and glance at the little tell-tale compass several times each night.

This particular compass had a history. It had been the main steering compass on the *QE-3*, the special dory-like rowing boat that Don and Jeff Allum had rowed across the Atlantic in 1969 or 1970. They had arrived in Barbados after 72 days at sea, and stayed with Jack and me in our home on Gibb's Bay for a week before setting off on the continuation on their marathon rowing adventure to row to the United States. Because of ill health, however, they were unable to complete the voyage and ended it on a nearby island. They gave Jack and me the *QE-3* in appreciation for our hospitality, but we left it in the hands of the local yacht club where Don and Jeff had ended their adventure. Jack and I each took one memento from the QE-3, and the steering compass was mine. It was the ideal compass to be my tell-tale compass on *Dart*.

Another superb innovation was two small windows in the top of the doghouse facing aft, one on each side of the companionway. Inside the doghouse, mounted in front of the windows, were the two main instruments that *Dart* carried, her fathometer and her electronic water speed indicator. The instruments were on brackets that allowed them to be faced either forward into the cabin, or aft to be read from the cockpit. So when I was sitting at the helm I had perfect visibility of the depth indicator, the water speed indicator, and the compass, all without moving in any direction. All the instruments were totally protected from harm due to impact or from the water. The genius of the design has to be experienced to be fully appreciated.

On the left side of the companionway, next to one of the instrument windows, was a heavy cast brass ship's bell. It hung from a heavy brass bracket, and inscribed into the surface of the bell were *Dart*'s name and date of "birth." This bell had no function other than appearance, but it was a very fine bell, so I took it with me as a memento when I sold *Dart* to Tristan Jones. Many years later, when I eventually connected with Rick Segal who was restoring *Dart*, I returned the bell to be restored to its former location on *Dart*.

Ventilation of *Dart's* interior was accomplished with her one tiny forehatch. It had a heavy mahogany frame that seated down on the gasketed hatch opening. When dogged down with its heavy brass latches it was totally watertight, even if fully submerged. The hinge was on the aft side, so it opened to the front, allowing us to rig up a nylon air scoop that tied to the lifelines. This provided plenty of fresh air in the cabin in all but a dead calm. On those rare dog days, when the sea was a glassy surface and not a breath of wind stirred, the cabin became horribly hot, but those days were very rare.

I upgraded the cockpit drains on *Dart* after I bought her just as I did the drains on several other boats. Any seagoing cruising boat needs sufficiently large drains and thru-hulls to allow the cockpit to drain completely in the space of time from one wave to the next if she is pooped in heavy seas. If the cockpit doesn't drain quickly enough, the boat is set up for disaster. Most production boats have very small cockpit drains, so changing them to larger drains is a necessity before going to sea. Also of importance is the size of the cockpit. *Dart*'s cockpit was very minimal in size, yet it was big enough to be comfortable when at anchor for extended periods. The size of the cockpit and the size of the drain holes and thru-hulls are directly proportional: bigger cockpit, bigger drains. To test the drain capacity you only have to plug them, fill the cockpit with water, and time how quickly they drain the cockpit when you pull the plugs. If it takes longer than 20-30 seconds, they are too small. A final point about cockpit drains — the thru-hulls should all be fitted with a valve so that it is possible to close the thru-hull and work on the drain system, which will be connected to the thru-hull with rubber or plastic tubing. Those valves could save your boat, as well as your life if the tubing fails.

Sea *Dart* had a bow pulpit and double lifelines down both sides, providing a lot of security when in rough seas. Although I wore a harness at sea which was attached to the base of the mast, the additional security of the lifelines and stout pulpit was extremely welcome. This was especially so when I was sailing solo after Fitz's departure. The double lifelines down both gunwales were thin galvanized steel cable when I bought *Dart*. They had seen better times and were quite loose, so when I came into possession of four 1/4-inch stainless cables having swaged eyes on each end, I used them to replace the original lifelines. These much stronger cables provided good security as well as a very taut attachment for the side dodgers. The dodgers were on *Dart* when I bought her, and had "Sea Dart" printed on them in eight-inch-high letters. To preserve them, I removed the dodgers until we moved aboard *Dart* to live full time. Dodgers have a number of functions that are appreciated by the cruising sailor. They provide a feeling of security from the sea. Even though it may be mostly mental, it is comforting. They also deflect a great deal of the spray that would come into the cockpit without them, as well as shielding the sailor from the wind and the reflected sunlight. Basically, they provide walls for the cockpit, making it a much more useful living space under a much greater variety of both weather and sea conditions.

An additional benefit of dodgers is they prevent items from rolling or falling overboard. Soon the space between the dodgers and *Dart*'s cockpit spray rails became a storage location for all kinds of things, including coconuts gathered on islands we visited. Dodgers are a must-have for the cruising sailor. They need to be made of the heaviest plastic-impregnated, sun-and-rot-resistant fabric you can find. Strength is very important because they may be subjected to the full force of a breaking sea when conditions get bad. That also means the stanchions and lifelines they are attached to also need to be very strong, and *Dart*'s were. When dodgers are installed on a boat they also change how she sails. They add a lot of wind resistance, so the boat will behave differently with dodgers than without them.

When I first sailed into the Grenadines and surrounding islands, I wasn't prepared for the scarcity of fresh water. It was almost totally unavailable. If you were planning to stay for an extended period, as I was, you had to have a way to catch water from passing rain showers when at anchor. The answer is a rain-catching awning that can be spread above the cockpit to catch and funnel the water directly into the water tanks. It also doubles as a wonderful sun shade, keeping the cockpit livable in the sometimes ultra-hot tropical afternoons. *Dart* had two spruce whisker poles that were attached to fittings on the mast. The upper ends clipped to the shroud lines when not in use. They were used when running downwind, wing and wing, when the two jibs were set on opposite sides of the boat, and the main was furled. These poles became of even greater value when used to span the cockpit and support the rain catching awning. They rested on top of the main boom, and were rigged to the aft stays and port and starboard shroud lines. The awning also had two canvas funnels sewn into it, one on each side of the boom, to drain the water directly into the water tanks.

This system proved wonderfully efficient. We didn't often get rain showers, so when they arrived we wanted to gather every possible drop of rain. If I was on board when the rain began, I would pull the connecting hoses from the water tank filler opening and allow the first water to dump into a tub for clothes washing. That kept the accumulated salt and dust on the awning out of the water tank. When the water was running freely, and I had collected enough in the tub, I put the hoses into the tanks and saved whatever nature provided. Only twice did we get storms with sufficient rain to completely fill the tanks, and provide additional water, too. One time we got so much that we filled the tanks, the wash tub, all our additional water bottles and jugs, and partially filled the dinghy, which we used for washing clothes and ourselves.

The water system on small boats in tropical seas can cause problems because of algae growth in the tanks. *Dart*'s tanks were heavy canvas-covered rubber bladders, secured under the two aft bunks. Whenever we added water to them in any significant quantity we would also add a teaspoonful of Clorox to keep algae growth at bay. Before we learned this trick we occasionally pumped out large clots of scummy algae when drawing water for coffee or cooking. It was disgusting but not dangerous to drink, and we just lived with it until we learned of the Clorox remedy. Once we added Clorox we no longer had the algae problems, but our water tasted of Clorox. We weren't sure which was worse.

As we learned how critical fresh water is in dry tropical locations, we developed ways to preserve the precious liquid. Whenever we got thirsty and needed a drink of water, we would first fill the glass or cup a quarter full of sea water, straight from the sea. Then we would fill the remaining portion with our fresh water. In the tropics, the intense heat and resulting intense sweating robs the body of salt and minerals, and the sea water replaces the badly needed salts. We found that if we drank only fresh water, we could drink water until we were totally bloated but would still be thirsty. One cup of the sea water/fresh water mixture and our thirst was quenched. It takes a little getting used to, but in short order it becomes second nature. We also washed all clothing, dishes, and ourselves in sea water. The only time we used fresh water for washing was when we had so much spare water that it would get dumped otherwise. That was very rare.

We had very little clothing to wash because we wore only bathing suits, and an occasional T-shirt. For personal washing we bathed in the sea while standing waist deep just off the beach if possible. Most soap will not foam up in salt water. There are a few kinds, however, that have special formulations that will work as well in salt water as fresh. We used a detergent called Mr. Bubbly. It was a British dish detergent, and it worked very well in salt water. We used it to wash our hair and ourselves, too. Today, saltwater soaps are more widely available. Most people think that washing in salt water has to leave you feeling sticky and uncomfortable, but nothing could be further from the truth. There is a trick to washing in salt water. You wash your body, leaving your hair for the last. After washing your hair, you get out of the water and immediately dry your hair and body extremely well with a towel. By drying thoroughly so quickly, you don't allow the sea water to evaporate and leave the salt behind on your skin or in your hair. Your skin will feel clean, and your hair will be very nearly as fluffy and clean as when you use fresh water. There is an additional benefit to washing in sea water in the tropics. It seems to help provide an increased immunity to skin fungus, which is always a threat.

I found that by bathing in the sea, as we did, we had almost no problems with cuts or insect bites becoming infected, and we never treated or cared for them in any manner. The only exception was when I was bitten by a poisonous spider on the back of my leg. It became infected, and was threatening to be my undoing until the kind actions of an English woman on another yacht saved my leg, and most likely my life. One night, with only the light of a single smoky kerosene light, and a bottle or rum for anesthetic, she operated on me, cutting the foul smelling mass out of my leg. Within a couple of days I was well enough to be back in the water again diving for our meals.

Cooking on a small boat presents its own challenges. Our stove was a pressurized, kerosene fueled, double burner, fully gimbaled, piece of fine British technology. It had fiddle-rails to hold the pots securely in place no matter how violent the motions were at sea. It had only one failing, but it was a failing of the operator for the most part. Kerosene would burn with a dirty smoky flame if the stove was started cold. So the stove burners had to be pre-heated by burning about a teaspoonful of "meths," or methylated spirits (alcohol) on the burner first. The operator squirted some alcohol into the little well around the burner and then lit it. When the alcohol was just about exhausted, the pressurized kerosene was turned on gently, and if the burner was sufficiently hot, a nice well behaved clean blue flame would result. However, if it was not hot enough, a roaring ball of black smoke and flame would be the result. Then, the burner would need to be shut off, and the pre-heating drill repeated. This complicated start-up procedure caused us grief only one time. Unfortunately it was right after we had repainted the interior of *Sea Dart*.

Fitz did all of the cooking. He was in the galley preparing dinner one afternoon while we were still anchored in Barbados. I was in the cockpit doing my evening chores, which included refilling all the kerosene lights and trimming their wicks, which involved simply lifting the glass chimney off the lamp, and with the wick just slightly raised, rubbing off the accumulated carbon with a finger to leave a smooth flat wick. While I was trimming the wicks, the sound of a muffled explosion suddenly came from the galley, and a big cloud of gray-black smoke issued from the companionway. A moment later, Fitz stuck his head out of the companionway. Most of his facial hair was gone, including his eyebrows, and his face was black with soot. Fortunately he was not injured, except for his pride. The boat was not so fortunate. The entire galley space and surrounding area had to be repainted, as it was as black as Fitz's face. I was not very happy about that, but it is funny to recall now. We were still getting used to the pre-heating routine, and Fitz hadn't done it right.

We had one other "tragedy" related to the galley. Once, while we had *Dart* on the pier in Barbados, we accidentally mixed up the kerosene and water bottles, and Fitz washed a fine, and rare for us, chicken in a tub of kerosene when preparing it for dinner. Fitz never used foul language, but on this occasion he let slip a rather surprising exclamation. He then asked me what he should do. I suggested he place the well soaked chicken in a tub of water and get out the trusty Mr. Bubbly, and wash the chicken in the detergent. He did so, then cut it up and made a pressure-cooked rice, vegetable, and well-washed chicken dish. The first bite went down easily . . . until the kerosene fumes reached our sinuses. The rest of the meal went overboard, and we went hungry that night. Suffice it to say, keep your water and fuel bottles well marked, and hopefully well separated.

We did without any kind of icebox. It is simply a waste of space on a small cruising boat, and it can become a chore to keep clean and fresh smelling. The space is better used for other purposes. You learn to have your drinks at "room" temperature, and that can easily be 95 degrees. We sailed with another yacht, as previously mentioned, and they often made beer in a soft sided plastic two gallon container. The beer didn't live long when we pulled into an anchorage together. We drank it warm, and it tasted wonderful. I soon became so used to my warm beer that even today I normally do not refrigerate my beer, preferring the much richer flavor it has when it's warm.

Toilet facilities on *Dart* were nonexistent. We used a rubber bucket in the privacy of the cabin for the more serious occasions, and simply dumped it over the side. We also had a "pee-cup" that was kept in a little shelf just under the tiller handle. It also was dumped over the side and given a quick rinse after use. On one occasion in Barbados I had a difficult guest on board who was not only very demanding, but who also made claims that he knew a great deal more than me on just about any subject you could name, including how to sail *Sea Dart*. We were sailing down the coast when I went below and handed him out a *cold* Banks Beer. He was at the helm, showing me how it's done, and I was doing something down in the cabin. When I came back up and sat down in the cockpit, he was happily drinking his beer out of the pee-cup! I almost gagged when I saw him, but I kept my composure and allowed him to enjoy the cup all afternoon. I stayed with the bottles. He may have known a great deal about everything, but his nose sure didn't work! You may want to mark your pee-cup, too.

Times have changed, and toilet facilities on boats are required in most locations now. We also threw all our trash over the side as the sun was going down each evening, but not unless the wind was favorable to carry it out to sea. We didn't want to foul the local beaches with our trash. We had very little trash, however, because the supplies and food we bought rarely came in store-supplied containers, other than an occasional wrapping of brown paper. Throwing trash over the side is also not an option today, legally or ethically.

Ultimately, living on a small boat is a constant balance and trade-off of living space versus storage of necessary supplies. Water is critical in some very dry locations, so preserving it in every possible way is also crucial. Also, cooking at sea can be not only difficult, but downright dangerous if a pot full of boiling water dumps on the cook when the boat takes a sudden violent roll. There is a simple solution to both the conservation of water, and the danger boiling water poses to the cook and crew. You cook with a pressure cooker. With a pressure cooker, only a tiny amount of water is added to the pot, and the food provides the rest. Also, the food and liquid is completely contained in a watertight vessel, eliminating the danger of splash burns.

We used small stainless steel pressure cookers that were made in England. I notice these same pots are still available here in the United States today in some specialty shops and co-ops, but at a rather high price. They have a flexible lid that fits down inside the pot and pulls up to lock and totally seal the pot closed. They are the answer to a shipboard cook's prayers. They not only greatly reduce the use of water in cooking; they also conserve fuel, and reduce the clean-up after the meal. Generally the entire meal is cooked in a single pot. Also, there is almost always a delicious soup left in the bottom of the pot. Fitz and I each had a big mug of soup with every evening meal. Although I am no cook, when I returned to college after my sailing adventures, I continued to use a pressure cooker to cook all my meals until I met and married my wife, Gretchen.

As with everything else, there is a downside to using a pressure cooker. Fortunately, like starting the kerosene stove, it is simply a matter of learning how to use it correctly. We had one incident where we put water and rice into the pot, as well as vegetables and fish to make a fish and rice dish. We put way too much rice into the pot. Rice expands at least double when it cooks. When our rice expanded it completely filled the pot and clogged the pressure release. Not only could this be potentially dangerous, it was also very painful for both Fitz and me. Suddenly the overpressurized pot vented the superheated rice through the escape vent, and it was like a machine gun shooting 250° rice grains at us at point blank range, and we had nothing on but bathing suits! There was no escape. Heroically, Fitz reached over and shut off the stove, and then we could do nothing but duck for cover until the machine-gunning pot cooled enough to reduce the pressure. For several days we both looked like we had chicken pox. Not only that, but the boat was riddled with rice grains. We were still finding them months later when we moved things to look for something or other. War is hell!

The berths on *Dart* were the absolute minimum in comfort and size. I am 5' 7" tall, and my berth on the starboard side was just long enough for me to lie down full length. It was also very much narrower toward the bow, so we slept with heads pointed aft, and it was just wide enough to clear my shoulders. It was adequate, but just barely. The two aft berths were not berths. The starboard side berth was the chart storage area, and the port side was blocked by the galley and the stove. In a pinch the chart storage area could be used to sleep in, but not comfortably because of the almost total absence of fresh air.

Handling *Sea Dart* was unlike sailing any other small boat I have ever skippered, and I started sailing as a young boy. *Dart* was slow, but she was very dependable. She would always get you to where you wanted to go. Because of her hard chines she would easily dip her lee rail under, and in fact sailing with her rail under was her best attitude. With her rail under, the lee bilge keel was in the best orientation for sailing to windward. She would make her best time with the rail under and a "bone in her teeth." When sailing *Dart* in good conditions you got used to living at a 45-degree angle. It just became a way of life. Also, with *Dart* laid over, the pressure of the wind in her sails prevented any motions other than up and down the waves. If a person is prone to being seasick, this goes a long way to prevent seasickness.

Even in the gentlest zephyrs *Dart* always responded well to the helm. In severe gusts the helmsman had to hold hard to windward to prevent her from rounding up, but otherwise she was easy to handle. This is the case for most yachts, and is caused by the imbalance of the main and jib in relation to the force center of the keel, so nothing new there. I did learn one interesting foible of *Dart*'s. In gentle air, with only the main up, she would not allow me to point downwind in order to sail out of a confined bay. Also, she would come to windward almost far enough to come about, then fall off, and you could try it again and again with the same results, so you were trapped; you couldn't jibe and you couldn't come about. The solution was to always hoist the jib first, then once underway, hoist the main. With only the jib up I could easily do a jibe, but not come about. *Dart* required the balance of jib and main to allow full control. *Dart* had her own personality, but once you became familiar with her she behaved very well.

The topic of anchors and anchoring is worthy of a book and, in fact, a number have been written. It is a very important part of sailing, and may in fact be the single most important part of seamanship. More about anchoring technique in a moment. *Dart*'s main anchor was a heavy CQR (plow) pattern anchor. It is a wonderful design, and in my opinion is the finest anchor ever. It has only one downside that I am aware of. It can become very firmly set into the bottom, making pulling the anchor very difficult without a winch. If I had been anchored in a location for an extended period, and the anchor was really firmly set, I would take up the anchor line until the line was vertical above the anchor. If there was any swell running at all I would pull in all the line possible in the trough of the wave and cleat it off, then let the rising wave crest provide the lift to break the anchor free. It sometimes took a little while to break it free, but it always worked, saving the back and arms.

As mentioned earlier, I had almost 1,800 feet of three-strand, 3/4" line on board *Sea Dart*. Once I actually had all of it in use when we anchored in ultra deep water off Barbados when huge seas were rolling in. The waves were monstrous and actually rolled right up in among the houses built along the beaches. They caused a huge amount of damage, destroying many boats and putting one ship ashore. I had never planned to use all my spare line at one time. It was purchased as a supply item to be used to replace line lost or worn as I was sailing around the world. Even so, it was certainly very much appreciated when push came to shove and I actually needed to use almost all of it one night to put out multiple anchors in very deep water to anchor *Dart* during the period those huge waves were rolling into Barbados.

Being in the tropics, I had the advantage of warm seas. I could dive in any time and not freeze. I had one unalterable routine to which I always adhered. No matter how tired or cold I was when I dropped anchor, I hand-set my anchor(s), even at night by using my diving light. I would sail in to the location I thought best and drop anchor. Once I had checked to see we were not dragging, if there was a strong wind blowing, I would put on my mask and fins and dive in to set the anchor manually. Also, if we were in murky water where I couldn't clearly see the bottom, I swam around the anchor at *Dart's* swing radius to check for coral heads or other objects that could foul the anchor line as the boat swung at anchor.

Another advantage to hand-setting the anchor was demonstrated one ultra-stormy night when I was anchored in Bequia. The winds were very strong all day, but during the late afternoon they reached hurricane velocity for an hour or so. The anchorage in Bequia sits in a natural funnel. The winds come over the top of the island, and then funnel down between the hills directly into the anchorage. The result is to amplify the winds tremendously under the right conditions. I had set my anchor as usual, and was confident in its placement and holding power. However, when the winds began to scream in the rigging I came up on deck to monitor what was going on. The bay was alive with activity. There was commotion on all the thirty or so yachts in the bay, and there was a lot of yelling that could be heard above the roar of the wind. *Dart* only had a short length of chain attached to her anchor to prevent chafing, then 3/4" nylon line to the boat. Earlier I had put chafing gear on the line where it ran though the fairlead. I was concerned because the stresses that the line was experiencing were now in the severe range. I went forward to inspect the line, and was awed when I watched it stretch to less than a half-inch in diameter during the peak of the gusts. The stretching was also subjecting the line to severe chafing action in the fairleads, even with the chafing gear in place. There was no significant damage to the line yet, but it needed to be watched carefully.

A few minutes later I heard a sudden cry to windward: "Prepare to fend off." When I looked out, I saw a large trimaran bearing down on us, dragging her anchor behind her. *Dart* had always been a lucky boat, and this night was no exception *Dart* was dashing back and forth in response to the winds and her bow string taut anchor line. She just happened to yaw away from the approaching yacht, clearing the passing trimaran by only a few feet as it dragged its anchor past us. Just as the boat was passing by us, the owner pulled his anchor up to reveal the point of his anchor firmly wedged inside a bucket! He had inadvertently dropped his anchor right into an old bucket lying on the bottom! If he had checked his anchor he would have been spared the embarrassment and danger of dragging his anchor through a crowded anchorage during a storm.

There was another procedure I always followed when setting anchor. Just as soon as the anchor was firmly set and checked, I always got out the hand bearing compass to shoot an emergency escape bearing. I generally shot two bearings, and plotted them on the chart. They provided the extreme navigational limits for safely escaping the anchorage if conditions became dangerous during the dark of night. As long as I held my course between those two bearings I could escape the anchorage safely in totally blind conditions. It was a tremendous comfort to have those two escape bearings plotted on the chart, just in case they were needed.

Unfortunately, the one time when I really, desperately, needed to make use of an escape bearing I was anchored inside a bay that required passage though a very tiny gap in the reef that was barely wider than *Sea Dart*. We had to wait for first light to attempt our escape, timing the wave arrival on the reef to allow us to run the narrow gap at the exact right moment. That was one of the more "white knuckle" experiences of my life.

GPS didn't exist when I sailed *Dart*, so we navigated the traditional way, with chronometer and sextant. Today most small boat sailors have never used a sextant. I have strong feelings about that. If I were to go to sea again today, I would most certainly make use of GPS, but I would also have a sextant, and the sight reduction tables and chronometer necessary to use it. The ocean is a big place, and a boat is very small. If you miss your mark because your GPS broke down, you better be able to navigate the old-fashioned way; your life may depend on it. Sadly, those who argue that the marine electronics today are foolproof may discover they are "dead" wrong. They have never had their boat go over the top of a giant breaker in a hurricane and come down upside down, mostly under the sea. I did, and when the boat eventually righted herself, we had waist deep water in the main salon, and four or five feet of water below that in the bilges. The engine, batteries, pumps, and all electronics, were under water, but the sextant was unhurt, although wet. Ten hours of marathon bailing saved the boat, and the sextant and compass saved us.

Today, I am long out of touch with what's available for provisioning a yacht in the Caribbean. When I lived in Barbados, the closest thing to fast food available on the island was a cheese-cutter at a rum shack. I understand that many Islands now have all the same fast food joints that plague the U. S. For me, that is a sad development and I wish the local governments had better protected that idyllic existence they once enjoyed. However, I am sure that all the pieces of equipment and supplies that were necessary for me to store on *Sea Dart* for long distance cruising are most likely easily available in most places today.

Today, I don't expect I will ever go to sea again. I am now landlocked in the dry desert of southern Idaho, and very content. I lived on, in, and under the sea as a boy on Okinawa. I think having experienced at least ten major typhoons while growing up on Okinawa, and surviving one major hurricane in a small boat somewhere east of the Dominican Republic and Haiti, I have experienced enough of the sea. When you experience the sea at her worst, you look at the sea, and life, in a different way, and time never changes that. The sea is not a gentle and forgiving place.

If one goes cruising thinking the sea is benign and friendly, one makes a huge mistake. Prepare for the worst but enjoy the best. If you live by that motto you will probably survive when the barometer drops out of sight, and the sea becomes a range of moving mountains that are mostly obscured by the wind-blown spray and rain. If you are lucky and skillful enough to come out the other side you will be a changed person. Life will be sweeter, and time will be much more valuable.

Debutante Mark I Specifications
Length Overall: 21'
Length of Waterline: 16'
Beam: 7'
Draft: 2' 3"
Sail Area: 155 sq. ft.
Center Ballast Keel Weight: 750 lbs.
Approximate displacement: 1,800 pounds

Editor's Note: *Sea Dart* must certainly rank as one of the world's most famous yachts of any size. That's because she was sold by Ron Reil to Tristan Jones, who would later truck the boat to the Andes, sail her on Lake Titicaca, and then manage to transport the little vessel across South America. This became the basis for Jones's popular first book, *The Incredible Voyage.* In 1981, I approached Tristan with the idea for a book of collected writings that was published by SAIL Books and called *Yarns.* At the time, Tristan was recovering from a leg amputation and was in Key West where the book's much-reproduced jacket photo was shot. Most within the nautical publishing community assumed that Tristan's writing was fictionalized to one degree or another, while offering sound advice and, at the same time, being highly engaging. The full extent of Jones's fabrications was not made clear until the publication in 2003 of *Wayward Sailor* and its disturbing revelations. Jones's obvious affection for *Sea Dart* would, however, not appear to be in doubt.

Sea Dart was built to the Debutante design created by British naval architect Robert Tucker during the late 1950s when high quality marine-grade plywood had been recognized as both an economical and durable boat-building material. The Debutante followed Tucker's

This is the restored Sea Dart as she appears today in Idaho.

immensely popular pocket cruiser, the Silhouette, and combined the shallow-draft virtue of a family cruiser with conformance to Britain's Junior Offshore Group seaworthiness standards.

Introduced at the London Boat Show, the Debutante made a solid impression on those looking for an affordable, compact cruising boat. It is estimated that 125 boats were built commercially by Blanks Boatyard between 1959 and 1961 when a more heavily ballasted Mark II version was introduced. Mark III and IV versions followed. Although the basic specifications resulted in a sturdy boat, *Sea Dart*'s builder increased the called-for 3/8" thick plywood to 5/8" for bulkheads. The rig was changed from the original sloop to cutter by the time Ron Reil bought the boat. Today, *Sea Dart* has been restored and is owned by the Idaho State Department of Parks and Recreation and is used for sailing programs on Lake Coeur d'Alene.

CHAPTER 5

Learning to Cruise

BY MARY LOU TROY

Mary Lou Troy is the director of a public library in southeastern Pennsylvania. She and her husband, Fred, sail their Rhodes 22, Fretless, on the Chesapeake Bay. They've been married 14 years and this is their 15th season sailing together. Between them they have five children and 10 grandchildren. Fred is a retired chemist and has a second career booking musical acts for a small theater and two large festivals.

THE CHESAPEAKE BAY IS A MARVEL of wide open spaces and hidden wonders. A drowned estuary 200 miles long with wide expanses of wild marshland, rural watermen's villages, urban waterfront, remote anchorages and small sophisticated boutique towns, it has enough coves and creeks for a lifetime of exploring. It's an ideal place for cruising in a small boat. With its many anchorages, harbors of refuge, and its soft mud bottom, the most dangerous hazards are storms and other boats.

My husband Fred and I sail our Rhodes 22, *Fretless*, out of a marina in Rock Hall on Maryland's Eastern Shore. She is the smallest cruising sailboat in a marina full of big boats: Sabres, Tartans, Cape Dorys, Island Packets, and Catalinas. There is even a Swan and a Hinckley. At 22 feet, we drag the average boat size in the Swan Creek Sailing Association down to 32 feet. All this exposure to larger boats, however, hasn't made us yearn for anything bigger. *Fretless* is our second home, and we live aboard most weekends in the summer whether at anchor or in the marina.

Sailing now plays a central role in our lives but we came late to it. By the time we started sailing regularly in 1988, we already had built lives and careers in the Philadelphia area — two hours from what we would eventually discover as one of the world's great cruising grounds. When we met, I was in my mid-thirties and Fred was in his early forties. We had common interests in the music business and surprisingly, in sailing. Fred had chartered a few times with friends and taken a couple of sailing courses but I had been sailing exactly once. My dad raced small sailboats as a boy on Long Island Sound but had given it up before I was born. He talked about it a lot but I only went sailing once as a child, a glorious all-day affair exploring a remote bay way downeast in Maine in a sailing dory built by a family friend. It sparked a lifelong interest in boats and in being on the water but it was an interest I never thought I would pursue.

When I met Fred, I was a single parent and he was newly divorced. He and I talked about boats in some of our early conversations. The idea of sailing sounded interesting but we both had other interests and obligations. We didn't want to invest a lot of money in something we weren't sure about. Fred had some knowledge and a little experience but it was all new to me. Then Fred got a small bonus and decided to buy a small boat, and I joined him in wandering through boatyards. I began to read a lot: Larry Brown's *Cruising on a Microbudget* and Bob Burgess's *Handbook of Trailer Sailing* and Lin and Larry Pardey's *Cruising in Seraffyn*. These books were a revelation to me. When I'd thought about sailing and cruising, I'd thought it was something for rich folks with big new boats or for less rich folks who poured their entire lives into their boats. Reading these books, I realized that this was something ordinary people could do.

We looked at a lot of small boats on trailers. We climbed all over them and stood on their decks. We thought about the possibilities — overnight camping and trailering to distant waters. We wanted something small enough to trailer easily and yet sturdy enough to be safe with a couple of novices at the helm. Finally we found a Com-Pac 16 that seemed to be just the right combination of size, price and solid construction. We bought it with the idea of using it to learn to sail and then seeing where the experience would lead.

The Com-Pac 16 proved sturdy, easily trailerable and it had a small cabin with room for a portable head. It wasn't fast but it was simple and forgiving. We outgrew the local lake in just two daysails. Other nearby lakes quickly came to feel small and limiting. Then we took the boat down to the Chesapeake. In no time we were trailering to the Chesapeake every time we wanted to go sailing. We also were tent campers so we would trailer the boat to Elk Neck State Park in northeast, Maryland, and Janes Island State Park in Crisfield, both of which had good ramps and camping facilities. It was a short leap from taking the boat along with the tent and the camping gear to packing our camping gear in the boat. Now, new anchorages were suddenly open to us — places where the big boats go and some where they can't.

We moved the Com-Pac to a marina with a good ramp on the Chesapeake's western shore north of Baltimore. There we could leave her completely rigged on the trailer. We could drive to the marina; transfer our belongings to the boat and then launch. Drysailing was simpler than towing everywhere we went, less expensive than a slip and it meant we didn't have to think much about the boat in between. We started camping out on the boat more often and occasionally going out for two nights at a time. We loved it but our middle-aged backs were beginning to complain. We decided to get a bigger boat.

What did we want? We wanted something that would be comfortable for two people for weeks at a time. We found we could afford a used 28–33 foot boat but we still liked the idea of drysailing. A trailerable boat still seemed to make sense. If it was sitting high and dry on its trailer in the marina we wouldn't have to worry about what was happening to it when we couldn't drive down for the weekend. The weather in July and August can be miserably hot on the Chesapeake. Some years there are three to five weeks in the middle of the summer when we don't want to be on the boat, or we might want to take the boat to a cooler place. What's more, with a smaller drysailed boat, the financial commitment wasn't so much that we would feel cheated if we missed a few weeks. Best of all, we could bring it home for winter for storage and spring commissioning. Parts would be less expensive and there would be less to maintain. So, we had our first criterion for the new boat: bigger but still trailerable.

Which boat? We liked the idea of a boat that was still in production even though we would be buying used since, because of our expected sporadic use, we couldn't justify the cost of a new boat. Besides, our Com-Pac had been 10 years old when we bought it and we'd sailed it for 10 years. It was in better shape at 20 years than it had been at 10! We also thought that with a boat still in production, parts and advice would be more available. Regarding advice, we were to learn that the Internet is a great source. There are now owners' groups on the Internet for almost any type of production boat, but that was a relatively new phenomenon when we were looking for *Fretless* and we were unaware of how widespread it was. If we were to look for a boat now, we would join the email lists devoted to the boats we were interested in. You can learn a lot just listening to how people talk about their boats.

We wanted a boat that would be comfortable for two people for weeks at a time. We wanted a boat at least as spacious as our tent. One of the issues on the 16 was how confining it felt after two days. The space issues are important when you consider going cruising. Fred and I are both small people and we are comfortable being in each other's space but we still wanted space to move around. Other people might need more space just to feel comfortable for a day or two. The other space concern was storage. In a small cruising boat, storage is critical. We weren't really sure how long we might be cruising but we didn't want the storage space on the boat to limit us to just a few days.

The new boat also had to be solid. The Com-Pac was built like a brick house and while some people claimed that it sailed like one, we'd pounded through some impressive powerboat chop at the mouth of the Middle River and never once felt we were in danger or that something might break.

Finally there were performance criteria. While we'd learned a lot about sailing trying to make the Com-Pac go, we decided that we wanted a boat that would sail well in the light air of the Chesapeake. We wanted a shoal draft boat because the Chesapeake is notorious for its broad shallows, sandbars, and narrow creek entrances. We liked the idea of a keel centerboard configuration because it would give us the shoal draft but would have the potential for better windward performance than a boat with simply a shoal keel. We also liked the idea of a keel-centerboard better than a heavy swing keel requiring a winch like those on the Catalina 22.

We quickly focused on three boats still in production that seemed to meet most of the criteria: the Com-Pac 23, the Precision 23, and the Rhodes 22. Most of the Com-Pacs we looked at were older. They were worn and we had doubts about their light air performance. Our experiences with the Com-Pac 16 led us to believe that the long shallow keel on the Com-Pac 23 would not provide good windward performance, particularly in light air. We looked at the Precisions. They were more of a performance boat but we were unsure about how they'd perform in chop and storms. The Chesapeake is a forgiving place to sail but sooner or later you will get caught in the sudden damaging winds and blinding rain of a summer thunderstorm. We also had doubts about storage and about making the Precision's big open interior work for cruising.

Then we saw the Rhodes 22. Phil Rhodes did the design for Stan Spitzer of General Boats (builder of the Rhodes 22) in the late 1960s. Stan was then looking for a small cruiser that would be comfortable for a couple and still be a great boat for daysailing. He had an aircraft design firm in Kansas City fit the interior into the Rhodes hull. For a while the boats were built by a succession of different builders under contract to General Boats. When the quality wasn't consistently up to his standards, Stan and General Boats became the manufacturer, first on Long Island and then in Edenton, North Carolina.

General Boats is a "mom and pop" operation with two products: new

Rhodes 22s and recycled (refurbished) Rhodes 22s. In addition to building new boats, Stan buys back used boats, refurbishes them, and sells them as "recycled". General Boats makes some fairly strong claims for the boat on its website like "uncapsizable under sail," "awesome storage areas," and "the amenities of a big boat in a small boat." The boat comes with a lot of gimmicks and gadgets: the in-mast furling (IMF) main, an unusual traveler arrangement, a home-built furling unit for the 175 genoa, a marine head and holding tank, and a General Boats-designed outboard motor lift. We were skeptical of so many unique features. Then there was the look of the boat. The flared hull gave the Rhodes 22 an unusual appearance that took some getting used to.

We looked at a few more Precisions and Com-Pacs and then at a few other used boats as they came on the market. Condition seemed to be a real issue with many of the used boats. We didn't want to buy a boat that we had to spend a lot of time fixing before we could sail. The General Boats recycling program started looking very attractive. When General Boats buys back a Rhodes 22, they take it apart, inspect it, fix what needs to be fixed, give the hull a shiny new paint job and give the boat a "new boat" structural guarantee. Options can be deleted or added just like on a new Rhodes 22, making every boat a semi-custom job.

We arranged for a test sail at the Annapolis Boat Show. General Boats sells directly to the public. Their only marketing tools are the boat shows, the Internet, and word of mouth. Stan Spitzer's salespeople are the owners of his boats. The day we went for a demo sail there was a four-knot breeze. Paul, the owner who took us out on his boat, told us about tying everything down and taking her sailing in some big waves off of Ocean City just to see how she would do. He said she did just fine in the wind and waves. She certainly did fine in light air. While we were looking for the secret trolling motor, Paul talked about sailing in heavy air. He demonstrated the in-mast furling, and demonstrated that by pulling a pin at the gooseneck you can drop the sail and the furling unit in the mast by about 18 inches — what Rhodes 22 owners call "the first reef." We quizzed him about the IMF sail and the traveler arrangement. He swore they worked under all kinds of conditions. We talked about dealing with General Boats and how they stood behind their boats. We talked to Stan and his brother Elton. We hemmed and hawed. We talked about what was available for recycling. We wrote a check.

Buying a Rhodes 22 turns out to be a lot like buying a new semi-custom boat. The options list goes on and on. General Boats can add most of the newer options to an old boat. We were still skeptical about the in-mast furling. Stan talked us into it by offering to swap it out for a conventional mast and main if we didn't like it. We decided to pay a little extra for new sails. While we went for a few of the options like the outboard lift and the IMF, we chose to go with the simplicity of a boat with a portable toilet in a curtained enclosure rather than an enclosed marine head. General Boats repaints most of their recycled boats with a two-part sprayed paint, so we got to choose our colors: white hull, red boot stripe, blue bottom paint, cockpit cushions and UV strips on the jib and main.

In May of 1998 we drove to Edenton, North Carolina, and returned pulling our Rhodes 22 behind our Chevy Blazer. The Blazer towed it well enough but if we were towing frequently in a mountainous area we'd want something a little larger. That year and the next we overnighted frequently, stringing together more nights when we could and sailing all over the northern part of the Chesapeake.

Our first overnight was in Worton Creek on the Eastern Shore. Worton is a lovely spot: well-protected behind a sandy spit of land but it is full of moorings. Many big boats anchor in the outer part of the creek outside the spit or pick up a mooring but our shallow draft allowed us to anchor in a small tributary called Mill Creek. It's quiet and very beautiful. Great blue herons stalk the shoreline among the tangled blowdowns below high wooded banks that rise abruptly on either side of the creek, offering shelter on three sides as the creek winds. Deer come down to the water to drink. Osprey, swallows, and an occasional bald eagle fly overhead. From the cockpit swinging at anchor in Mill Creek you can watch the boat traffic heading up Worton Creek to the marina but be untroubled by the swells. At night as we swung at anchor with the tide, we watched the stars overhead and reflected in the water. We still weren't sure where she would take us but it seemed clear that we had found our boat.

From the start we had eased into the sailing lifestyle. We thought sailing was just going to be another thing we would do in our busy lives filled with work, family and our music business hobbies. The Com-Pac 16 had given us a small, relatively inexpensive platform for learning. It was a way to get out on the water when we could without a large commitment of time and financial resources. Now, sailing was becoming more and more prominent in our lives. We found that the more we sailed, the more we wanted to sail.

No sooner had we gotten comfortable with the new boat than we decided to move from drysailing on the western shore of the bay to keeping the boat in a slip on the Eastern Shore. We already spent a lot of our time overnighting on the Eastern Shore. The driving distance was the same but half of it would now be off of I-95. We had thought about continuing to drysail but couldn't find a suitable facility on the Eastern Shore so we decided to take a slip. That move brought unexpected changes to the way we used the boat.

The marina is home to a sailing association that sponsors races and serves as an informal social club. Many of the members are retired or have found ways to live in the Rock Hall area. Others commute from Philadelphia or southern New Jersey. Many of them spend every weekend from May to October on their boats. Like them, we have come to regard our boat as our summer home, our waterfront property, our home away from home. We sail more than ever, but we also find ourselves going down to the boat to use it as a base for other activities. We do a lot more daysailing because it's easy to go out for a few hours and come back to the slip. We will sometimes do a weekend of daysailing, staying on board overnight at the marina. One of the hazards of keeping a boat in one of your favorite destinations is that it is harder to go somewhere else. Most of our friends who use their boats similarly, as weekend retreats, have much larger boats but it is a lifestyle that also seems to work very well on a Rhodes 22.

We weren't planning on these lifestyle changes when we bought the boat so you could say that reality has far exceeded the promise. We had originally thought in terms of overnights at anchor and short cruises. We never seriously considered living on the boat for weekends as a matter of course. We never thought about falling into a big boat lifestyle with a little boat but once we did, it seemed to make perfect sense.

We are now so comfortable on the boat that it's easy to throw our gear in the car and go. Once we are aboard it is easy to let go the docklines and sail. It's nearly as easy to be out overnight as it is to be at the dock so we spend a lot of nights at anchor and visiting ports like St. Michaels or Annapolis. Cruises that take in more than two nights demand a bit more planning in terms of provisioning, packing and arrangements for reprovisioning, ice, showers, and sanitation. Still, every time we've returned from a five- or six-day cruise we've felt that the other commitments in our life are the limiting factor to the length of our cruises, not the boat.

We bought the boat because we expected that it would be comfortable, fun to sail and easy to maintain. It proved to be all that and more. The unexpected pleasures have been how truly at home we feel on the boat and the expansion of our social life to include the social scene at the marina and the camaraderie with the other Rhodes 22 owners, most of whom I first met on the Internet. The Internet has led to numerous get-togethers with the chance to compare notes, experiences, and solutions to problems. This has been enlightening to say the least and has given us the opportunity to meet many people with whom we already have at least one thing in common. We have joined raft-ups with other Rhodes 22s and gone on short cruises with our sailing association. I am still amazed at how sailing has filled up our life. I am convinced that had we initially thought that we wanted to cruise the Chesapeake, we would have focused on a larger boat and then probably decided against the entire endeavor as just too hard to fit into our lives.

The Rhodes 22 has a lot of characteristics that make her a good choice for a couple who want to trailer, daysail, live aboard for short periods of time, or just take off on a cruise in protected waters. At first glance the Rhodes 22 is an unusual looking boat. Some people immediately love the flared-hull look while others find it disturbingly reminiscent of a powerboat. We were somewhere in the middle.

According to Stan Spitzer, even Phil Rhodes was at first reluctant to put the flare on a small sailboat. Stan had admired the shape in the 505, a racing dinghy. The flare gave the racing crew a broad surface for hiking out, and deflected waves keep the cockpit dry. Stan felt that the shape would help a larger boat resist capsizing in extreme heeling situations and that the compound curves would add strength to the fiberglass hull. In addition, the flare would provide support for the wide side decks. On the other hand, the cabin is narrower than it would be if the hull dropped straight down from the toerail, and the flare does create some additional windage.

But it is the rig and sails on a Rhodes 22 that are probably the most controversial. Basically the boat is a masthead sloop with a loose-footed main. While some Rhodes 22s are sold with conventional masts and standard battened mains, many of the boats are sold with the General Boats-designed in-mast furling (IMF) main. Five years after Stan Spitzer talked us into trying it, we can safely say that for cruisers, casual sailors, and single-handers, the IMF main is very convenient. Properly maintained and lubricated with a dry lube, it seems to function well even in difficult situations. The extrusion for the mast has a broader section than a conventional mast in order to contain the furled sail. This and the sail itself add weight aloft but the R22 is such a stable boat that it does not seem to make much difference. To accommodate furling, the loose-footed main has a straight cut leech (no roach, no battens) which limits sail area and shape and contributes to a tendency toward lee helm in light air and a very neutral helm in moderate winds. This can be more easily tuned out on some boats than others. These disadvantages are balanced by the convenience and the infinite adjustability of the sail.

The main is controlled by an outhaul that cleats at the end of the boom and a furling line that exits on the underside of the boom. The outhaul cleat configuration has changed many times over the years but the design on the new boats seems to be the most successful. The outhaul goes over a roller and through the boom to a cam cleat mounted on the underside of the boom so that it can be easily reached by the helmsman or crew. Our older-style outhaul just went around a block and was cleated on a horn cleat. After seeing the new system at an Annapolis boat show, we bought the parts from General Boats and retrofitted them to our boom.

Another unique feature of the IMF main is the ability to lower the height of the sail without changing its area. This is accomplished by pulling a pin at the gooseneck and can be done with the sail powered up. This "first reef" reduces heeling by lowering the center of effort and is the first action we take in building winds. Further reefing is accomplished by partially furling the main.

Most Rhodes 22s are sold with a roller furling 175 genoa which, until recently, was mounted on a home-built furling system designed by General Boats. While they now sell boats with an off-the-shelf furling unit, ours is the older system consisting of a tube over the forestay with the sail permanently attached to the tube. It works remarkably well considering that the usual headsail is a 175 genoa with no luff pad. The system is simple and nearly bulletproof. It always furls. It is very difficult to get an overwrap on the open drum. The downside is that you don't have a halyard to tension the luff and, if you need to get the sail off the boat, you have to drop the mast. The 175 is a lovely sail in five- to 10-knot winds but the sailcloth is so heavy that it collapses on itself in lighter air and chop. In stronger breezes it works well partially furled from 10 to about 18 knots. As the wind increases, the poor shape of the furled sail makes pointing more of a problem. Many owners in windier places than the Chesapeake have gone to a smaller sail and conventional roller furling units. When it comes time to replace the sail, we will probably go with a furling unit that allows us to change sails so that we can have a couple of headsails more closely suited to a variety of conditions. After several windy seasons on the Bay, we find ourselves wishing we had a smaller sail for winds over 15 knots.

The genoa sheets are usually run outside the shrouds through fairleads on genoa track cars to single-speed winches. If the sail is partially furled the sheets can be led inside the shrouds to a fairlead on the track on the side deck next to the cabin or if reefed way down they can be led to cam cleats on the cabin top. The various sheeting positions help to compensate for poor sail shape as the 175 genoa is furled smaller and smaller.

The Bay is notorious for light winds in summer. Once the wind drops to under five knots, the big 175 starts collapsing under its own weight, so to improve performance in light air we've added a Doyle UPS sail, a tri-radial drifter made out of spinnaker cloth that flies behind the furled genoa. The tack of the sail is clipped to a mini-furler that in turn gets clipped to a padeye just aft of the roller-furling unit. The sail has a high tech line sewn into its luff, flies from a spare halyard and is controlled with the mini-furler. We immediately found we could sail in winds less than five knots, where, previously, we would have been motoring to overcome the chop or the tide. We can use the drifter downwind instead of a spinnaker. When we fly the UPS, we run the sheets alongside the genoa sheets through the fairleads on the genoa track. It's a very forgiving sail and a lot of fun to play with.

Another unusual aspect of the rig is the traveler, a stainless steel tube secured between the twin backstays. The main sheet attaches to a car that slides on the tube. The car is controlled by two lines with a 2:1 purchase that cleat on jam cleats at the ends of the bar. This arrangement probably caused us to hesitate more than any other feature of the Rhodes. We were concerned about its integrity in an uncontrolled jibe but were reassured when we talked to a number of the Rhodes 22 owners. We've had no problems with it. Like many other things on the Rhodes, it is simple and unconventional and it works.

We use a Honda eight-horsepower four-stroke outboard to get in and out of the slip and for going places when there's not enough wind to fill the sails. Though we call ourselves sailors, we've certainly enjoyed many a long ride home on a still Sunday morning with the motor quietly pushing us through glassy seas. Sometimes just being out on the water is enough. When we were looking at outboards, the Honda 8 was one of the few four-strokes that had been made over a period of time. The model we have is lighter than later versions but still a heavyweight at 80 lbs. There are now more choices. We decided on a four-stroke primarily because it is quieter and cleaner than the equivalent two stroke engines. The outboard motor mount on a Rhodes 22 is one of General Boat's nicest gimmicks. It's a molded plastic mount that rides a pair of aluminum rails controlled by a 6:1 or 7:1 block and line system. It makes raising the 80-lb. motor possible.

One of our favorite improvements to the boat was the addition of cockpit mounted controls for the outboard. It was a long reach to the outboard from the normal steering position by the tiller. It was acceptable to us to have a hand on the outboard tiller to steer with the motor when backing out of a tight slip. But the long reach was a problem if we had to be reaching back over the transom for the throttle and shift when there were boats all around in a crowded harbor. While we wanted the controls to be easily reached we also wanted them out of the way when we were just lounging around the cockpit. Rather than cut a hole in the coaming or gunwale, we mounted the controls on a piece of wood attached to the removable cockpit table leg. The leg fits in a socket directly under the tiller. This puts the controls on the centerline and allows us to remove the controls along with the table leg and stow them under the seat when they are not needed.

We generally carry six gallons of gasoline in two three-gallon tanks. The Honda snap fitting makes it easy to change tanks while motoring. For extended trips we carry a 1 1/2-gallon jerry can. We conservatively calculate 1 1/2 hours of motoring per gallon at just above half throttle. Depending on tides and conditions this gives us a range of 50 miles if we motor at 4 1/2 knots, enough for most trips on the Chesapeake, where fuel docks are fairly common.

The cockpit on the Rhodes 22 was an unexpected bonus. It is large, nearly eight feet long, and the seatbacks are incredibly comfortable. The only drawback to the size is that the distance between the seats makes it difficult for short people to brace themselves in boisterous conditions. I've learned to hang on to the winches. We've talked about finding a way to give me a few foot rests but mostly we just try to sail flatter and anticipate the gusts.

The cockpit's bench seats have good storage under them. We keep our two three-gallon gas tanks for the outboard on one side. On the other are three large plastic containers that hold safety and rain gear in one, propane for the grill, fuel canisters for the cook stove and other miscellaneous equipment in the next and a small plastic dinghy in the third. There are coaming boxes on either side. There is a fitting for a table leg in the center of the cockpit. The tabletop stores in the cabin but is easily brought out for entertaining or for a meal in the sun. The lazarette is very large, encompassing the entire stern of the boat. We use it for docklines, fenders, and ground tackle.

We have a large bimini that shades most of the cockpit. We can sail with it up as long as the winds are under 10 knots. At that point it starts creating a fair amount of windage and we will lower it against the cabin top. It also helps keep us dry on drizzly days and will help shield the companionway in pouring rain at the dock.

The cabin has a settee to port and a galley to starboard. The settee can be made into a small double berth with the addition of the tabletop, which stores above the v-berth. There is a storage drawer under the cabin step and storage under the settee. The galley has a large storage space under the counter, which is fronted with sliding doors. There is also storage with sliding doors at the back of the countertop against the hull. Under the counter there is an upright RV style icebox aft of the storage space. There is also a small sink and a single burner stove set into the countertop.

The pop-top covers the area from the settee to the countertop and allows standing headroom in this portion of the cabin. Forward of the main cabin is a partially enclosed area for a portable toilet and forward of that is the v-berth. We took the cushions out of the v-berth and use it strictly for storage. We have a canvas enclosure with large clear vinyl windows that fits over the raised pop-top and snaps to the exterior sidewalls of the cabin. The enclosure, which we bought used from General Boats, provides privacy at the dock and protection from the elements. With the enclosure in place, the entire cabintop becomes short-term storage.

The enclosure has screened windows on each side. The windows have a clear vinyl outer flap so the windows can be opened or closed. The companionway entry is canvas with zippers on either side. The front wall is clear vinyl with a zipper so it can be fastened forward of the mast. We are scheming to get screening on the front as well. The ports on the front of the cabin open, which is useful because we need all the ventilation we can get for hot nights on the Chesapeake. We have shore power so we can use an electric fan help keep things cool at the dock. It is usually cooler at anchor but we have a small battery powered fan that helps keep air moving. We also have a mosquito net enclosure that just drapes over the pop-top. We've used this on hot nights at anchor instead of the pop-top enclosure when no rain protection was needed.

We sleep in the settee/double berth in the main cabin. The interior was engineered so that the three-inch thick foam cushions from the back of the settee fit the other half of the double berth, which is made up of the companionway step, the table, and the flip-up seat by the head. Rather than use sleeping bags, we made a bedroll out of two sheets and two fleece blankets. The two fleece blankets are sewn together at the foot as are the sheets. The sheets can be snapped to the blankets at the foot to keep everything in place and allow for quick stowage and bedmaking. It also allows the sheets to be removed easily for cleaning. The bedroll rolls up and stows in a duffel in the v-berth when not in use. We use full-size pillows, which get stuffed into square pillow shams during the day and double as throw pillows for the settee. The more things you have that serve more than one purpose, the more comfortable you will be on a small boat.

The Rhodes 22 has a 15-gallon freshwater tank but we use bottled water for drinking and cooking. Spare jugs are kept under the settee. The jug in use stores in the sink. The boat came with a battery-powered faucet but we never got it to work well. We use a hand-pump faucet and added a foot pump with flexible water lines so that it stores under the sink when not in use.

The head is a portable toilet with a 2.6-gallon holding tank. When the water pump bellows on a previous toilet gave out, we purchased an identical model and saved the holding tank from the old one so that for longer trips we have a second holding tank. If we use both, we put the second in a large plastic bag and stow it under the cockpit seats until we can empty it. The Rhodes 22 is available with a regular marine head in a full enclosure with a small holding tank but we decided that the cabin seemed roomier in the boats with a semi-enclosed head. We chose a portable toilet because it was simpler than a marine head. While pumpouts are widely available on the Chesapeake, there is always the chance we might want to trailer to places where pumpouts are not available. The portable toilet is easy enough to bring home to clean and we don't have to bother with fixing head problems at the marina.

Some marinas (often ones that cater to a lot of smaller boats) have dedicated dump facilities for portable toilets. At others, I just empty the head in a restroom. I do try to pick times when it's not busy and make sure I clean up well when I'm done. The fancier the marina, the more likely that I'll carry the holding tank up to the restroom in a plastic bag late at night.

We do not have shower facilities on the boat. Marinas are so plentiful where we regularly sail that our general rule has been no more than two nights at anchor before a marina stop for showers. If we wanted to stay out longer we would use a sun shower or following a tip I read on the Internet, rig a large pump spray bottle (like a bug sprayer) with a shower head for a miniature pressurized water system.

Cooking on a small boat presents all kinds of problem-solving opportunities related to preparing meals on a single burner stove with limited refrigeration and limited facilities for cleaning up. I look for meals that need only one pot or that can be cooked sequentially. We have a gas grill that can be set up on the stern rail and used for grilling or as a spare burner. If I get inspired to cook something complicated we have a small two-burner propane camp stove that stows flat and uses the same gas canisters as the grill. We only use it in the cockpit and only in the calmest of anchorages.

Fretless's stove is a single-burner backpacking stove set into a stainless steel pan in the countertop. The original stove used the valveless canisters that are punctured on first use and then must remain in place until empty. When the fuel for that stove became hard to find, we replaced it with a newer stove from the same manufacturer that uses the same butane-propane mixture but the canisters have a valve and are readily available at sporting goods stores. The new stove fit into the original stainless steel pan in the countertop with only a minor modification. Newer Rhodes 22s use a butane stove, but I have no complaint with ours. The flame is very hot and we've never had a canister leak. Spare canisters are stowed in a plastic container under the seats in the cockpit. The stove's only drawback is that it does not have potholders to keep pots on the burner in any kind of wave action. For that reason we never cook while under way and watch for wakes from boats motoring through an anchorage while we are cooking.

I try to plan meals that are easy to prepare and easy to clean up. I use more canned goods aboard than I do at home and am always on the lookout for packaging that suits life on the boat, such as pancake mix that is mixed in its own container or vacuum packed tuna that you don't have to drain. I repackage items bought in bulk into servings for two. We use an 8" x 15" x

9" plastic container with good handholds and a lid with a snug fit to hold most of the nonperishable staples that we regularly take to the boat. We call it "the pantry". It fits under the shelves in the galley and makes it simple to haul spices, oils, rice mixes, and canned goods back and forth. It's easy to pack at home, carry out to the dock to the boat, and requires no repacking once it's aboard.

I freeze meats in marinade to avoid having to mix sauces on the boat. We often boil leftover marinade to kill bacteria and then add it to the cooking water for rice. Salad mix in bags has made making a salad on a boat much easier and the bagged salad keeps longer unopened than greens purchased separately.

If we have time, we will make a fancier breakfast on the boat than we ever eat at home. There is something memorable about pancakes with real maple syrup, sausages and orange juice on a brilliant morning while the wisps of fog are still rising off the water. For quicker meals we'll toast bagels on a long fork over the open flame of the stove or just have muffins I've brought from home. If we have a long distance to travel and we want an early start, we'll make our tea, put it in travel mugs and have homemade breakfast bars that we can eat out of hand while underway. I make these in large batches at home and freeze them. They keep for months in the freezer and for days in the cooler. They seem to survive thawing and refreezing. Most are a combination of dried fruits and nuts in an oatmeal or oatmeal and peanut butter batter. Lunches are generally eaten under way. We'll have finger foods or easy-to-eat sandwiches.

Longer trips require more careful planning. If ice will be available, I'll plan meals that require refrigeration throughout the cruise but I always plan to use my most perishable items first. I always have some extra meals, which require no refrigeration on board so if something spoils or we end up spending an extra day or two holed up in a protected creek waiting out the weather, we'll have something good to eat. Good food seems to make bad weather more tolerable. Some of our favorite meals require no refrigeration. I'll often make a pasta sauce from a can of stewed tomatoes dressed up with canned mushrooms, olives, and sun-dried tomatoes. Then there are noodle and rice mixes with additions of canned or vacuum-acked tuna, salmon or chicken, rice mixes with canned Chinese vegetables and corned beef hash. Such supplies can also be used to stretch a meal if you have unexpected guests.

I try to plan meals so that the cleanup will be easy, because discharging soapy water over the side is legal in the Chesapeake. We use paper towels as napkins and then use them after the meal to wipe plates and cooking pots before washing. This way we mix less debris with the dishwater. We put a little hot water in the largest dirty pot and dispense dish soap from an eye dropper bottle to reduce the amount of soap used. We rinse with small amounts of hot water from the tea kettle using the additional soapy water to wash the larger items. We save the dirtiest items for last. You can do a lot of dishes with very small amounts of soap and water. The secret is using really hot water.

Fretless's icebox is an old, upright RV icebox of the sort they used to use in pop-up campers. It's not particularly efficient or well-insulated but it does the job. We use block ice that we freeze at home in half-gallon plastic milk containers with screw tops. We supplement this with ice purchased dockside. The icebox doesn't hold everything we need for a longer trip so we will bring an additional well-insulated cooler, pack our frozen goods in that and open it only once a day. We also have a small six-pack-style cooler that we use for drinks during the day so we do not have to keep opening the other coolers. Since our general cruising pattern on the Chesapeake is to stop at a marina every second or third night, we can replenish our ice on a regular basis. If we had to make our ice last longer, we would have to replace our primary icebox or at least improve its insulation.

We have set up the galley storage space so that everything is organized, yet secure so that things don't get flung about. We use the space under the sink for perishable dry goods and there is usually room there for a bottle of wine or two. The pantry is in the space under the stove on the bottom shelf next to a set of nesting pots and the teakettle. Above that is a narrow shelf with a box for utensils such as spatulas, knives, mixing spoons, and the corkscrew. Next to it is a tubular plastic bag of the sort used to deliver newspapers that we keep stuffed with plastic grocery bags used for trash bags. The top shelf has room for a flat box with our eating utensils under the stove and the electric teakettle that we use at the dock.

The items on the shelves are held in place by the sliding doors of the cabinet if the boat is heeled to port and the hull if the boat is heeled to starboard. Both of the utensil boxes have lids so that if they should slide off the shelf they won't spill their contents. There is a six-inch-high storage space at the back of the countertop fronted by sliding doors. Here we store plates, bowls, and miscellaneous equipment such as an electric light on a gooseneck that we use at the dock, and citronella candles. On top of this space is another shelf with a rail. This space is deep enough for mugs, wine glasses, plastic cups, and a jar of peanut butter. Our eyedropper bottle of dish detergent lives here, as do containers of sunscreen and bug repellent.

The large amount of storage and living space make it possible for us to live aboard for days at a time without ever setting foot on land, but there are times when we just want to get off the boat. It is not absolutely necessary to have a dinghy on a 22-foot boat with a 20-inch draft, but our first season with the Rhodes 22 found us occasionally feeling trapped aboard in an anchorage. We looked at others zipping about in their dinghies and began to think about a dinghy for *Fretless*. Often what lay between *Fretless* and the shore was only 20 or 30 feet of muddy bottom. We knew that for the most part we didn't want to tow a dinghy. An inflatable seemed more reasonable but they can be quite expensive. As with other outfitting decisions, we went for the simplest, most inexpensive solution and found it so workable that we've never progressed beyond that point. We bought a plastic inflatable three-person dinghy for less than $100. It is really more of a pool toy than a working dink. It weighs less than 15 lbs. and stows in an 18" x 20" x 10" high plastic container with a lid under the cockpit seats. It inflates in 10-15 minutes and deflates in a little less. We are careful about where we beach it but otherwise don't give it any special treatment. We figured we could buy one a year for the next 10 years for the same cost as a real inflatable but we are now into our fourth season with the same plastic pool toy. It does not row especially well but it gets us from one place to another. We upgraded the oars after a couple of seasons and that improved its rowing characteristics. We've used it to explore an anchorage, to row into a restaurant from the anchored boat, to get to shore from a mooring, and as comic relief in dinghy rowing races.

Our primary anchor is a nine-pound Danforth with six feet of chain and 175 feet of rode. This anchor was the storm anchor for the Com-Pac. We kept thinking we would replace it with something a little heavier but it has held so well in the Chesapeake mud that we decided to improve it by just doubling the chain. When it comes time to replace the rode we'll increase the length to 200 feet. Our second anchor is a Danforth-type that came with the boat. It is slightly heavier, has broader flukes, 10 feet of chain, and 200 feet of nylon rode. Rather than a storm anchor we think of it as a spare and would probably set both in a storm situation. If we were traveling out of the area we would want to consider another anchor more suited to different conditions.

One of the features I like least about the Rhodes 22 is the arrangement for storage of the anchor and rode. With the anchor stored on the bow pulpit, the rode is fed down a cowl vent on the foredeck to a tray in the forepeak. This tray sits on runners above the v-berth and is open to the cabin of the boat. Often when we haul an anchor the chain and rode are very muddy. As they dry, the rode gives off a musty "eau de bay" smell. After considering our options, we finally decided to abandon the idea of keeping the anchor on the bow. We store the anchor and rode in a large mesh bag with twill handles designed for the purpose. Such bags can be found at marine stores. They have a grommet in the bottom so you can thread the bitter end through and tie it off to the cleat without fumbling around for it in the bag. We keep the anchor in the bag with the rode neatly coiled so that it will always pay out freely. We keep the bag in the lazarette. In an emergency anchoring situation the anchor can be dropped off the stern and the line walked to the bow when it is convenient. In most situations I walk the anchor forward, tie off the bitter end on the bow cleat and drop the anchor from the bow as Fred maneuvers. Our never-used second anchor is kept in a similar bag, stored in the forepeak and is ready if we ever need it. With the cowl vent no longer being used for the anchor rode, we installed a solar-powered vent in the deck opening.

The smaller the boat, the more of a factor weather becomes in the planning and enjoyment of cruising. A safe cruise requires knowledge of the weather and the ability to plan around it. When planning a cruise we usually build in weather days so that if we need to be back by a certain date, we have a bit of leeway in the schedule. We carry a dedicated weather radio that has a standby mode and will produce a warning tone when storm warnings are issued. It doesn't take the place of watching the sky and heeding the forecasts, but it is an added measure of protection.

On the Chesapeake, sooner or later you will be caught out in a thunderstorm. We have been fortunate and have been caught out in a squall only once. We had less than a season on the new boat. One minute we were sailing under an even gray sky and the next we could see a wall of rain approaching us. We had time to don our foul weather gear, furl the sails, start the motor and not much else. There was no lightning but the winds were so strong the motor could barely keep the bow of the boat pointed upwind. Fortunately, it rained so hard that it flattened the waves and it was over in 15 minutes or so. In truth, we were more frightened by the after-the-fact realization that we had forgotten to close the companionway hatch and don our PFDs than by the storm itself.

The experience led us to develop a weather drill that we use to batten down for a storm. We start by making sure everything is secure in the cabin and cockpit. The pop-top has a tiedown so that it won't lift or bang if we roll. We secure the companionway hatch. We get the anchor ready to deploy and lower the motor so that it is ready to start if we need it. We don our foul weather gear and our PFDs if we are not already wearing them. We note our position, course, landmarks, and hazards. If we are on a lee shore or if there are other boats or shipping in the vicinity, and we have time, we may start the motor and try to gain sea room. One of the things we learned in that first storm is that when it is raining and blowing that hard it is difficult to hear each other. It is best that we both just know what we need to do.

Good foul weather gear is important if you are going to be comfortable when a storm or rain shower catches up to you. We keep ours stowed where we can get at it quickly. We find that if we manage to keep our clothes mostly dry under our foulies, we stand a better chance of keeping the interior of the boat dry. A dry boat is a good thing anytime, but especially on a longer cruise. Once we anchor or take a slip for the night we do everything we can to keep the interior of the boat dry. The pop-top enclosure does a good job of keeping rain out of the interior. The bimini helps keep rain from blowing in and keeps the cockpit somewhat drier. Lacking a wet locker, we often hang our foul weather jackets from the center of the bimini where they can drip dry. Miniature woodworking clamps work wonderfully as secure clothespins. For long periods of heavy rain, we also have a tarp that we can rig over the bimini to give more protection to the cockpit or over the opening ports on the front of the cabin so we can have some ventilation and still stay dry.

The bimini's prime purpose is to keep the sun off the crew, a must in a Chesapeake summer. It works well but we also have broad-brimmed hats and dark wraparound UV protecting sunglasses. I'm particularly sun-sensitive, so I generally wear lightweight long pants and a loose long-sleeve shirt over a tank top for additional sun protection. At anchor, the bimini provides shade but when the sun is low in the early morning or late afternoon we will use the miniature wood clamps to hang large beach towels from the bimini or the rim of the pop-top to provide additional shade. The towels are stored in dry bags under the settee and are also available if anyone wants to go swimming.

We sail in cool weather too. We generally launch in late April and sail through October. We have a small portable electric heater that keeps us warm at the dock when the temperature dips into the 40s. We looked for the safest, most stable one we could find. We have a heavy fleece blanket that we use for cool nights at anchor and of course bring many layers of warm clothes.

Sailing is not a particularly dangerous sport, but safety precautions will help you avoid the incident that will ruin your day. Drowning is always a possibility. A surprise jibe could crack your skull or at least raise quite a welt if you don't get your head out of the way. Even a small cruising boat is surprisingly heavy. Get between one and a dock or another boat and you could lose a digit or crush a limb. Avoidance of these hazards is mostly common sense, but Fred and I found that a good basic boating course and a lot of reading about safety issues raised our awareness and increased our safety on the boat.

There are some safety factors specific to the Rhodes 22. It has positive flotation and won't sink even if holed. I talked to a Rhodes 22 owner whose son had grounded the boat on a sandbar with the centerboard down. A wave lifted the boat and then dropped it straight down on the centerboard pushing the board up through the fiberglass cap on the centerboard trunk. The trunk is below the waterline and the boat filled to the level of the settee seat but it floated well enough to be safely towed into port and repaired.

The Rhodes 22 has significant form stability. As it heels the water presses up against the flare of the hull and slows further heeling. In the only instance I know of a capsize, a Rhodes 22 was motoring toward a marina when it was caught on the stern quarter by a wall of water being pushed ahead of the downdraft of a microburst. The stern rose with the water and then the wind turned the boat over. Many larger boats were sunk in the same incident. The Rhodes 22 floated low, upside down with its crew clinging on. It did not right itself until the stays were cut, but it was afloat. The mast may have been stuck in the mud or just weighed down by the water filling the furled main inside the mast. The boat was totaled by the insurance company, rebuilt by General Boats, and is still sailing.

The old axiom "one hand for yourself, one for the ship" applies to all boats. Many Rhodes 22s, *Fretless* included, do not have lifelines, but they do have numerous handrails, and the stays can be used as handholds. The molded toerail also aids significantly to moving sure-footedly about the deck. With the furling jib, it is rare that you need to go forward while sailing but we occasionally snag a sheet on a cleat or have some other reason to go forward. The step from the cockpit to sidedeck is easy. The sidedecks are wide for a boat this size and have that generous toerail. There is a handrail on the cabin top and then there are the shrouds and stays to hold on to. If you are going all the way forward there is only one step beyond the cabin that does not have a good handhold. I never take that last step without knowing what I will grab and how. The bow pulpit and the furler are both possibilities. It would be possible to rig a jackline from the mast to the padeye for the drifter but we have not done so. The Rhodes 22 comes with a swim ladder and we added a Lifesling to aid in man-overboard recoveries. We carry all of the Coast Guard-required safety equipment.

Most of our navigation is coastal piloting. We rely on paper charts and a compass and use a handheld GPS for backup. On a small boat, paper charts can be unwieldy wind-catchers and we have come to rely on a chartbook in a plastic envelope. The charts are much smaller than a full-size paper chart and the plastic protects them from rain and spray. The only drawback is the fact that we frequently sail off the chart and have to calculate courses from page to page. The book we use has some courses pre-plotted and we've been known to use those courses and the GPS to help us over a particularly troublesome transition. The GPS is also useful for telling you distances to a mark and speed over ground. Ours is a simple handheld that we use to confirm our navigation on the paper charts. If we sailed in more remote areas we would probably add a knotmeter and practice our dead reckoning. We did add a fishfinder a few years ago as a depth sounder and that has given us another valuable piece of navigational information. The Chesapeake has extensive shallow areas that are accessible in a shallow draft sailboat. There are many times when a small, shallow draft boat can arrive somewhere before a faster, deeper draft boat because of this ability to cut across the shallows. It's helpful to know what's under your keel if you are taking the shortcut.

Most of our sailing remains daysailing or overnights. We make the two-hour drive to the boat most weekends. My job is flexible enough that we can often leave on a Friday afternoon and come home early on a Monday morning. Some of my neighbors who have houses at the shore do the same thing. The highlights of our sailing season are the long weekends and the five- to seven-day cruises. On a long weekend we'll generally go where wind and whim take us. From Rock Hall there are destination anchorages in almost every direction as well as the ports of Annapolis and Baltimore. On the longer cruises we'll get out the cruising guides and the charts and decide on a possible itinerary. We won't plan a day's sail longer than 25 miles (in a straight line). After six or seven hours we find ourselves more than ready to anchor or tie up. We generally plan to take a slip or a mooring every two or three days, so we can get a good shower, empty the head, and walk around.

We've been accused of sailing from restaurant to restaurant. We could plead guilty and argue in our defense that there are so many good ones so why not, but the truth is that we cook aboard a great deal as well. For a long cruise, I will have enough food aboard in planned meals and emergency rations to eat every meal on the boat. This gives us a lot of flexibility and puts us under no pressure to find places to reprovision. Our emergency rations are nonperishable so if we have the opportunity to shop, we can do so without worrying about wasting food already on board.

In planning our cruises, we try to leave a couple of extra unscheduled days so that if we get held up by weather we still have a chance of making it home on time. If, toward the end of the cruise, it looks like the weather will be good, we'll stay an extra night in a favorite port or stop in another anchorage or just get home a day early and do laundry.

We've stayed on the Chesapeake even though we could put the boat on the trailer and go cruising somewhere else. The limiting factor is once again, the other things in our lives. If we had more time or could rearrange our lives to give us more time, the list of potential destinations is practically unending. At the top of the list is a trip around the Bay, top to bottom and bottom to top. I think it would probably take two to three months to do it right. Then there's Maine, Lake Champlain, Lake George, Long Island Sound, the North Channel or Charlotte Harbor, and the Florida Keys. They are all possible in a 22-foot boat set up for cruising. Now, if we can only find the time.

Specifications for the Rhodes 22:
Length Overall: 22' 0"
Length Waterline: 20' 0"
Beam: 8' 0" (less at the waterline)
Freeboard, Average: 3' 0"
Cockpit: 7' 4"
Pop Top headroom: 6' 4"
Mast length: 26'
Bridge clearance (min.): 31'
Displacement: 2,900 lbs. Ballast: 700 lbs.
Draft: 20"/4'
Sail Area: 300 sq. ft.

CHAPTER 6

Offshore in a 22-footer

BY MICHAEL MEIER

Born in Portland, Oregon, in 1950, Michael Meier grew up on a farm before his family moved to California when he was a teenager. He has worked in broadcast television, as a professional musician, policeman, grocery clerk, construction project manager and now as a sales representative. Michael's involvement with boats began at age seven and has continued ever since. He currently lives aboard a 32-foot Nordic tug in Seattle with his wife, Helen.

T HE STORM HAD BEGUN DURING THE PREVIOUS DAY at about three o'clock in the afternoon with winds building to 50 mph and gusting to 75. At first, we thought little of the deteriorating conditions. We had encountered the usual rough sailing on our initial leg from our home port in Seattle down to the California coast. Upon leaving San Diego, however, we had expected smooth sailing. In fact, that's what we got for three days. Jogging along about 50 miles offshore, the seas had been limited to four- or five-foot swells at 15-second intervals, and we had progressed on this leg of our cruise nurtured by dreams of cold Pacifico Beer and palm trees on the horizon. How suddenly things had changed! What's more, it soon became apparent that this was to be no mere passing squall.

The waves were more like 30 feet high and higher, and I have to tell you when waves seem as high as your masthead it can get pretty scary. There were times when it seemed as if our Falmouth Cutter might not be big enough to withstand these screaming monsters. Thanks to El Niño, that once little-known weather phenomenon that causes excessive wind and sea conditions, even the area that was supposed to be nice had severe wind and sea conditions. Before we left on our dream cruise, I had never heard of El Niño, but now I surely understood that El Niño was not just some strange name, but a weather threat to take very seriously.

When we encountered the storm about 30 miles off Cabo San Quentin, we did so as part of a six-boat fleet headed south along the Pacific Coast of the U.S. bound for Mexico. All of us were seeking warmer climates with palm trees and sunny beaches, and we shared dreams of paradise. Somehow, in all the stories and dreams one comes up with, really rough times seldom enter into the equation. I, at least, tended to minimize concerns of dangerous weather and focused instead on the more positive aspects of cruising. In truth, cruising is wonderful but stormy sea conditions make the best of us a little nervous.

Even though we had spent considerable time prepping for the trip, learning everything about our boat, ourselves, and studying marine weather and storm tactics, I soon learned that nothing really prepares one for the eventful day when you are actually caught out in a storm. It was at that point, amid those big seas that I understood nobody would be coming to help us cope. It was a sobering insight but the one thing that comforted us was our belief in our boat.

Our Falmouth Cutter was by far the smallest boat in the little storm-tossed fleet that included a 50-foot custom cold-molded schooner, a 50-foot Endeavor sloop, a Whitby 42 ketch, a 33-foot Freedom cat ketch, and a 30-foot Cape Dory. Each skipper developed a different plan for handling the storm conditions. Some ran with the seas and wind. Some hove to, trimming their boats so they would lie at about 45 degrees to the wind and slowly slide backward, creating a slick in the water from the disturbance of the hull that helped to smooth down the biggest waves. Others just tried to keep moving and remain in control.

At first we kept moving toward our destination, trying to steer a comfortable course through the huge seas. However, as conditions deteriorated, we started thinking of heaving to ourselves. We tried it several times, but could not keep the head of the boat up into the waves. Finally, I determined that I needed more sail to heave to in these large seas because I needed more power to hold her head up. That said, trying to talk yourself into putting up more sail in 50-75 knots of wind is *really* hard, so we opted to keep moving, working toward our intended destination. As a last resort, we still had a nine-foot diameter sea anchor, essentially a reinforced parachute, on 400 feet of heavy line. Even so, the idea of parking our little boat in the middle of the sea lanes from Panama to Japan via the great circle route

— we were then 40 miles west of Isla San Geronimo — didn't appeal to me, especially since we couldn't see anything in the blowing spume and salt spray.

Our Falmouth Cutter now demonstrated an uncanny ability to press ahead through all of this foul weather better than the bigger boats we were with, which seemed to push through the waves, rather than ride over them like a duck. Most skippers complained of pounding terribly heading into the seas and discovered that running offered the only reasonable comfort to be found. Our boat, with no flat spots on the hull, slipped gently along with an easy motion and a surprisingly comfortable ride. Together with one of our buddy boats, *Salty Dog*, the Cape Dory 30, we worked up a plan to move closer to shore where it was reported that the waves were smaller and where we might even enter Punta San Carlos at the north end of large Bahia de Sebastian Viscaino, which lies just short of half way down Baja Mexico. We had hoped it could provide a somewhat sheltered anchorage. Getting there required us to sail just south of Sacramento Reef, which is known as one bad place to be on the Pacific side of Mexico. However, when we finally did arrive at Punta San Carlos, we found huge breakers and numerous lobster pots. The bay, which lies just short of halfway down Baja Mexico, offered no haven of security and, as sheltering there was completely impossible, we immediately put back to sea.

We weathered that nasty storm for five more days. When the wind finally settled down, the storm was labeled the worst off the west coast of Baja Mexico since 1949. Ours was the last boat to arrive in Bahia San Bartolome and we were received with some pretty nice greetings as we circled the anchorage looking for the right spot to anchor. With that accomplished, we were soon made to feel welcome with gifts of fresh-baked bread and other treats. We were "the little boat that could" and we had survived with ourselves and our vessel intact and ready to enjoy our new surroundings.

I have often asked myself how it was that I found myself aboard an ocean-going small yacht on the Pacific Coast in a gale! The answer to the question is found in my childhood. TV shows like "Adventures in Paradise," books like *The Venturesome Voyages of Captain Voss, Trekka 'Round the World, Through the Roaring Forties* by Vito Dumas, Slocum's *Sailing Alone Around the World* and *Kon-Tiki* all helped influence my desire to explore by sailboat. When my friends went water skiing on the local lakes, I went sailing. Some of my friends didn't think sailing was macho enough — where's the vroom and the wake? That changed, however, when I took them sailing on a blustery day that soon had my Sunfish skimming along at some six knots on Whiskey Town Lake in Northern California. Most of my friends then thought I was simply nuts to be out there. In my youth I spent many a day in the water trying to right a capsized boat, and repair my dripping wet relationships with fair maidens.

As a young adult I was landlocked in the high desert of central Oregon and sailed the lakes with an occasional trip to the San Juan Islands. More serious sailing had to wait until vacations on the Columbia River aboard a Ranger 20, and a 25-foot US Yacht. My cruising experience on the Oregon and Washington coast exposed me early to some really rough sailing thanks to the big swells, dangerous river bars, and the bad weather typical of the area.

On one trip from Portland to Barkley Sound on the Western side of Vancouver, Canada, with a boatload of kids all around 12 years old, we hit a storm that blew out the main sail and damaged the diesel engine by shearing off the oil filter housing. That allowed the oil to escape, forcing us to sail back to the Columbia River Bar, cross the bar, and enter a small boat harbor, all without the help of an engine, and with the kids as crew. Once, on a delivery trip with a new owner on board, we rounded Cape Flattery headed south in zero visibility and rough conditions, hoping to break out of the weather. Instead, we had to sail all the way to the Columbia and cross the bar without ever seeing any aids to navigation, the jetties, or anything else – a total of 40 hours of blind sailing! On another delivery trip from Seattle to Portland with a green crew aboard who had never sailed, we were almost put on the beach while I tried to get some sleep. Then, we had to wait at sea when the Columbia River Bar was closed because of heavy conditions.

I also tried a little racing but was always drawn to far horizons, not marker buoys. By age 35, my sailing career had taken its toll and I found myself divorced. I bought the largest boat I had owned to date, a 32-foot Fuji ketch, and moved aboard with my two kids. The ketch got small quickly with three people living aboard, especially when two of them were preteens! Still, the boat provided a home for us all, a place to heal and grow emotionally healthy again. It also served as that very special place where some of my own passion for sailing could be passed on to my children, so they too could have dreams and romance in their souls.

As always, the kids grew and we all moved on in life. In 1991, I met my new sailing companion, best friend, and future wife, Helen. When we met, my first question was how she felt about sailing and could she cruise and live aboard a vessel. Fortunately, the answers were "yes" to all the questions. She was someone who understood and also heard the voices calling to all of us irresponsible sailors. Like me, she had also watched "Adventures in Paradise" as a child and, oddly enough, had a house full of sailboat art. We were without a boat when we met, since I sold the Fuji to buy a house, which seemed like the right thing to do with two children in high school.

Then one magical day when we were between boats doing what sailors do best, walking the docks to admire all the beautiful boats, we came across *Mariko*. This, we learned, was a Lyle Hess-designed Falmouth Cutter. She was hull number nine, built by the Sam L. Morse Company in 1981. Among the things that set the boat apart was her rare, factory-finished interior versus a home-built version. Helen said she did not know what kind of boat it was, but if she was going to buy a boat, this would be the one. For my part, I thought the boat's long, sturdy bowsprit, substantial bulwarks, and boxy cabin with three bronze ports on each side made her a classic beauty. Three days later *Mariko* — the very first Falmouth Cutter I had ever seen — was ours! At that time there were only 27 of them in the world, so they were (and still remain) rare. We felt like we owned an heirloom that could not be replaced.

Now that I owned *Mariko*, all those boyhood dreams of cruising seemed within my grasp. The primary issue seemed to be the boat's size. Everyone always said the same thing when inspecting *Mariko*: "What a cute boat, but she sure is small." I wondered to myself if their comments were not entirely correct. Still, to me, the boat seemed perfect. I moved aboard and started prepping our little vessel for cruising.

Initially, we docked and sailed the boat at Big Oak Marine on Multnomah Channel on the Columbia River. This gave us lots of experience going upstream or downstream, but not much in the way of real ocean sailing. We worked on getting to know our little beauty and planned a relocation to Seattle, which would require an off-shore passage. In fact, it was on that trip that we experienced our first foul weather with the boat.

When we departed the Columbia River, the forecast was for southwesterly winds of 15 – 20 knots. These proved to be 30-35 knots winds accompanied by 13-foot seas on the port quarter. Being our first experience with this boat offshore, we had contacted the Coast Guard just to let them know our location, heading, and speed in case something should go wrong. The Falmouth handled those conditions wonderfully and provided us our first glimpse into the great sea-keeping ability of the boat. During the night the Coast Guard put an hourly position check on us to make sure we were okay. We were forced to put into La Push, Washington, where nobody in a sailboat goes, but with a wife's medical emergency caused by food poisoning from our last meal on shore, we had no choice.

To this day, I remain thankful to the gallant Coast Guard crew that escorted us into the entrance of the bar at La Push for that emergency. The Coast Guard works in the worst of weather, doing an often thankless job, with little or no reward other than the relief they see in the faces of the people they save and help. Imagine my shock when I learned that the men of that motor lifeboat were killed just a few months later when their 42-foot surf boat was rolled over and thrown against the rocky sides of Anderson Island outside La Push.

Helen and I finished our first ocean passage with little drama. Once settled in Seattle we found ourselves docked among blue water boats, salty marine stores, and numerous sailors who were highly experienced. We set some goals and time lines, went to work at our new jobs, and dreamed of cruising within a few years. And we enjoyed ourselves immensely. When you put more than one small cruising boat in the same neighborhood as another, they always seem to end up next to each other. Soon, *Mariko* was joined by new sailing friends that included the owners of a 20-foot Flicka, a 24-foot Dana, and several others. Together, we spent many a wonderful afternoon sailing Puget Sound. We were surprised to find that, even loaded with all our live-aboard stuff, *Mariko* could always out-point and outrun all of them. Gradually, we began to believe that, small as she was, our boat was well up to our planned cruising. When we met Lynn and Larry Pardey, the cruising couple who had so effectively championed the virtues of their own Lyle Hess cutter, *Seraffyn*, I asked Larry if the Falmouth was strong enough for deep-sea cruising. His answer: "Heck, yes! It was plenty strong for anything we could throw at it." With that recommendation, nothing was going to stop us. Later, the Pardeys used one of my wife's photographs in one of their books about storm tactics.

In June 1995, we started to prepare the boat for our adventure by tackling the expensive and tough things first, and we soon learned that a 22-foot boat posed some special engineering challenges simply because of size constraints. We wanted to re-power *Mariko* because we'd been hit by a large following sea that forced salt water into our engine through the exhaust outlet. Diesel engines are wonderful things but they make terrible water pumps! Yanmar had a replacement engine for our now "salt-water injected" single-cylinder, eight-hp BMW, which was of similar dimensions. However, while checking prices, I found a two-cylinder, 15-hp Yanmar for the same price as the single-cylinder model, so I bought it and started the engineering to make it fit.

Mariko was the first Falmouth to get a two-cylinder diesel. During installation, I added a shut-off valve in the exhaust line to keep any future sea water out of the engine. Needless to say, our two-cylinder Yanmar gave us plenty of power with very little additional fuel use. We used a three-blade prop to give us the highest transfer of power possible. Because the prop was tucked in a hidden aperture behind the full keel, our sailing did not suffer as much as one might think. The extra horsepower also allowed us to install a high-powered alternator and smart regulator for battery charging which kept running times to a minimum when topping up the batteries.

For additional electrical energy, we mounted a 55-watt solar panel across the cabin top. Solar panel placement should be in a safe location to avoid breaking seas and foot traffic, so the housetop was about as safe as it gets. It was also a location that minimized shadows because, when sailing, the boom was seldom centered over the panel, so we got full output. At anchor, I just swung the boom out over the side to clear the panel of any shadows. We could generally stay at anchor for days and days without running short of electricity to run the computer, lights, and the ham radio that we used to say in contact with family and friends back home.

With all of our new-found electrical output, we could now power a water maker. This we installed under the sink. I plumbed the fittings to mate with the existing drains and water inputs, limiting thru-hull fittings, which is always a good thing, I think. The unit could run all day while we were sailing or anchored using solar power, and it required us to use the engine only occasionally to top up the batteries. The success of this water maker is demonstrated by the fact that we never shore-filled our water in our two years in Mexico. Nor did we ever have any problems with our water maker, which I attribute to the fact that we used it all the time. When buying a water maker, the trend is to buy big with high outputs in the 10-20 gallons and hour output. These bigger units make much more water than one can use in a day. Our unit made 1 1/2 gallons per hour, so I could run it daily, which also had the advantage of keeping the filters clear of bacteria and other impurities. Just as our boat would prove that bigger is not necessarily better, so did our water maker.

Once the new engine and the water maker had been installed, I turned my attention to the boat's rigging. Considering that we were heading out for up to 10 years, we did not want any rigging failures, so we replaced all the standing rigging with new wire and Sta-Lok fittings. Running rigging was replaced with Sta-Set X for low stretch. Rather than have a rigger do the work, we had a rigger teach me how to splice braided line and measure standing rigging. I also learned how to replace the existing swaged fittings — which tend to dramatically fail at the wrong time — with Sta-Lok fittings that can be repaired at sea if needed. The rigger taught me what kind of wire to use, and how big, and how to upsize the bottle screws to match what I needed. I learned that these fittings are usually totally incorrect on most boats. I learned how the toggle pin used to support the bottle screw is usually too small for truly reliable performance and I also learned how to tune the rig for optimum performance. By the time the rigger left, I was able to complete all the rigging changes.

The Falmouth is cutter-rigged, meaning two head sails ahead of the mast and a main sail aft of the mast. One of the advantages of this rig is the ability it provides to shorten sail by moving it constantly in toward the center of the boat and down, closer to the deck. In lighter winds you do just the opposite and hang large amounts of sail up and out. The boat's bowsprit allows a good-sized genoa jib to be set while also having a staysail that is actually of some size and power. The genoa was mounted on a roller furler at the tip of the bowsprit, and could be quickly reduced to any size. The spinnaker was tri-radial in design with its own luff wire so we could set it on a pendant and tack it back and forth like a genoa, if needed. The spinnaker pole is the Pardey style, with a continuous line running a car and slide up and down the mast, continuously adjustable, lockable at any height, and a secure place to store a normally unwieldy pole in rough weather.

During foul weather, our typical sail reduction would be to reef the main first at around 15 knots or less. Since it did not affect speed much, why not be comfortable? At 20 knots, the roller fuller was rolled up halfway, and at 25 knots to 30, the genoa was rolled up completely. Bt the time it was blowing over 35 knots, it was time for a second reef in the main using a standard single line jiffy reefing system. Once the wind increased much more, we used the staysail alone and, if it looked like conditions would get worse still, we would set the storm jib on the inner head stay normally used for the staysail. The storm jib was carried in 50-plus knots of wind, although in anything over 50 plus, I think it is time to consider heaving to and taking the strain off the rig and crew.

One of the disconcerting things we discovered about our boat's sail plan was that it produced a serious amount of weather helm when the wind increased. To counter this, our sail maker suggested we take some of the rearward tilt out of the mast, and add a more efficient staysail with a few extra square feet ahead of the mast. What's more, he recut the genoa by raising the clew slightly for improved forward visibility, which also powered up the larger staysail better. The effect was immediately noticeable and the boat was much more manageable and better balanced. It is absolutely amazing how little changes in the sail plan can make huge benefits for the performance of the vessel.

With the rig complete, we turned our attention to steering. For offshore sailing, one would love to have an extra crew member to steer and stand watches. In a Falmouth Cutter, two people can handle the watches, but the steering gets really tiresome. "Radcliff," as we nicknamed our self-steering vane after its manufacturer, was a servo pendulum in design. It was a wind-powered vane manufactured by Radcliff Marine in Penobscot, Maine, for Falmouth Cutters. The vane could steer a better course than Helen or I and, of course, required no food, drink, or sleep. The addition of a self-steering vane makes a boat more efficient and safe, and gives one the needed rest to stay alert.

Once we were hit by another boat in a marina and our vane paddle was damaged. We called Radcliff and asked about a replacement and were told they were not just run-of-the-mill parts and that every paddle had to be the exact weight as the counterweights to be "zero biasing." Zero biasing means that both the wind vane itself, and the counterbalance weight used to center the vane straight up and down must be the exact same weight. When that is the case, the unit is not influenced in any direction other than wind force on the vane itself. During my phone call with the manufacturer, I could hear, in the background, the calculator punching out numbers for the fiberglass costs, shop costs, grinding costs, and shipping. To our surprise, the cost was minimal. In fact Radcliff talked us into another spare set of bushings for a pittance compared to other systems. Radcliff Marine manufactures wind vanes for small boats on boat-by-boat basis. They are very effective vanes at very reasonable prices.

The trick to any vane use is proper trim of the boat itself. A Falmouth Cutter with her cutter rig, full keel, and balanced helm can be trimmed to almost sail herself. About all the vane needs to do is make small adjustments for swell and wind shifts. The true test for a vane is the ability to sail downwind, and still steer a steady course.

For periods of extended motoring times, we carried two tiller-pilot type autopilots, both named "Auto." We destroyed one pilot and buried it at sea, and used the backup for the remainder of the trip. If you can imagine crossing an eight-foot swell every eight seconds for six months, just think of all the small adjustments the autopilot would make during that time. No wonder they don't last!

After buying everything else, we could not afford radar, and so opted for a radar detector. This gave us the relative direction and signal strength of broadcasting radar. The theory here is that, in fog, everyone would have radar running, so all we needed to do was avoid those guys and we would be okay. In practice the unit did work well. In fact, there were a few times, including one in the Santa Barbara Channel, where all we could see was fog interrupted by the occasional offshore oil platform, which came looming out of the fog with their attendant crew boats running around at 30 knots. All the boats around us running radar could not see those low-riding wooden crew boats, but I could see the approximate location and distance to them with the detector since they were all running their radar.

Our other electronics included a digital depth sounder, GPS with a handheld backup, a VHF radio and a SSB/Ham radio for HF use. We used a notebook with a small demodulator for downloading weather fax to the notebook computer off the HF radio. This allowed us to develop our own amateur weather forecasts and certainly gave us something to talk about with other sailors. Our greatest pleasure was using the ham radio to call home and check in with family and friends. Several of my old ham friends back home maintained radio schedules for us so we could phone patch to loved ones and report in. Our antenna consisted of an insulated section in the back stay that we fed through a manual antenna tuner. I highly recommend that anyone going cruising should spend the time to get a ham radio license before departure, and know how to operate the radio gear as well as they know how to run the boat itself.

In May 1996, I quit my job to work full time on the boat and in July, we had our pocket cruiser all decked out with every possible sailing trick available Of course, we still needed to be able to stay put when we anchored. We carried a 35-pound CQR and 275 feet of 1/4" high-tensile chain as our main working anchor, with two Danforth backups, and a 75-pound fisherman anchor in the bilge as a storm hook. We had chain and line for each anchor. All this ground tackle was stored out of the way, yet in accessible places so that we could get any of the anchors and rodes quickly, if needed. Try that in your average 22-foot boat! All the chain is kept in an ample, open-top chain locker in the bow. The open top was important, because it allowed the chain to breathe and not smell badly as most messy chain does with time. It also made it easy to clear any constrictions or tangles in the chain that may occur while anchoring or hoisting anchor.

To handle the anchors, we had a Simpson Lawrence manual windlass with the appropriate chain gypsy and rope gypsy on the opposing side. We installed a handle holder on the side of the cabin house so that we did not need to carry a handle each time we went forward, which is the major reason all those windlass handles now lie in Davy Jones's Locker.

For those who have ever visited La Paz, Mexico, and understand the "La Paz Waltz," our heavy working anchor system would make perfect sense. In La Paz Bay, the current runs four to five knots in one direction, and the wind in the other. The anchored boats blow forward on their anchor chain, turn sideways, and then the keel catches the current and off they go, sailing back and forth on the anchor chain, swinging from side to side. Now imagine 65 boats doing that, all at different rates in different directions and you have the La Paz Waltz. We actually had all the chain rode out in 16 feet of water several times, and we *still* stayed up all night at anchor watch just to make sure we stayed put and stayed anchored.

What do two people do on a 22-foot boat when cruising? The answer is the same thing you do on a 50-foot boat. You can only be in one place at a time so look at all the extra room you really have! Most of one's time is spent on watch. Our watch schedule started at six PM and lasted three hours on and off throughout the night. I started so I could prep the boat for night sailing, and prepare for any weather circumstances planned for that night. In the daytime we shared the deck duties, so whoever was on deck had the watch. All in all it was a fairly workable schedule except that at five AM each morning, it always blew up and my rest periods were always cut short since we would both be on deck for that morning's weather surprise. One advantage of a small cruising boat is that the off-watch person can readily hear the other person on deck. Should there be a problem it is immediately evident because there is a change in motion. In addition, on a small boat, everything on deck is just a short distance away.

We were very comfortable in *Mariko*. We each had our own particular space separate from the other's, and to be used by that person alone. This matter of separate space soon became a sacred thing with us. I do not infringe on Helen's space, and she stays out of mine. When invited, we would share, but keeping each other happy is of great importance to us, so we always kept the sacred space rule. To identify our special places, we each spent some time alone in *Mariko* when we bought her. We'd sit, read, lie down, and just reflect on the entire interior to identify that one special location. After we identified several possibilities, we discussed them and compromised on those areas that were in conflict so that we each had our own special spot that was somewhat private only to that person.

Many cruising couples with small boats develop the same philosophy, and ultimately this consideration for each other gives sailing couples a giant leg up over the landsman when it comes to respect for individuals and caring for another human being. Have you ever noticed how close cruising couples are? Ever wonder why and how they could be so close living in such tight quarters? I have often been very thankful for the opportunity to raise my children on a sailboat so they could develop that respect for people and space.

On *Mariko*, the companionway hatch slid under a canvas sea hood. This kept water from seeking that certain drip point that always catches the off-watch person as they are sleeping. As a further protection against water intrusion below, an eye was installed in the back of each drop board so a lanyard with a snap could be snapped in and locked in a jam cleat mounted inside the companionway. If the cockpit ever flooded or, worse still, if the boat ever capsized, the lanyard would stop the boards from floating away. It also gave us the additional security of being able to lock the boards in place when at anchor at night.

The seating/sleeping arrangements on our Falmouth Cutter proved to be perfect for two people. The two quarter-berths are settees, which face center with a sliding table that pulls out from over the engine lid. We could sit together for meals, to play cards, to read, and still had the room to spread out and have space. For sleeping — to keep the settees comfortable yet easy to make up or clean — we used the Travasak brand system. This is similar to two quilts joined by zippers on each side, with Velcro sewn into the edges for securing specially fitted sheets. You end up with a bed-like feel and look, including sheets. There is even a summer and winter side as one quilt is heavier than its summer cousin, allowing for seasonal changes.

During engine maintenance times, the table was removed from the center section, revealing the entire top of the motor. Access is further gained by opening the cover in the front of the engine.

We found *Mariko*'s interior layout overall to be vastly more user friendly than most boats, including the larger Bristol Channel Cutter, whose interior seems broken up with bulkheads and rather strange angles. Aboard *Mariko*, we served dinner for six people several times and everyone had a spot to sit that was fairly comfortable. Our little boat continuously became the meeting place because she was comfortable and homey, and she made everyone feel welcome.

The galley, which lies amidships facing port, is secure for the cook in a seaway since the food locker to starboard is close enough to lean against and stop any falls as soon as they begin. Rather than use an electric propane solenoid we installed a manual gas valve just inside the bulkhead, right at the cook's shoulder. This provided a safe way to turn on the gas without either an electrical switch or going on deck. With only one bronze fitting where the gas line and valve fit together inside the boat, gas leaks were very unlikely and very testable at that one spot. The propane bottles were stored in nesting bases on each side of the mast with a canvas cover and then secured to the deck.

All bulk food in dried form was in the food locker under the chart table. Noodles, flour, rice, spices, and beans were stored in plastic bins in large quantities, which extended our cruising range. We carried 300 tins of canned goods under the floorboards over the keel, low and centered where the weight should be.

We did not use any refrigeration. We had experimented with several icebox arrangements but each took up valuable space with all the insulation required to make a box that would be efficient, so it was decided to go without cold storage other than in the bilge close to the sea water. While we sometimes missed a cold drink or beer, we got along fine. Our ancestors managed without refrigerators and ice makers, so why can't we? It took a little adjusting but we learned to handle foods differently. We learned which foods lasted longer, such as cabbage instead of lettuce, white bread instead of wheat, and powdered instead of whole milk and changed our diet slightly. It all worked out just great. There are at least 356 ways to cook Spam!

We also learned to carry our vegetables in nets to allow for air circulation. The gentle swinging in the net kept them from being bumped and bruised against one another. We also found that products that had never been under refrigeration did not need to be refrigerated at all, but once they had been in cold storage the shelf life was destroyed. Eggs kept for months as long as you rotate them weekly so the inner lining of the egg did not dry out, causing it to rot. Cabbage can be used for very long times if you remove the outer leaves one a time exposing fresh surface continually. Unfinished meals could be left on the stove and rewarmed for several days as long as you warmed them to boiling temperatures and kept them at that temperature for 10 minutes to kill anything that might have started to grow.

Once we caught a large dorado and cooked the entire fish in one day, rewarmed it and later ate from that same fish for about a week with no ill effects. When we bartered with the locals for shellfish we often would be completely overwhelmed with quantities like 187 tiger prawns that were slightly frozen. We kept them wrapped tightly in damp towels and took out enough for a meal at a time and did not disturb the balance still wrapped in towels. They lasted for a week. Not having refrigeration did not mean going without; we had it all, and often.

Forward in the Falmouth Cutter are the head and a v-berth. We used this area for storage. On the port side a pullman berth was made up of several slide- in-and-lock panels, which we found cumbersome when sailing, so it became our main large item storage area. The very large forward hatch allowed easy removal of items stowed below, like the liferaft and ditch bag. Very few boats have adequate storage for really large items. The goal is this: after you get them stored, can you get them out of the boat in a hurry? The boat's hanging locker had been converted to hold a Sigmar diesel cabin heater for keeping warm in the northern climates, so all of our clothes were rolled, stowed in plastic bags, and put into the quarter-berth lockers.

Have you ever tried to use the average marine head while dressed in 15 layers of clothes looking like the Michelin Man or Pillsbury Dough Boy? Most head compartments are very small, unlike the Falmouth, which has the head sitting on the starboard side in the forepeak, under the large opening hatch. This wonderful arrangement gave you a large area to wrestle your clothes on and off while using the facilities. A simple modesty curtain pulled across the hatchway between the main cabin and forepeak for the shy but, for us, looking aft and up the companionway was a nice way to keep an eye out for the on-deck watchkeeper.

Most sailboat interiors are quite dark and often remind me of what it would be like to live inside a log. *Mariko* had a wonderful deck prism, which flooded the entire front section from hanging locker to chain locker with light, creating a zone that was cheery and bright. We installed fluorescent double tubes in the center cabin top. This effectively illuminated the entire cabin while, at the same time, was very electrically efficient.

New Falmouth Cutters have wooden strips affixed to the exposed parts of the hull for a finished, dressy look that is efficient for controlling moisture and mildew. The older boats like *Mariko* had sheet cork installed, which sounded like a good way to go but as we cruised we discovered the cork tended to absorb some moisture and then hold on to it for a long time. We considered various coverings and methods of changing the liner, but finally decided extra ventilation was cheaper and better in the long run for controlling moisture. We added two large cabin-top dorade boxes made of teak, each with a bronze cowl ventilator. Facing one forward and one backward greatly increased air flow below. We then installed Dri-Dek brand rubber grating, which comes in one foot squares that snap together, on all cork surfaces, all locker bottoms, and under our berths. The grating held everything that all-important quarter-inch away from the surfaces, and allow some ventilation. We also installed one tube-type electric dry air heater in each clothes locker so that, when docked and shore power was available, we had the ability to dry those areas and increase air flow.

Tankage aboard the boat was well thought out. The fuel tank was located directly under the cockpit sole, with filler located in the center of the sole. This puts the tank fairly central and on the hull's centerline, so trim does not change with fuel levels. Much the same is true of the water tank, which is located under the engine, deep in the keel so the weight is kept where it should be. The tube filler was located in the cabin, in front of the engine under the inspection lid. This did make for some exciting filling until we learned it was a very good way to check the bilge pump. We'd let any excess water drain into the pump well, causing the pump to run.

The smaller the boat, the greater the need for a good bilge pump. Because the volume of the interior is comparatively less than that of a bigger boat, a two-inch hole could quickly become a serious issue. We installed the largest electric bilge pump that we could fit into the bilge. The pump had an internal float switch. The outlet was located in a controversial location in the cockpit, which constantly got comments about the installation. Many sailors install a light or meter that registers each cycle the pump runs to identify when it is running. I went one step better by installing the outlet behind my right leg, which got soaked every time the pump went on, so I knew immediately if there was water entering the boat. For a backup, we installed a manual bilge pump accessible in the aft storage locker.

Dinghies are always a challenge for the cruising sailor. Our tender was an Avon 9.5 inflatable roll-up. This we kept rolled and stowed ahead of the cabin top, aft of the forward hatch in a nice little recess designed in the deck. Secured with a couple of tie-downs, the inflatable traveled well in its bag, ready for deployment. To inflate, we simply pulled the boat from the bag, swung it fore and aft and inflated it on the foredeck. We then hoisted it and lowered it with a halyard. This allowed us to store the dinghy on deck at night by simply hoisting it out of the water to deter any thieves. When rolled up, the boat did not interfere at all with *Mariko*'s operation. Using an inflatable in a beach landing through the surf is much easier than a hard dinghy, because they are more stable and still float when full of water. Since inflatable boats generally do not row very well at all in current or wind, we used a 3.5 Nissan outboard to power it.

As our cruising experience broadened, we found *Mariko*'s small size to be an advantage in smaller bays where swinging room on the anchor was limited. What's more, we could often anchor in shallow water close to the beach. We also were a smaller target for bandits and thieves who looked at us as just a little boat. What could the owners of so small a vessel have that would be worth stealing? Being small also meant that many marinas could find a spot for us where the bigger boats would be out of luck. Our offshore insurance was based on the size and experience of the crew, which made for lower premiums, although some concern was expressed about the boat's short length.

Our trip down the coast from Seattle to Mexico lasted for 120 days, including a variety of stops. When we arrived, we found that we were accepted quite readily by the Mexicans, since we lived in a smaller space than they did. We were not considered "rich Americans" and this was great. We were never hassled by officials, and were treated with great respect by harbor masters, port captains, and naval personnel. The only nasty remarks were by Americans sailing their huge mega yachts claiming we were a nuisance that would require rescuing by the Coast Guard soon.

We sailed Mexico and the Sea of Cortez for two years. We wandered in and out of bays, snorkeled every day if we wanted to, and lived off the sea. When we did use marinas the cost was less because of our size. We were actually somewhat of a celebrity since we were the smallest boat in the fleet, and one of the most active.

Our actual cruising costs were fairly low and averaged around $950 monthly, which included offshore boat insurance, health insurance for us, all maintenance costs, all food and fuel costs, and any entertainment expenses we might incur, including meals out, airfare home for visits, and calling cards for the telephone. A very good suggestion from the Pardeys was to put your monthly expense money in an envelope for that month only, spend what you need, and put the remainder in another envelope for a rainy day. Never, but never, use more than your envelope allowance for that month!

We used an American Express card to transfer funds, and watched the exchange rate daily and only exchanged dollars to pesos when the rate was in our favor. We would typically carry a $1,000 in Mexican pesos hidden around the boat in various places. We never used dollars in Mexico, we never exchanged funds in small towns, and we never carried large sums of money, fancy jewelry, or cameras, and we never had a problem.

Only once during our trip were we confronted with an official that wanted a bribe, or "mordita" as it was called, and that was at a roadside stop where the police flagged you down using spikes across the road. They inspected our papers, and asked us to unload stuff for inspection, or pay dollars to avoid inspection. I simply got out of the van we were traveling north in and slowly, very slowly started unloading all the stuff in the van. The Mexican cop got tired of waiting for me and said to go ahead and go. He got no mordita from us.

Our cruising plan had been to sail Mexico until it wasn't fun anymore, and then head across the Pacific. But we hit a small snag. It gets really hot in the summer, and Helen, who is from Maine, wilts. Each day, as the Mexican summer got closer, she faded further and further away until, finally, she was "done," and so was our plan to cross the Pacific. So when the right time came, we put the perfect cruiser on a truck and hauled her to Seattle and home. We negotiated with a Mexican hauler to Tucson, Arizona, and an American driver from there to Olympia, Washington. I asked both haulers that they please let us know when they had a trip going in that direction to pick up a boat. That way, we would give them our boat to haul, giving them some profit going north, which saved us half the usual rate. All I needed was a few days advance notice to prepare the boat for shipping.

When the allotted time came I rode with the driver to Tucson, watched as *Mariko* was unloaded, and waited for the American driver who arrived the next day. He fell in love with our boat and called *Mariko* his little girl. Later, when we sold her, the same driver showed up to haul her to California and hugged the boat, and again called her his little girl, and asked if she had missed him. The man was obviously a boat owner and lover.

Thus did we put *Mariko* on a truck in San Carlos, Mexico, and ship her back to Puget Sound. At the same time, we prepared to re-enter life as most people know it. Needless to say, before a month had passed, Helen and I were both dreaming of sailing again. This time, however, to preserve our marriage, we planned on heading north to Alaska. When looking at Alaskan cruising, one has to consider certain things like rain, cold, snow, and wind. Because we did not want to spend all our time on deck with the elements, we started looking at pilothouse sailboats and soon found a Fisher 34. Suddenly, we became two-boat owners, in love with both boats, but for different reasons. We prepped the new boat, and took off for an exploratory trip north to Princess Louisa Inlet for a month. We had a great trip, enjoying fresh snow, and beautiful scenery all from the inside of the pilothouse.

When we returned to Seattle a month later, we needed to move *Mariko* to another slip across Puget Sound for storage, so we piled aboard and headed out. We immediately noticed the little boat's easy motion and her better handling. It was dramatically clear that *Mariko* was by far the better sailboat, despite her much smaller size. So now we wrestled with the choice – big open pilothouse, or great seaboat? The Fisher, which is admittedly designed as something of a motorsailer, won out, but to this day we keep a picture of *Mariko* in every boat we own.

As this is written, four years have passed since we sold *Mariko*. The Fisher 34 has worked well for us on several trips up north, and it has been a very nice live-aboard boat. It has also been my home office, and I have entertained guests and clients on board. But once again we are thinking of distant destinations, most of which are up north. We have learned several important things about sailing north: a lack of dependable winds, high currents, and narrow channels prevail. It is for these reasons that we have sold the Fisher and just purchased a 32-foot Nordic Tug.

Am I through with sailing small boats? Never! We have a nine-foot Ranger Minto sailing dinghy that we sail frequently to ease the need. I am also asked to deliver sailboats here and there for owners occasionally. But once you have cruised aboard a small boat, you realize that a certain feel and excitement can be lacking aboard a bigger vessel. If I were to go to sea again it would be in a Falmouth Cutter.

Looking back now, it seems to me that Lyle Hess knew exactly what he was doing when he created the Falmouth Cutter. For one thing, the boat has an undeniably salty look about her, thanks to her graceful sheerline, substantial bulwark (unusual on most boats today) a boxy cabin, bowsprit, boomkin, and boom gallows. As befits a blue water yacht, there is only a very small foot well in the cockpit to reduce flooding in a following sea. The stepped deck – the foredeck was six inches lower than the deck around the cabin – does much to shed head seas while the full keel and outboard rudder are clearly marks of a boat intended for offshore work.

The mast is deck-stepped mast for easy removal and maintenance. The shrouds attach to huge, stainless steel chain plates that are on the outer edge of the hull, thru-bolted using ½-inch stainless steel bolts to equally sized backing plates. The location of these sturdy chain plates provides clear side decks, and decent sheeting angles.

Many people confuse the Flicka and Falmouth only because they are less than 25 feet long and have bowsprits. The differences are immense, especially when it comes to sailing ability. The Falmouth Cutter is a powerhouse to weather and can carry much more cargo, which is needed for the long-range cruiser.

For us, *Mariko* was the little cruiser that could and always *did.* In her, we departed on time, arrived safely, survived the storm, used less fuel, and served as a meeting place for other cruisers. She was in fact, a "sailor's sailboat" with a seakindly hull and an easily managed sail plan. At our mountain cabin, we have an area dedicated to boats. We call it our "sailor section." On the wall is a photo of *Mariko* sailing off the California coast. It is one of my favorite possessions, and *Mariko*, long gone though she is, will forever be the most important boat I have ever owned.

Editor's Note: for specifications of the Falmouth Cutter, see Chapter One.

CHAPTER 7

A Canoe Yawl in the Bahamas

BY DAVID BELLOWS

David Bellows is a psychologist who learned to sail at summer camp at age 11 and has been at it ever since. His family owned a pair of 28-foot cruising boats and these, together with his reading of Joshua Slocum and Irving Johnson, inspired a lifelong dream of someday making his own voyage in his own boat. The dream persisted through poverty-stricken student years until a move to Maine, where David acquired a 17-foot O'Day Daysailer that he outfitted with a cockpit tent and camping gear. He cruised hundreds of miles of Maine's coastline in this boat before finances permitted him to order a new Rob Roy 23, the vessel that carried him on the journey described here. "At some point," he said, "I could have afforded a larger boat, but Tryphena *met my needs. I liked the responsiveness of a small boat. I enjoyed being close to the water and more in tune with the elements. There is also something to be said for having a boat whose bottom can be painted with a single quart of paint."*

Tᴴᴱ LIGHTS ON THE DARK HORIZON AHEAD WERE CONFUSING. I struggled to hold the binoculars steady against the motion of the boat and stared intently at the irregular straggle of lights, trying to wring more clues out of them. The low-lying land beneath them was invisible on this black, overcast night. There should be two islands ahead. The lights must be on Cat Cay, I thought, since it is a rich-man's private club, while Gun Cay — the more northerly — is uninhabited. According to the cruising guide, Gun Cay has an anchorage along its western shore with no offshore obstructions.

It looked fairly easy to enter at night, but I still had to find my way in.

I had rejected the island of Bimini — 10 miles to the north — as a landfall because the entrance to its harbor is through an unmarked, narrow, dogleg entrance channel that runs between a shoal and the beach. It seemed too dangerous for a stranger to try in the dark. Through the binoculars, I could see no sign of the lighthouse that the chart showed on Gun Cay. I had expected the light to guide me directly into the anchorage. Yet, I wasn't entirely surprised, having been warned that, in the Bahamas, aids to navigation are often inoperable or missing.

Despite these misgivings, I was thrilled to make my first landfall after the 62-mile passage from Miami. Finding my way into an unfamiliar anchorage in the dark is not my idea of fun, but there was no way to make the crossing within the span of daylight provided by a short winter day. Crossing the Gulf Stream, that great river in the sea that flows north between Florida and the Bahamas with a current that sometimes exceeds four knots, can be dangerous if you get caught in the strong northerly winds that accompany a front. Then the wind blowing against the swift current creates steep seas that can quickly cause survival conditions for a small vessel. The prevailing easterlies, however, can mean a long slow beat while you are swept off course by the current.

I had seized the best weather window available, a dead calm, and had motored across. With her new engine kept at less than full revs to slowly break it in, my 23-foot yawl *Tryphena Chandler* would make only 4 1/2 knots,

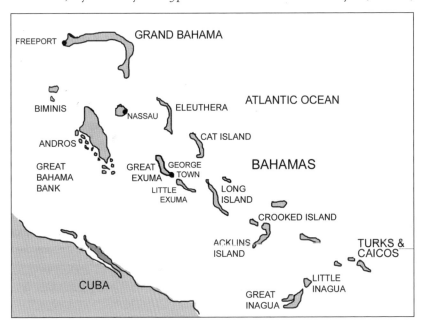

so I had to aim as much as 40 degrees south of my intended course to keep from being swept north by the Stream's current. During the crossing, I had kept on course by monitoring my progress with the GPS and hourly plots on the chart. Now the lights gave me my first glimpse of the Bahamas.

I had set up a waypoint in my GPS at a point off the entrance to the channel between Gun and Cat Cays, and from there I expected to be able to turn north into the anchorage. Now, still exhausted from a recent bout with pneumonia, my early morning departure, and the strain of the passage, it seemed like an eternity between when I first sighted the lights and when I approached the actual waypoint. A half-mile out, the depth sounder began to pick up the bottom, but the lights ahead still confused me. They extended much too far north. I expected that the northern end of the lights would mark the passage between the islands, since uninhabited Gun Cay should be dark. Did I believe the GPS that the passage was at the waypoint, or my eyes that told me it should be well to the north, at the end of the lights? This distinction was crucial, since there was a point of land jutting out from the northern end of Gun Cay that I didn't want to hit.

Finally, I realized that the lights to the north were all well above the water. They were the lights of boats anchored off the island! More confident but still anxious, I turned north at the waypoint and felt my way gingerly into the anchorage, passing several boats, watching the depth sounder and trying to judge the distance to the unseen beach by the sound of the surf. When I thought I had reached the place I wanted to be, I circled cautiously to check for obstructions and anchored. The price of an easily entered anchorage was a swell that came around the island and caught little *Tryphena* on her beam and made her roll violently. I tied a long mooring line to the anchor rode 30 feet out from the bow and brought it to the stern to use as a spring. Tightening it brought the yawl's bow into the swell, a trick I had learned from Horatio Hornblower and Jack Aubrey who used it to bring their cannons to bear while at anchor. It was nearly midnight and I was beyond exhaustion. My crew and I had a celebratory scotch and went to bed.

Like many sailors, I had long dreamed of sailing in my own boat to exotic tropical islands. During the 16 years I had owned *Tryphena* — a real cruising boat though a diminutive one — I cruised the coast of New England for 16 years from Newport, Rhode Island, to Grand Manan, the first island in Canada. When I wanted to sail farther afield, I went in other people's larger boats. I made several trips to Nova Scotia and Newfoundland with a friend in his 30-foot cutter, and sailed across the Atlantic in a 34-foot cutter, and in the eastern Caribbean on an 80-foot schooner.

But the dream of making a long voyage in my own boat endured, and finally the opportunity came when I could take the time for some extended cruising. By now I knew from experience that the trade winds in the eastern Caribbean were too boisterous to comfortably and safely sail in little *Tryphena*. Her beam of less than seven feet, her shallow keel, and less-than-3,000-lb. weight (empty) would mean that she could get thrown around on the passages between islands. A deeper, heavier boat would fare better in those conditions, but would sail less well in the gentle winds of a Maine summer. I didn't want to go to the trouble and expense of buying a bigger boat just for this cruise and end up with more boat than I wanted afterward. I wanted to avoid the trap of having more boat than I wanted simply because of the occasional cruise.

Because *Tryphena* was too petite to fulfill my long-term dream, I decided to modify the dream. The year before I had done some sailing in the Exumas in a little camper cruiser, a 21-foot Sea Pearl cat ketch owned by Exuma Bahamas Sailing Expeditions. They run beach-cruising trips up the island. This had been a wonderful introduction to the Bahamas. Here, I realized, was a cruising ground that was still exotic and tropical, but one that could be reached without long ocean passages and where *Tryphena*'s small size and shallow draft would be an advantage rather than a disadvantage. A new dream was born. I couldn't get away until January, a bad time to head south from Maine, so I decided to truck *Tryphena* south to Miami. I spent much of the summer preparing her and had her ready to go by the end of November. I had told the trucking company to pick her up before December first, but they delayed several weeks and by the time they finally loaded her, she had six inches of snow on her and a seventh was coming down hard. When I arrived in Miami in January, I fitted her out and headed east on the first of February.

As dawn broke over us on our first morning in the Bahamas, we awoke to find ourselves anchored 100 yards off a long beach, in the shelter of the point I had feared. A half-mile away the inoperable lighthouse was resplendent in new red and white paint. We motored through the channel between the islands to the marina on Cat Cay to tie up and, for the "token" fee of $50, to clear Bahamian Customs and Immigration and to buy some gas. After lunch we headed east across the Bahama Banks.

From the Bimini Island chain to the next group of islands, the Berry Islands, is a passage of 75 miles. This would be the longest passage without sight of land in my entire cruise, but I had once done an overnight of 130 miles up the Maine coast in *Tryphena*, so I felt fairly confident that she could do 75. It is strange sailing across the Banks since, although the land is far away over the empty horizon, the bottom is very close — only six to 12 feet

— and the crystalline water makes it seem even closer. A bit of weed or a starfish on the bottom is clearly visible as you pass, even in the moonlight. We began with a good breeze, romping along on a reach.

After a few hours of sailing across the banks the wind died away to an almost dead calm. Not wanting to prolong this passage until the weather turned sour, I decided to motor. *Tryphena* ground along under a pale blue sky dotted with occasional puffy white clouds. The water was a pale turquoise over a pale sandy bottom almost devoid of sea life. Motoring was monotonous, but it was slowly getting us there. We passed only a single fishing boat all day. At dusk we passed through an unusual area of light fog. This created a surreal landscape, where it was impossible to judge distance with no land as a reference point. Above the water, the gray fog was reminiscent of Maine and my eye instinctively looked for forested islands in it, but looking down I could see that incongruously aquamarine water. The sun sank, leaving brush strokes of pink in the west, and it was night again. The common practice among boats crossing the banks is to anchor for the night, but we still had far to go and I knew we would be unlikely to hit anything with only two feet of fixed draft, so I elected to keep going.

Motoring through the darkness with no land around anywhere and my crew asleep, I had time to think and reflect on the journey that had brought me to this place in this boat. Before I bought *Tryphena*, I spent several years thinking about what I wanted and looking at different boats. I sought a boat for day sailing and coastal cruising on the Maine coast. The summer winds are usually gentle — around 10 knots — but they can blow hard, and the cold water and granite ledges are unforgiving. I have seen people cruise the Maine coast in everything from a sea kayak to the ocean liner *Queen Elizabeth II*, but I wanted something more seaworthy than my Daysailer, an unballasted centerboarder which was quite capable of capsizing and staying there with its mast pointing toward the ocean floor. At the bare minimum, I wanted a boat with a weighted keel that would right her if she were knocked down, a self-bailing cockpit, a rig set up for easy reefing, and an enclosed cabin with fixed berths.

As I looked at various boats I realized that it is true that every boat is a compromise, or, more precisely, a series of compromises between competing and often mutually exclusive characteristics. In choosing a boat, I had to weigh and decide between a number of competing factors. I wanted the following:

1) A boat that was small enough to be easily handled and fun to sail, but large enough to be seaworthy and have decent cruising accommodations.

2) A boat that had the traditional lines and beauty of a wooden boat,

but the ease of maintenance of modern fiberglass.

3) A boat with a draft shallow enough for gunkholing, but deep enough to provide the stability of a ballasted keel and enough lateral plane to go to windward well.

4) A boat with enough lines and sails to keep me from getting bored, but still easy enough to handle that I could readily sail her single-handed, even up to a mooring or a dock.

5) A boat simple enough to not have too much to break down, but sophisticated enough to do its job easily and efficiently.

6) A boat that I could afford but that had top quality design and construction.

Among these trade-offs my personal tastes leaned in the direction of an attractive, small, shoal-draft cruising boat with a traditional design but built of fiberglass that would sail well. My requirements for traditional looks and high quality construction ruled out most of the production boats of the time. My budget and desire for easy handling meant I was looking in the 21- to 24-foot size range.

I looked seriously at the Sea Sprite 23 and Cape Dory 22, both Alberg-designed sloops with almost full keels and attractive sheer lines; the Crocker-designed Stone Horse, a 23-foot cutter with a full keel and a raised deck; and the Cornish Crabber, a 24-foot English cutter with a shallow full keel, centerboard, and gaff rig including a topsail. All of these boats came close to what I wanted in size and traditional looks, but all had berths for four, leaving little room for much else in the way of cruising accommodations. I joked that most boats in that size range had bunks for four, as long as nobody was more than 10 years old and had no more duffle than a handkerchief. I chose the Rob Roy 23, a yawl, because it had a traditional beauty, the least draft with a keel-centerboard design, and an interior with only two bunks that allowed for better accommodations. Since my wife is a militant nonsailor, I do much of my sailing solo and didn't plan to take more than one other person with me overnight anyway.

I first learned of the Rob Roy 23 from a small ad in the now-defunct magazine *Small Boat Journal*, and first saw the boat when I drove down to Newport, Rhode Island, for the first annual Small Boat Show sponsored by that publication. I studied the yawl and decided that this was the boat I wanted. I was immediately taken by her unique and traditional look; the beauty, function, and attention to detail in her design. I also liked how she was built, including things like foam core construction, teak trim, and quality fittings. Marine Concepts in Tarpon Springs, Florida, built her, and they were dedicated to turning out a quality product on a low-volume basis.

I decided that if I was going to have a new boat built for me, I might as well have her built the way I wanted her, adapted to my needs and desires. I sent for detailed plans from the designer, Ted Brewer, and consulted with him about some of the options I was considering. I also corresponded with the builder, sending drawings of my ideas, and even traveled to Florida to sail the boat and consult about details. The result was a semi-custom boat built with a number of options and modifications. These included the anchor mounted on deck, leading all the lines leading aft from the mast to winches on the cabin top, different head, forepeak, and ice box arrangements in the interior; a compass mounted in the after cabin bulkhead; painted spars, and other minor details.

Looking at the Rob Roy 23's specifications, I realized that she has only 800 pounds of ballast, and that her hull contained a significant amount of foam in its core. I wondered if she could be made unsinkable by adding additional foam. I wrote to Ted Brewer about this question and he sent back a drawing showing various dead spaces in the hull that might be filled with foam to make her unsinkable, and I had her built that way. This feature has never been empirically tested, and I'm not sure the foam in *Tryphena* is sufficient to support all the things I have loaded into her, so if I ever get a serious leak you can bet that there will be a lot of canned goods and anchors flying overboard. In retrospect, I can see that my relationships with both the designer and builder were very collaborative and productive, and I remain thoroughly pleased with the boat. Even after 18 years, there is practically nothing I would change about her.

Ted Brewer designed the Rob Roy 23 after the English canoe yawls, a type of boat that evolved out of sailing canoes in the shallow waters on the east coast of England in the 1870s to 1890s. They were some of the first "pocket yachts," intended to be maintained and sailed by their owners rather than professionals. They ranged in size from 15 to over 30 feet, from little daysailing boats to ocean cruisers. In a letter to the Rob Roy owners' newsletter, Ted said that his greatest inspiration for the design came from Dixon Kemp's *Manual of Yacht and Boat Sailing,* circa 1878. "Kemp's has a section on canoe yawls ranging from the small canoes with sail rigs to the larger Humber yawls such as the *Viking.* I fell in love with them all, so when I was asked to design a boat that was not just another white plastic bath tub, the canoe yawl was the answer."

Like her ancestors, *Tryphena* has the rounded, double-ended hull reminiscent of a canoe, with a relatively long waterline and a springy sheer line. Under water, Brewer gave her a keel-centerboard design, with a long shallow keel that gives her only two feet of fixed draft. A boot-shaped centerboard increases her draft to 4 1/2 feet, but, other than the toe of the boot, the board is entirely housed in the keel and doesn't intrude into the

cabin. She has a kick-up spade rudder tucked under her canoe stern. With a fairly narrow beam, rounded cross section, and high ballast, this sort of hull is not overly stiff, so like her ancestors, her rig is kept relatively low and extended fore and aft with a bowsprit and a boomkin. To make her more weatherly, Brewer gave her a taller Marconi rig rather than the gaff rig of her ancestors. The little mizzenmast is stepped in a socket on the cockpit combing, and its boom is sheeted to the end of a boomkin, which projects several feet beyond her pointed stern. Interestingly, some of the original canoe yawls sported the "modern" feature of roller furling on their jibs. They were intended as coastal cruisers, and for longer trips were carried on freight trains or steam ships, so my hauling *Tryphena* overland to Miami was entirely within the tradition.

Some might ask, "Why put a yawl rig on such a small boat?" Indeed, I once read a quote of the famous yacht designer Olin Stephens where he said that a 39-foot boat was too small for a yawl rig. I have found that the Rob Roy 23's yawl rig has a number of advantages. Perhaps the major advantage

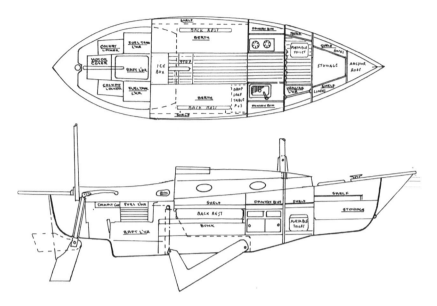

is balance: adjusting the trim of the little mizzen can increase or decrease weather helm. Trim can be adjusted so that, in many conditions, the boat will sail itself with no hand on the tiller. In strong winds the boat can be sailed under jib and mizzen with much better balance than a sloop under jib or mainsail alone. On a light-air reach, a mizzen staysail can be flown to increase sail area. At anchor, or when raising sail, the mizzen sheeted in hard can help the boat lie pointed into the wind. I use the mizzen staysail halyard to raise my sun shower when I want to use it, and have even, when there was only one other boat in the anchorage off my beam, stepped behind the mizzen and used it as a shower curtain for privacy.

I had *Tryphena* finished with forest green topsides, a gelcoat color which I knew would not be the most practical, but one I like and is traditional in Maine among Friendship sloops, schooners, and lobster boats. As I expected, it shows dirt and scratches more than a white hull, and as the years went on, the gelcoat faded and chalked. After more than a decade I had the topsides professionally painted with the same color Awlgrip. Her bowsprit, boomkin, toe rails, handrails, and other exterior trim are teak, currently finished a honey-brown color with Armada. Her deck, cabin, and cockpit are a yellowish off-white.

To further maintain a traditional look, I had the masts and booms painted with Awlgrip, the traditional buff color with cream tips. Her sails are a rust-red "tanbark" color. I chose this color because it is traditional among English working boats, the color coming originally from linen sails that were boiled with bark to preserve them, and because they would stand out better in Maine's frequent fogs. The result is, to my eye at least, a very pretty boat, and one that stands out, even on the horizon, in a world of white sloops with white sails.

I wanted a distinctive and somewhat quaint name for a distinctive and somewhat quaint boat. So I named her *Tryphena Chandler*, after an ancestor who was the daughter of a captain in the American Revolution.

The engine installation on the Rob Roy 23 is very well engineered. The engine is an outboard motor, a two-cylinder 8-hp Honda four-stroke, set in a well under the tiller at the aft end of the cockpit. It sits low enough in the well to be unobtrusive under a cover the height of the cockpit seats. The outboard well is located three feet in from the stern so that the propeller comes out just where it would be with an inboard engine. This placement has real advantages over boats with outboard motors on a bracket or attached to the transom, where the prop can more easily foul lines or come out of the water if the boat pitches in a head sea. The opening in the bottom of the well is of minimal size and is mostly filled by the engine's cavitation plate, which minimizes underwater drag. A hose directs the exhaust overboard just below the rail, so the engine doesn't choke on its own smoke in the well.

The forward side of the well can be closed off with teak drop boards, but I leave the top one out so I can easily reach the choke and starter cord to start and run the engine without raising the cover. The engine's tiller arm, with its twist throttle, is swung vertical to come up through a hole in the engine cover where it is easily reached. A five-amp alternator helps charge the batteries (supplemented by a flexible solar panel on the cabin top).

Forward of the engine, on either side of the cockpit, are two molded-in lockers designed to hold standard six-gallon fuel tanks under the cockpit seats. These are sealed off from the interior, so no gasoline fumes can get below, and are open to the cockpit for ventilation, the tanks being held in by three teak slats. I modified one of these lockers slightly by putting spacers behind the slats, which allows it to hold a nine-gallon tank, so together my two tanks have a 15 gallon capacity. If the throttle is only opened about three quarters of the way, the boat will cruise near hull speed in flat water making about eight miles to the gallon, giving me a motoring range of around 120 miles, ample even for a trip through the Bahamas. In short, this engine arrangement has most of the advantages of an inboard engine with the lower cost and weight of an outboard and the added bonus of being able to easily remove the engine to free a line around the prop or to work on it. The engine well also serves as a high capacity cockpit drain. About the only disadvantage of this design is a little more drag from turbulence around the opening in the bottom of the well and dragging the prop through the water when under sail.

On either side of the motor well are deep cockpit lockers. The starboard locker contains all of my deck gear: dock lines, fenders, fender board, telescoping boathook, the second anchor and its line, hatch dropboards, mainsail cover, and chafing gear. The port locker is dedicated to safety equipment: life jackets, a waterproof box containing enough flares for a respectable Fourth of July celebration, a sea anchor, a fire extinguisher, and — new for this trip — a Pains Wessex 406 Emergency Position Indicating Radio Beacon (EPIRB) to call for help in an emergency.

Beyond this basic equipment, I have always tried to incorporate consideration for safety into all of my planning and sailing, in my selection of equipment, and how I have set up *Tryphena*. Maine's frigid water, fog, and unyielding granite ledges serve as constant reminders of the need for safety. As preventative measures to keep me out of trouble in the first place, I have my Garmin fixed-mount GPS, knotlog, depth sounder, and the best of charts and cruising guides to help me navigate accurately. To avoid or minimize problems with the boat, before I shipped *Tryphena* south, I had gone over both the boat and gear very carefully to make sure everything was in good working order and that I had spares and repair manuals for things that might break down. My friend Don says that it is usually not the first problem that kills you. But if it isn't managed quickly, the first problem often leads to a chain reaction of other problems, one of which may prove fatal. Trying to anticipate possible problems so they could be quickly controlled, I had installed a second bilge pump and brought along epoxy putty to fix leaks, had a good collection of engine spares, two fire extinguishers, battery powered backups for my GPS and VHF radio, and a first aid kit. As a final line of defense I have a "crash bag" in my tender containing additional life jackets, flares, horn, knife, and other safety gear. Before this trip, I researched life rafts, but found that even a small and minimally adequate one would be quite expensive and difficult to stow, so I had abandoned the idea, a decision I hoped I wouldn't have reason to regret.

One of my favorite pieces of safety equipment is a pair of Mustang Air Force automatically inflatable life vests with built-in safety harnesses, for me and for my crew. The old adage "The only life jacket that does you any good is the one that you wear" contains some profound truth. I had always carried conventional Mae West life jackets but had never worn them because they were so bulky, uncomfortable, and movement-inhibiting. When I accepted that they wouldn't do me any good in the locker, I went in search of a Personal Flotation Device (PFD) that I could stand to wear, and found that the lack of bulk in the inflatable vests meant that I would wear them, maybe not always, but a lot more than I ever had the old style. I always wear one when it is rough or I am venturing out of the cockpit. A strong stainless steel inverted U-bolt is mounted on the bridge deck, just outside the companionway hatch. This is the attachment point for the tethers. If I go overboard, the vest will inflate even if I am unconscious. And if I am in the water separated from the boat, I can attract attention with a whistle, flares, mirror, and dye marker carried in a pouch on the belt of the harness. So as I motored through the night, I was tethered to the boat by my harness, and wore a strobe light strapped around my upper arm to make me more visible if I went overboard in the darkness.

Around 11:30 P.M. we passed the Russell Beacon, a lighthouse on a metal tower far from everything in the middle of the banks. Amazingly, it was lit. We began to see a few other lights of boats anchored for the night, but we continued on. At the eastern end of the Banks a tongue of deep water reaches in from the east. At the edge of this deep water the chart shows a line of coral reefs, but neither the chart nor the cruising guides gave any indication of depth over these reefs and I was loath to cross them in the dark. I anchored, therefore, at 2 A.M. a few miles from the reefs, about a half-mile north of Northwest Channel Light, also lit, in 11 feet of water. It seemed bizarre to anchor for the night far from any land, but at that point I was too tired to care.

Five hours later we were under way again in gray morning light. When we crossed the line of reefs at the edge of deep water we had no soundings less than twenty-five feet and in a quarter mile the water turned from the aqua color of the banks to the indigo blue of deep water. By mid-morning we reached Chub Cay, in the Berry Islands. At last I felt that the long passages were behind us and I had truly arrived in the Bahamas, and the tension began to drain out of me. From here on there should be no passage of more than 35 miles between islands.

I decided to lay over a day at Chub Cay, and moved the next morning into the marina in the inner basin. Here I began to learn about weather and cruisers in the Bahamas. By now I was well out of range of the American NOAA weather reports I have always relied on and have come to take for granted. I learned to my dismay that I could not get an intelligible forecast from the little multiband radio I had brought along. So I asked around among the other cruisers how they got weather reports. The best reports seemed to come through the single sideband frequencies I couldn't get, but a brief, crude, report could be obtained from Radio Bahamas on the AM band, sandwiched each morning between the preachings of a long line of evangelists. In a few of the more popular areas like Nassau, a more detailed report is rebroadcast by cruisers on VHF.

My survey of how people got weather reports allowed me to begin to get to know my fellow cruisers. I learned that the typical cruising boat in the Bahamas is between 35 and 45 feet long, or longer, and is sailed by a married couple who are retired or can afford not to work. Most live aboard their boats and cruise south in the winter and north in the summer. Because they live aboard year-round, carry all of their possessions with them, and want a lot of things and creature comforts, these people need a larger boat.

I stood out among the liveaboards because I still had a house to go home to, I didn't have to carry all my possessions with me, and my wife was not with me. This meant that I was liberated by not having to carry so much and could get by with a much smaller boat, which might not have so many amenities but would still meet my needs.

As I got to know my fellow cruisers I was shocked by how many people bought a boat, usually used, and took off cruising in it after only a few weeks or months, without a thorough shakedown. I was repeatedly glad that I had sailed *Tryphena* for 16 years and knew exactly what she could do, and not do, and how every piece of equipment worked.

Among the vessels at Chub Cay I found two small boats which, interestingly, were also owned by people who still had a house ashore. One was a 30-foot catamaran sailed by a family from Vermont with two children. Like me, these folks were on a sailing sabbatical. A Cape Dory 27 was sailed by a couple from Michigan who spend their summers running a marina on the Great Lakes and their winters cruising. These two boats were to become my friends and allies.

My crew and I managed to get two forecasts, from AM radio and the telephone, both for winds from the southwest at ten knots, becoming northwest after the passage of a weak front. After reading and hearing many stories of fearsome winds around a front, I was nervous about sailing. But this forecast didn't sound too bad, and so with some trepidation, I decided to sail. Other boats listened to different forecasts and called boats already underway on the radio to learn conditions firsthand. Eventually, most decided to sail. Outside the anchorage I set the mizzen first, as usual, and sheeted it in tight to keep *Tryphena* headed into the wind while I set the mainsail, then fell off onto our course for Nassau and unfurled the roller furling genoa.

I believe that a good sailboat should be able to easily vary its sail area to suit the wind conditions. Toward this end I have set *Tryphena* up with a variety of light sails and reefing gear. Since she is too small to carry effective lifelines, I don't have any. Instead, to minimize the need to climb around on deck and for safety and convenience, I have set her up so most sail handling can be done from the cockpit. All halyards are led aft through blocks at the base of the mast, fairleads, and rope clutches, to a pair of winches on the after corners of the cabin top. The jib sheets are also led to these two winches, the smallest and cheapest that Lewmar makes. I consider roller reefing/furling for the jib to be essential, since I have no desire to go forward on *Tryphena*'s narrow side decks and climb out on her skinny bowsprit to tame a flailing jib, especially in rough conditions when I am sailing single-handed. Instead, I simply pull a line and the jib rolls up.

Over the years I have added light air sails to supplement the yawl's basic complement of mainsail, working jib, and mizzen. I started with a cruising spinnaker, since it adds the most sail area. It really moves the boat in light air on a reach without a pole, or on a run poled out with a telescoping pole which is normally stowed in chocks on the cabin top. But I find I don't use it much, since setting it is usually more work than I want to do, especially when sailing alone. I brought it to the Bahamas but never used it, being unwilling to take it out of the tight bundle into which I had folded it to save space.

Next I had a genoa made, which for years I set flying as a light-air-only sail, keeping the working jib on the roller furling. This sail adds power on all points of sail, including poled out before the wind. Since my old jib furling gear was shot, on the advice of my sailmaker I had a new Schaeffer Flexible Furler installed for this trip, and had the genoa modified for roller furling with a sewn-on sun cover and a luff pad to make it reef better. This worked well. I began reefing with the mainsail first, and never used the working jib.

Finally, I bought a mizzen staysail. I had hesitated to buy this sail since it only adds 55 square feet of sail and can only be used on a reach, but I find that I use it a lot, since it is so easy to set and can be flown in anything from a close reach to a broad reach. It is essentially a jib for the mizzen and is set flying. The tack of mine fastens to the U-bolt on the bridge deck. It is raised by a halyard on the forward side of the mizzen mast, and sheeted to the end of the mizzen boom. It takes me about a minute to set this sail, and is so easy to do that I often set it when sailing single-handed. It adds extra push on a reach, and somehow transforms *Tryphena* into a little ship when she is carrying four sails.

When I use the cruising spinnaker and mizzen staysail in combination, along with the main and mizzen, *Tryphena* is flying 175 percent of her designed sail area. I once passed a Sabre 30 carrying a main and masthead genoa with this combination, slowly walking past her on a parallel reach. The sloop's skipper was so chagrined that he started his engine, furled his jib, and motored off in the opposite direction. One advantage of a smaller boat is that the cost of such a wardrobe of sails is more modest, and, for popular classes of boats, can often be obtained used.

As I began the 36-mile passage to Nassau I set the mizzen staysail and was sailing well on a "four-sail reach." Around mid-day, towering dark clouds began to approach from the northwest, the promised front. I wasn't sure how much wind there would be under these ominous clouds, so as they came close, I took in all sail. The rain came in torrents, blocking out all visibility, and it was accompanied by strong gusts, which were no problem since I was carrying no sail, and I continued on, motoring. The gusts didn't last long, and when the rain ceased after an hour, I stopped *Tryphena*, pulled my little rowing dory alongside, and leaned precariously over the side to bail out the rainwater. I then reset the mainsail and motored on in a calm, waiting to see what the weather would bring next. A northwest wind soon began, and as it strengthened, a sea began to build up and I was glad I hadn't waited to bail the dory. We were now halfway to Nassau, making good time. The wind gradually clocked from northwest to northeast, on the beam, and increased. As it got stronger, I progressively reefed the mainsail and unrolled some jib to balance it, leaving the mizzen furled to reduce weather helm.

I have outfitted *Tryphena* with a single-line reefing system on the mainsail. To reef, I ease the sheet to luff the sail and take the strain out of it, ease the mail halyard by the depth of the reef, and winch in the reefing line. This line starts near the outward end of the boom, goes up through a reefing cringle in the leach of the sail and back down through a cheek block on the boom, then forward along the boom to another turning block on the mast, where it turns up to pass through a reefing cringle in the luff of the sail and down to a block at the base of the mast and aft to a rope clutch (a device that will hold and release a line under strain) and the winch. When the two reefing cringles are hauled down to the boom, I fasten the reefing line with the rope clutch, tension the halyard if it needs it, and trim in the sheet. The sail is reefed in little more time than it takes to explain how, without leaving the cockpit. I consider the ability to reef quickly and easily a major safety requirement of any sailboat. I had a new mainsail made after 16 years and the new sail has three reefs, each set up as above. So far I haven't needed the third reef much, but I'm glad it is there.

Tryphena's mizzen furls by hauling the clew of the loose-footed sail in on the continuous outhaul line that runs the length of the boom, unclipping the snaphook that holds the sail to the outhaul, and wrapping the 35-square-foot sail around the unstayed mast, then refastening and tensioning the outhaul. The sail can be reefed — without leaving the cockpit — using the same process, but only rolling one or two turns around the mast. The genoa can be reefed by pulling in on the furling line.

In ever increasing winds and seas *Tryphena* was racing toward Nassau under a double- reefed main and a little scrap of jib. Steering was a challenge. A strong weather helm told me she would have done better with more jib and another reef in the mainsail, but I was too busy trying to keep on course to want to go through further sail changes and in the deteriorating conditions I didn't want to delay reaching a safe harbor.

In mid-afternoon New Providence Island appeared as a faint smudge off the starboard bow and gradually resolved into a long, low, island topped with the square blocks of hotels. *Tryphena* was surfing off the seas at 6.5 knots and occasionally more. That is fast for a boat whose theoretical top steed is 5.2 knots. My arm ached from wrestling with the tiller and I was tired, wet, and cold. The entrance to Nassau Harbor is hard to see, but was easy to find by spotting the emerging cruise ships and following the other boats funneling into its mouth. At long last we were safely in the arms of its breakwaters and I could relax, having learned that I shouldn't sail when a front is predicted.

I had only planned to stay in Nassau for a day to reprovision, but I ended up staying for several days to let the strong winds after the front die down and to wait for my next crew to arrive. I was learning that in the winter the Bahamas can, at times, have stronger winds than I had expected. The prevailing winter winds are the southeast trade winds, which blow fairly steadily. When a front approaches, the wind can clock around to the south and west, often lighter, or it can go calm as it had when I crossed from Miami. But a front usually brings strong winds from the north, which can then clock around and blow strong from the northeast and east before returning to the southeast.

My days in Nassau allowed me to spend time with my new friends from *Woodchuck,* the Vermont catamaran, and *Saiorse,* the Michigan sloop. Together we hiked downtown to see the cruise ships, tourist shops, and straw market; and across the bridge to look at the big hotels and beaches of Paradise Island. One day we went to a lunch for cruisers at a local restaurant. There everyone was complaining about Nassau: If they had anchored in the harbor they were afraid their anchor would drag in the poor holding bottom or their boat would be run down by one of the many out-island freighters or fishing boats moving through the anchorage. If they had tied up in one of the marinas they complained about the high dockage charges of $1.50 per foot of boat per night, which could quickly add up for a large boat.

"I don't have those problems," I replied, "I'm staying at East Bay Marina, where the fee is 60 cents per foot, and for 23 feet the cost is less than 15 dollars per night, not enough to worry about."

I was happy at East Bay, a ramshackle little marina between the two bridges that cross the harbor to Paradise Island, which can be reached only by going under the end of one of the bridges with only fifty feet of clearance. It is half the price and closer to downtown than the other marinas. True, I was glad that I had made a four-foot fender board out of an old two-by-four that, backed by a pair of fenders, let me lie against a rusty piling without damage. I had to put up with fewer amenities and more local color than the fancy marinas, but this is what I had come to the Bahamas to see. East Bay is right next to Potter's Cay, the transportation hub of the Bahamas, where all the inter-island freighters and mail boats bring the produce and passengers from the out islands to Nassau and return laden with goods and people from the outside world.

Both Steve from *Woodchuck* and I needed parts for our boats that we were unable to find in the chandleries of Nassau. So I got out my West Marine catalog and my Pocketmail, and sent an email to my next crew, whose office is close to a West Marine store. When Michael arrived to crew, he had the needed parts, some vents I wanted to install in the engine cover for better engine breathing, and for Steve a cowl ventilator to replace one lost overboard.

As soon as Michael was refueled with conch fritters, we left Nassau headed for Allen's Cay in the Exumas, some 35 miles southeast of Nassau. To reach this island took us a day's passage through shallow turquoise waters, watching out for the dark spots that are coral heads, in a freshening breeze that had us reefed by the time we arrived. I entered the anchorage expecting to find no more than a half-dozen yachts, but to my horror, I found 18. I had underestimated the anchorage's popularity, not only as the gateway to the Exumas, but also as the home of a famous population of friendly iguanas. I wondered where we could find space to anchor in the crowd, but right where I wanted to be there was a sandbar with only four feet of water over it, which kept out the larger boats, and there we anchored next to *Saiorse*. Although the sloop has twice *Tryphena*'s displacement, both boats looked dwarfed by the surrounding yachts twice their length.

The Exumas are the stuff that dreams are made of. This archipelago of more than 130 islands, strung in a line like a strand of green pearls, starts thirty miles southeast of Nassau and stretches 120 miles south and east, with rarely more than a mile between islands. To the east, to windward, lie the deep blue waters of Exuma Sound. To the west are the shallow aquamarine waters of the Exuma Banks. Most larger boats travel down the string of islands out in the deep water of the Sound or far out on the Banks where the water is not so shallow. But a smaller boat without much draft can, with care, follow a winding channel through the shallows close in the lee of the islands where there is protection from wind and seas and the beauty of the islands, and the underwater world can be more fully appreciated. The islands tend to be low, with rocky shores and long sandy beaches, covered with low green scrub vegetation and an occasional palm or feathery casuarina tree.

But it is beneath the water that the greatest beauty of the Bahamas lies, in the shades of indigo blue and aquamarine in the water and in the brilliant colors of the corals and fish on the reefs. Michael and I began to work our way down the string of islands, drinking in this beauty.

One of the things I like about the Rob Roy 23 design is that it is more of a larger cruising boat scaled down, with a fully functional interior, rather than a daysailer scaled up with a few bunks shoehorned in as an afterthought. The space inside *Tryphena* is small: the main cabin, including the galley, is about six-and-a-half feet long, six feet wide, and has a maximum headroom under the hatch of about four feet. The boat doesn't have full headroom, but if you think about it, how much time do you spend standing up anyway? Better to be comfortable sitting down where we spend most of our time.

In the main cabin are bunks port and starboard, with the galley forward. About 18 inches of the foot of each bunk run back under the bridge deck, leaving about five feet of the bunks exposed in the main cabin. Behind each bunk are comfortable backrests. The backrests unfasten and are stowed forward to make the bunks wider for sleeping. Alternately, the floor panel between the bunks comes up and can rest on some higher cleats. The backrests fit neatly on this surface making a bunk the width of the boat.

The "toe" of the boot-shaped centerboard comes up in a short trunk behind the companionway steps. This allows its pennant to exit the trunk well above the waterline and be led aft to the cockpit. Under the bridge deck is a good-sized built-in icebox, a custom option. This isn't the most convenient spot for an ice chest, but it was the only place the builder and I could find for a box that met my requirement of being tall enough to stand up a quart of milk. With two inches of foam this chest will hold ice for a week in Maine, but I had added extra insulation around the outside and an interior insulated blanket over the food for the Bahamas. There, 20 pounds of block ice would last about five days. I was able to find ice most of the time when I needed it. If not, I carried a squared bucket. On a few occasions when ice was otherwise unavailable, I was able to persuade someone to fill it with water and put it in their freezer overnight to make ice for me. In the space between the ice chest and the companionway steps live my sea boots on one side of the centerboard trunk and the garbage bag on the other. I didn't really need sea boots in the Bahamas, but one boot normally holds a bottle of scotch and the other a bottle of rum, and where else was I going to find such a secure place for my booze? Under the steps is space to stow shoes.

There is a lot of storage space under the bunks of a Rob Roy 23. At the head of the starboard bunk is the water tank, a 13-gallon flexible Nauta tank. Aft of that live my toolbox, some boxes of spares, extra rope, my bosun's chair, and other bosun's supplies. Under the port bunk I stow food: bottled water and other drinks, an extensive collection of canned goods, and dried foods stored in plastic bags, as well as more spares. Narrow shelves up under the deck the length of each bunk hold small things that need to be accessible. The port shelf holds my spices at its forward end, handy to the galley, then a flashlight, the GPS and other navigation stuff, tapes for the AM-FM cassette player mounted under the deck above it and, back under the bridge deck, my autopilot when it's not being used. At the forward end of the starboard shelf is the main electrical panel, handy to my bunk, then a flashlight, hats, flags, safety harnesses, winch handles, tiller extension, and finally, the screens for the opening ports. On the after bulkhead to port of the hatch are the VHF radio and a rack for the hand-held VHF, and to starboard is a rack for my binoculars where they can be easily reached from the cockpit.

Forward of the bunks is the galley, with the stove on a counter to port, and the sink in a counter to starboard. The builder told me that when Ted Brewer was designing the Rob Roy, he decided to buy one for himself. His wife, I was told, said, "I don't care what you do, but I'm not working that galley on my knees." So Ted designed a very clever seat that pulls out like a drawer from under the head of the starboard berth and spans the space between the berths, creating a thwart-like perch on which you can sit facing forward with your legs between the two galley counters. From this seat you can easily reach anything in the galley.

To port is the two-burner Origo nonpressurized alcohol stove hung in gimbals. This may not be the most efficient stove, but I like it because it has only a few moving parts and can't flare up or explode. The gimbals keep the stove level when the boat heels and allow it to function under way. With pot dogs to hold the pot on, it will cook in rougher conditions than I care to be in down below. Behind the stove is a bin that I use for dried foods like cereal, pasta, crackers, and rice. Beneath the stove are two drawers. I have put dividers in the after drawer and it holds a complete set of flatware for four, decorated with a shell motif, plus a can opener, chef's and paring knives, a spatula, a large serving spoon, a lobster cracker, and a corkscrew. The forward drawer holds navigation equipment: my back-up hand-held GPS, lead line, compass and protractor, hand bearing compass, and miscellany like pens, pencils, and boat cards. Beneath the drawers is the pot locker containing a frying pan and a variety of pots up to the largest lobster pot that would fit into the opening. One item I particularly like is a perforated half-moon of metal on a handle that serves as a colander. Held against the lip of a pot it allows you to pour the water out of the pot without dumping your pasta in the sink, yet it takes up almost no space.

To starboard, a small stainless steel sink is set into the counter, served by a marvelous Fynspray brass hand pump, which draws water from the tank under the bunk just aft of it. Behind the sink is a bin containing a complete set of stoneware dishes for four, plus mugs and plastic glasses. In 18 years and thousands of miles of sailing, thanks to being stowed securely in the bin, I've chipped only one cup. Above the sink is a paper towel holder, to the left of the sink under the counter is my miscellaneous drawer, and under the sink is a locker in which I keep my cleaning supplies and plastic bags.

At the head of each berth are small drop-leaf tables that swing up to make extra counter space for the galley or to serve as eating tables. A centerline table would be nicer for dining, but just wouldn't fit in the small space. This galley is simple, but has all the basics and has turned out some excellent meals.

Forward of the galley is a bulkhead, which provides support for the main mast, mounted on the cabin top just above it. The bulkhead has an opening in the center that can be curtained off. On this bulkhead to port are a barometer and a clock that has a red third hand which tells the state of the tide. On the starboard side of the bulkhead is mounted a small brass Fastnet kerosene lamp in gimbals. I hung it over the sink since washing dishes is often the last activity of the evening. Forward of the bulkhead are a hanging locker to starboard and a portable toilet to port.

It is an unusual luxury to have an enclosed head on a 23-foot boat. I like the privacy, much appreciated by female crew. Nor is the head located between v-berths a few inches below your pillow, which is common in many boats of this size. Using enzymes to treat the waste minimizes the smell. Initially I wondered how I would like a portable toilet as compared to a regular marine head. However, sailing with a friend, I once spent an afternoon listening to the swearing skipper as he disassembled and overhauled his nonfunctioning marine head. My portable toilet, which has only two moving parts, has never let me down.

The standard Rob Roy had a smaller portable toilet in the forepeak, but I specified a larger one moved aft to get greater capacity and to free up the forepeak for stowage. My portable toilet has a storage capacity of around three gallons. I follow the practice, and encourage my male crew to follow suit, that number one goes over the side wherever decorum permits. This means the portable toilet fills more slowly. When it does fill up, it is a fairly simple process to separate the lower half and take it ashore to dump into some marina toilet, which I think beats trying to find a pump-out station or fouling the anchorage with waste. The few times I have been unable to find a toilet to pour it in, I simply dumped it overboard offshore in deep water.

Forward of the head is another partial bulkhead and the forepeak, about four feet long. On the standard Rob Roy, this area is used for the portable toilet and anchor stowage. But since I keep my anchor on deck and moved my portable toilet aft, the whole area of the forepeak is opened up for storage. Here I keep clothes in small duffle bags, and further forward, light air sails in bags. Above is a shelf a foot below the deck. On the starboard shelf I keep sheets and towels, and on the port shelf is the ship's library, consisting of 25 volumes ranging from cruising guides and manuals for the engine and all the other equipment aboard to nature guides and novels. Forward on this shelf, separated by a water-tight baffle, in the point of the bow is the anchor rode storage.

If you are getting the impression of "A place for everything and everything in its place," you are right. Good organization and neatness are very important to living successfully in a small space where just a few things out of place can make the cabin seem cluttered. It takes thought to be able to fit everything you want in a small space, organization to be able to find it, and discipline to keep it organized on an ongoing basis. It is my custom to straighten up the cabin and stow everything in its place every morning before I get under way.

On a small boat space must not be wasted. Whenever I buy anything for the boat I must decide whether it is important enough to take up space, what it weighs, where it will go, and if it will fit. Before I bought my Garmin fixed-mount GPS, for instance, I had to measure it to make sure it would fit on the shelf where I wanted it to go, which was about the only place I had space for it. When I was planning to go to the Bahamas I took everything off the boat, and only those things deemed essential to the trip were allowed back on. In this way I got rid of 16 years' worth of accumulated stuff and took only what was most important.

If this seems austere compared to the way most people live on land, it is, but compared to backpacking or traveling in a sea kayak, it is the lap of luxury. The fact is that almost everyone, even those living aboard a 50-footer, have to live in less space than they have ashore, and must make decisions on what to take and what to leave behind. In seven months of living aboard *Tryphena* I rarely felt deprived. Instead, I was surprised at the things I could happily live without and enjoyed living a more simple and uncomplicated life. I did accumulate things along the way, particularly books, but periodically I would box up things I wasn't using and ship them home.

A necessity for the Bahamas was the awning that gave us relief from the relentless sun. Custom-made by my sailmaker, it ties to the two masts at each end, has four telescoping poles to keep it extended out to the rail, bridles that attach to the mizzen staysail halyard and spinnaker pole lift to hold up the center portion, and side curtains that extend down 18 inches on each side to provide protection from oblique sunlight. It shades the cockpit and much of the cabin, making the boat much more livable in the heat. I also have a fabric scoop that goes over the forward hatch to force more air below. For insect protection I have screens for *Tryphena*'s four opening ports and two hatches. Screens made of mosquito netting and attached by Velcro cover the hatches well and fold up to store in almost no space with negligible weight. With all of these arrangements my yawl was well adapted to the tropics. The only drawback to the awning was that it could be used only at anchor. If I were to sail a lot in the tropics, I would want a bimini to provide shade over the cockpit while underway. Fitting such an awning on a boat with a low boom like the Rob Roy 23's is tricky, but it can be done.

Navigation in the Bahamas is done much by eye. GPS will help with longer passages between islands, but close in you will soon get in trouble if you rely solely on electronics, since the charts are neither accurate nor detailed enough to save you from all the rocks, reefs, and shoals. You must instead keep a close lookout and read the water, mostly by color. Deep blue means deep water. Aqua means a sandy bottom and the lighter the shade, the shallower the water, to the point where the water becomes "gin clear." That's when, in *Tryphena*, it is time to brace yourself for the impact of grounding. Mottled aqua means there are rocks in the sand; brown — usually a brown smear — means a rocky bar; and an intense black spot means a dangerous coral head.

We crossed a rocky bar at the corner of Norman's Cay and found a wrecked airplane, sitting incongruously with water up to its waist, slowly crumbling from its years in the sea. From this wreck I turned south, across some shallow sandbanks, where the chart indicated we should have enough water. This turned out to be a mistake, and we ended up in a nightmare of shallows with Michael forward pointing out where the water had the slightest aqua tinge. We meandered for what seemed like an anxious eternity with less than a foot of water beneath *Tryphena*'s keel and seemingly no way out of the shallows. But we never ran aground and eventually we saw the darker color of a channel ahead, worked our way laboriously toward it, and having reached it, made our escape.

The next island we approached was Shroud Cay, the first island in the Exumas Land and Sea Park, the jewel of the Exumas, a wonderful nature preserve that stretches for 10 miles along the island chain. Shroud Cay is usually bypassed by cruisers, however, since it is mostly mangrove swamp. The few boats that do stop anchor off its western shore, and the braver among them will explore the channels through the mangroves in their dinghies. I had been told that the most northerly channel is the deepest, and figuring that it was two hours before high tide, I decided to try it. There is only about 2 1/2 feet of tide range in the Bahamas, a mere trifling for someone used to Maine's tide range of 10 feet and more, but even this small range can make a major difference in shallow water.

We found the rather obscure entrance to the channel, passing over a very shallow sandbar to reach it, and entered the interior of the island. Dense green mangrove bushes line each side of the 25-foot-wide channel, rooted in a soft mire almost awash at high tide. Within the channel the deeper water wandered randomly back and forth and we were obliged to pick our way carefully to find enough water, touching the keel several times.

On the far side of the island, 50 yards inside the shallow inlet to Exuma Sound, I found a pool of water deep enough to float *Tryphena* at low tide. I anchored there using both bow and stern anchors and a line to the mangroves to keep her in place. Just as we were finishing anchoring, a family arrived paddling inflatable kayaks. They had come up the same channel and had seen *Tryphena*'s masts across a switchback. Unable to judge her size by just the rig, they couldn't believe their eyes that an ocean-going sailing yacht could be traveling up such a shallow channel. After a few hours the kayakers had left and the tide had fallen enough so that even dinghies couldn't get up the channel, so for the rest of the day Michael and I had the two long beaches on either side of the inlet and the hills behind them – including "Camp Driftwood" the former hilltop home of an eccentric hermit – to ourselves. We spent a peaceful night there with the masthead anchor lights of the larger yachts just visible over the mangroves a mile away. We visited several more wonderful islands in the park, but for us, none held the magic of Shroud Cay.

After Michael's departure a few days later, I was a bit nervous sailing alone in the Bahamas for the first time. Still, I had a very pleasant sail to Little Farmer's Cay, where I went to the Ocean Cabin Club, a great little bar-restaurant, for some company and dinner. On this particular night, Terry Bain, the proprietor and an ardent local conservationist, had lured the yachties in by advertising on the VHF radio that he was conducting hermit crab races. These small land crabs live in a borrowed mollusk shell. A group of people each placed "their" crab in the center of a circle, and whoever's crab made it out of the circle first was the winner. As is usual in such small places, there is no menu. The cook gives you a choice of several things available and then you wait while she prepares your order. This time I chose fried grouper, which came with the Bahamian staples of cole slaw, macaroni and cheese, or beans and rice, all washed down with a Kalik, the Bahamian beer.

A front was due to come through and I spent over an hour the next morning trying to get a weather report, but Radio Bahamas gave me an unbroken string of evangelists, since Sunday is the weatherman's day off. I finally gave up and pushed back the hatch to find a line of clouds marking the front directly overhead. I should have looked first. This front seemed to have no particular winds associated with it, so I spent the day sailing on down the Exumas, even slipping out of an inlet for a gentle sail just off the beaches on the deep water Sound side of the islands. I came back through another inlet onto the banks to anchor for the night at Barreterre, a little village at the northern end of Great Exuma Island. That night I learned that the winds can be delayed behind a front when I found myself anchored 50 yards off a rocky lee shore in 25-plus knots of wind. Barreterre, open to the north and northeast, is no place to be in the strong northerlies following a front. However, in the morning, I found that *Tryphena*'s small size and shallow draft allowed me to hide behind a tiny cay, where I put out two anchors and rowed ashore to spend the day with a friend.

I grew up with Danforth anchors, have always had good experience with them, and usually carry several of them. *Tryphena*'s working anchor is a 12-pound hi-tensile Danforth, advertised to hold up to a 35-foot boat. This anchor may be a bit oversized for my boat, but I sleep better with bigger anchors, and even with ten feet of chain, it still weighs a very manageable 20 pounds. I keep it in chocks on the foredeck, instantly available, with 250 feet of 3/8-inch nylon rode, far more than I needed in the shallow waters and low tide range of the Bahamas, where at times I could anchor with seven-to-one scope and only use 35 feet of line.

The only situations where I have found that a Danforth doesn't work well in Maine are in rock or kelp, both challenges for any anchor. For these situations I carry a 33-lb. folding kedge whose greater weight and sharp downward point will punch through kelp and hook rock when other anchors can't. I keep this seldom-used anchor — with its own chain and rode — stowed amidships in the bilge, where it usually functions as ballast.

For my trip to the Bahamas I wanted another alternative type of anchor and bought a plow. When I called Simpson Lawrence to get the exact dimensions of their anchors to see whether they would fit into my cockpit locker, the man I talked to recommended the Delta plow over the CQR, so I bought a 14-lb. Delta and put 12 feet of chain and 100 feet of nylon rode on it. This anchor, which is good-sized for the size of my boat but still manageable, became my second anchor, and I never used the kedge or second Danforth in the Bahamas. With these two anchors dug in, I didn't mind leaving *Tryphena,* even in high winds.

Several days later, when I arrived at George Town — the only town, and yachting capital of the Exumas — I was invited aboard a large sloop for cocktail hour, along with the crews of several other boats. The talk turned to problems, and it seemed that everyone was waiting for parts for something, parts hard to come by in this remote location. One boat needed a replacement for the propeller of their dinghy outboard destroyed going over a reef, others needed parts for a broken water maker or generator. I listened to this conversation and realized that the things that had broken were all items considered normal and essential on liveaboard boats in the usual 35–45-foot size range. But they were things that I didn't have on my smaller and simpler boat. My mind formulated a new rule: "If you haven't got it, it can't break."

Many of the boats in George Town had come south for the winter, arrived in the harbor, put down several anchors, and didn't move. In contrast, I used George Town as a place to reprovision, change crew, and see friends, and tended to be in and out and moving around to different parts of the anchorage to explore and see friends rather than stay in one place. I noticed that although there were, at the peak, close to 500 boats in the George Town area and a steady wind, mine was one of the few boats ever seen under sail in the large harbor. I sailed when I shifted anchorages, or when I took friends out for the day. I think part of the reason I moved more than other boats was that *Tryphena* is so much easier to get under way than a larger boat.

While I was in George Town I wanted to do some work on the boat, including scrubbing out the cabin and putting another coat of finish on the exterior teak, and to do this I put *Tryphena* in the marina. Since she draws so little water I was assigned to the slip closest to the land where the water was too shallow for other boats. That meant that everyone coming on or off the dock complex, everyone tying their dinghy in the designated place across the dock, and everyone walking along the waterfront, came by me. It was often hard to get work done with a constant stream of people saying, "Oh, what a cute boat," and asking, "What is she?" or "Did you sail her all the way from Maine?" At one point I stood in the cockpit with a brush full of Armada in my hand that I was trying to get on the toe rail, talking to a man on the dock while a second man in a dinghy waited to talk to me. The guy in the dinghy introduced himself as a writer for *Cruising World* magazine and asked if he could interview me for an article on the four smallest boats in George Town harbor.

The largest of these boats was an Albin 27 sailed by a young man I hadn't met, but I had met the others. Sandy and Bill are from Peaks Island in Casco Bay, very close to *Tryphena's* home port. Their Columbia 22 is a few inches shorter than *Tryphena*, but with more beam and draft and 1,000 pounds more displacement. It is a much simpler boat than *Tryphena*, and would be cheaper to buy used and to maintain without wood trim or so much equipment. But they had brought her down the Intracoastal, sailed across to the Bahamas, and planned to return to Maine in the spring. Dave had built his 16-foot Bolger-inspired lug-rigged sharpie himself and had sailed it with his wife Mindy and their parrot down from their home in North Carolina. Their boat is so small that it has no cockpit and is sailed from the hatchway of the tiny cabin where they sleep on the floor. They had sailed around a good bit of the Bahamas and planned to do more. I admired their courage and fortitude but their boat provided less margin of safety and fewer creature comforts than I could live with.

Mike Savage, the writer, looked around *Tryphena* with her teak trim and high level of equipment and asked me an interesting question. "You look like you could afford a larger boat. Why do you sail in one so small?" I explained that it is the ease of handling, simplicity, and ability to poke into shallow areas that makes me hang on to *Tryphena*, not the inability to afford a larger boat. My time in the marina and this interview brought home to me how unusual it was to sail the Bahamas in such a small boat. I had always sailed among larger boats, and since the Bahamas seemed well within *Tryphena's* capabilities, I hadn't thought about my cruise as anything that remarkable.

I wanted to sail among some of the more remote and less-developed islands of the Bahamas. Some 20 miles below the last island in the Exumas lies the first cay in the Jumentos, another string of islands that trail off to the south in a gentle arc for seventy miles. The Jumentos are like the Exumas in that they are a string of islands lying roughly north and south with deep water to the east and shallow banks to the west. They are different, however, in that the islands are smaller, there are often much wider gaps between them, and they are seldom visited. The Jumentos are uninhabited except for Duncan Town, a village of around 50 people at the southern end of the string, which lies closer to Cuba than to the nearest other Bahamian settlement. If I went to the Jumentos I would be on my own, with no place to get any food or fuel, or even water, unless I reached Duncan Town; no guarantee of seeing any other boats; and out of range of communication by VHF radio or cell phone.

I was excited to go to the Jumentos, also known as the Ragged Islands, but nervous about it. This part of my cruise would be the ultimate test of self-reliance, and I obsessed over being prepared for anything. I had a strong crew, my friend Don, the man with whom I had sailed to Nova Scotia, Newfoundland, and across the Atlantic. I checked and rechecked my gear and spare parts. Before Don arrived, I packed the boat with as much food as she would hold. I had lots of rice and pasta for starch, canned tuna, salmon, chicken, turkey, and lunch meat for protein, and many types of canned vegetables and fruits. I would also take as much ice and fresh food as I could fit in the cooler, and fresh bread.

Water was a major concern, since like food, we would be unable to get any water in the Jumentos for several weeks, longer than I was used to going without replenishment. In the Bahamas you can get water from wells, from rain catchment systems, or from the desalinization process called reverse osmosis — generally referred to as "R.O. water." I made a practice of using only R.O. water because it is the purest, even though there is a charge for it. Since my water usage is modest, the cost was reasonable and I had less worry. *Tryphena*'s 13-gallon tank doesn't hold a lot, so I had brought along one 5-gallon and two 2 1/2-gallon collapsible jerry cans to supplement the main tank. The cheapest place to obtain R.O. water in George Town turned out to be the snack bar on Stocking Island where there is no wharf or hose, but the jerry cans allowed me to lighter the water out to the boat in my tender. With the tank, the jerry cans, and a few gallon jugs I had a total of 27 gallons of water stashed in various places all over *Tryphena*. This water was supplemented by Gatorade, beer, and other bottled drinks. For washing I had two sun showers filled with the slightly brackish tap water at the marina, adequate for bathing.

With *Tryphena* loaded and ready to go, she was definitely down on her marks. I later figured — based on weighing everything I took off the boat when I returned to Maine — that when I left for the Jumentos, I had at least 1,400 pounds of gear, provisions, spares, crew, and personal effects on board. Since, according to the builder, the Rob Roy 23 weighs 2,800 pounds empty, this is a load factor of 50 percent, quite a lot for any yacht. This was the heaviest I loaded her, and *Tryphena* handled it well, but I wouldn't have wanted her any heavier.

One of the reasons the Jumentos are seldom visited, despite being close to a major yachting center like George Town and the recent availability of decent charts and cruising information, is that they are not easy to get to. The usual route is a difficult and circuitous 65 miles around the islands and shoals at the southern end of the Exumas, but I could save 21 miles by cutting through an inlet only three feet deep, and known for its fierce currents.

Don arrived and we set off, picking our way through the shoals at the eastern entrance of Elizabeth Harbor. Don is a blue water sailor, and I'm afraid he was initially very uncomfortable with the close proximity of the bottom in the Bahamas. "Better your boat than mine," he kept saying, shaking his head as *Tryphena* skimmed along with every detail of the bottom clearly visible through crystalline water so shallow that his 34-foot cutter would have been hard aground. His confidence probably wasn't improved when I strayed a little too far off Little Exuma Island and got us into a maze of coral reefs.

We reached Hog Cay Cut late in the afternoon. I had planned to anchor there for the night, but the only spot with protection from the wind and seas was in the cut itself, a narrow channel curving around an island. Like many cuts, the one at Hog Cay has such strong tidal currents that the bottom of the channel is scoured clean, leaving a smooth hard bottom with very poor holding. At the side of the channel it shoals to a sandbar, which is above water at low tide, in little more than 50 feet. I anchored in this transitional zone, where there was a little less current, using a "Bahamian moor," with an anchor off the bow in either direction. With this arrangement the boat could swing when the tide current reversed so the bow always faced into the current, but it was held in pretty much the same spot regardless of which way the current was flowing. Even for *Tryphena* this situation was a bit tenuous, and I doubt a larger vessel with much more draft could have successfully anchored there, but it worked fine for us.

There were still several hours of daylight left and we decided to explore a beautiful shallow cove to the south. We did this in my tender, a 12-foot light rowing dory. I had thought long and hard about a tender for this cruise. My first thought had been that for crossing the Gulf Stream and the Bahama Banks, I wanted a tender that could be carried on board. But *Tryphena* is so small and her main boom is so low that I couldn't find a rigid dinghy that would fit on her deck, even a folding or nesting one. I then thought of an inflatable dinghy, which is standard for at least 98 percent of the yachts cruising the Bahamas. I could carry a small inflatable, deflated, in the cabin, but they row very poorly and I had no place to stow a second outboard on board, not having the stern pulpit on which most outboards are carried. Nor did I want to tow an inflatable with a mounted outboard for any distance.

In the end I came back to my little dory. It meets my criteria of a two or three-person boat that rows and tows well, and can be easily manhandled up and down a rocky Maine beach so it wouldn't be swept away by the tide. My 12-foot dory was designed by Francis Kinney. Its lines were published in Skene's *Elements of Yacht Design*. The boat was built of plywood sheathed in fiberglass using the "stitch and tape" method by Portland Yacht Services in Maine. It weighs only 100 pounds and has a great deal of flare in its sides thanks to double-chine construction. This means that it has a very narrow waterline beam when lightly loaded — only about two feet with one person aboard — making it feel tippy because it has low initial stability, but giving it good speed with a long narrow underwater shape. Powered by a pair of Shaw and Tenney 6 1/2-foot curve-bladed oars, it will do a steady four knots with the rower in the bow seat and a passenger in the stern seat, as fast as some low-powered inflatables with outboards. Its flared shape means that it becomes more stable as it is loaded or tipped.

Painted white, with a light gray interior and varnished mahogany seats, the dory is a beautiful and elegant little boat. In order to use it as a tender, I added a good rub rail all the way around its gunwale. Since it would have to be towed, I worried about losing it if it was rolled by a wave or swamped crossing the Gulf Stream, so I bought a collection of inflatable bags used for floatation in canoes and kayaks and lashed them into the dory so it would float high even if full of water. These were good insurance, but not needed and were removed when I reached Nassau. I have to remind passengers unfamiliar with it that they must step into the middle of the dory, but once they are in it they are conveyed well and I get exercise, and don't have to worry about an outboard breaking down. It tows well, rarely shipping even a teacup of water in thousands of miles, with no more drag than my old eight-foot rigid dinghy and much less than an inflatable.

The Jumentos were all that I had hoped for. Don and I spent most of our time there at Flamingo Cay, enjoying the beaches, snorkeling on reefs, exploring a cave and a wreck, and evenings with a delightful English couple on a catamaran eating barracuda, conch, and lobster. We romped back to George Town on a marvelous four-sail reach, arriving just ahead of a gale.

I wanted to go east from George Town to Long Island, but my first attempt was too soon after the gale and I was forced to turn back by strong winds and steep seas, which left me discouraged. When I left again early in the morning two days later, I was motorsailing in light air, but still nervous over the possibility of bad weather on this run of 32 miles without a sheltered anchorage. Around mid-day a group of larger boats came up from astern and passed me, headed in the same direction. One was a very rugged 44-foot cutter, the kind of boat I would want if I were sailing around Cape Horn, a boat that would have none of my worries about bad weather. I spoke with her skipper on the radio as she passed, expressing my concern, and discovered that he had his own, more pressing fear. His boat drew 6 1/2-feet and ahead lay an area of shoals with little more than that amount of water over them.

When I anchored in Thompson Bay I called on the radio to see whether my English friends were in the area, and later to obtain a weather report from another boat. Then I rowed ashore and caught a ride to the village with a friendly woman who also gave me a ride back with my 20 pounds of ice on her return from an errand. Long Island is much larger than any island in the Exumas. It is a pastoral place of green rolling hills, more agriculture than most of the Bahamas, and only a few resorts.

One place I particularly wanted to visit was the Thompson's Bay Inn, since the cruising guide said it is run by a woman named Tryphena and I had never before discovered a living woman with that name. I arrived after dark and found a modest bar-restaurant with a few locals playing pool and a few more at the bar. When I asked the woman behind the bar if there was anyone there named Tryphena, she said, "You must be from that boat! My cook likes to listen to the marine radio in the kitchen and twice today she said, 'Tryphena, there's somebody calling from a boat with your name,' but by the time I got there, there was no one talking and I thought she was playing a trick on me."

According to an eminent Greek scholar, "Tryphena" comes from the Greek and means a woman who likes fine things and good times. With an outgoing personality that would make her the life of any party, this Tryphena lived up to the name.

My one serious problem with the boat occurred while sailing between Nassau and Eleuthera. I left early reaching on a westerly breeze predicted to be 15 knots. By mid-afternoon it was over 20 and I had the mizzen furled, the mainsail double-reefed and the genoa partly reefed. A sea had built up, and after a wave slapped *Tryphena* on her quarter, the steering suddenly went all rubbery and I had to keep the tiller at almost a 45-degree angle to keep on course. Something was seriously wrong, and looking over the side I could see that the rudder was bent at an odd angle. After a few minutes the rudder broke off entirely and was dragged astern by its retrieving line. I hauled it aboard and discovered that the two stainless steel plates on the bottom of the rudder post —which held the rudder bolted between them — had broken off, though they were a quarter inch thick and six inches wide. I had thought that this was one of the strongest parts of the boat. The stress of the wave hitting wasn't very great, so there must have been a crack and some crevice corrosion to cause such a failure.

I quickly assessed my situation: I was alone, out of sight of land, in strong winds and choppy seas, with no rudder. It was 10 miles to the nearest land and 12 to the nearest harbor, and to reach it I had to steer between the sunken wreck of a ship and a large reef, both just awash and hard to see but very dangerous. I found that I could control the direction of the boat to a considerable degree with the trim of the sails: trim the mainsail and it would head up into the wind, trim the jib and it would head off. The outboard motor is not designed to turn in its well, but I found that by freeing its tiller arm from the cover above, I could turn it approximately 10 degrees in each direction. By turning and gunning the engine I could get a little steering action from it, but this required me to crouch awkwardly in the bottom of the cockpit. With this combination I could just barely keep control of the boat in the wind and seas. Occasionally I would have to let go of the engine's tiller to stick my head down the hatch for a quick glance at the GPS below to see how I was doing toward my waypoint between the wreck and the reef.

After what seemed like an eternity I passed between the hazards and eventually saw land ahead. I passed Egg Island and approached Royal Island, my intended destination. Outside the harbor entrance at Royal Island I made a difficult decision. The shelter beckoned, but I realized that the island is uninhabited and could give me no assistance with repairs. I decided to go on to Spanish Wells on St. George's Cay, six miles farther on, since it is a large enough community that I might be able to get some help with repairs, even though the wind was increasing and the harbor entrance there is narrow and difficult. But my yawl refused to steer toward Spanish Wells! The new course was farther off the wind, and even with the mainsail luffing and the engine turned I couldn't get *Tryphena* to steer the new course. I hauled the mainsail down and roughly furled it, and she fell off to the new course, still traveling at hull speed in winds now up to 25 knots.

I approached Spanish Wells barely in control with *Tryphena* surging off each wave. Now I had to face how I would get into the narrow harbor entrance. I called ahead on the radio to the pilots on Spanish Wells and asked for assistance. I was told that one was away guiding a vessel through the dangerous passage around the northern end of Eleuthera past an infamous reef called The Devil's Backbone. He would not return for several hours and I was advised to anchor and wait for his arrival. This was the last thing I wanted to do, since there was no shelter and the weather was still deteriorating with stronger winds and higher seas, and night was not far away. The other pilot said he couldn't help because he only had a small Boston Whaler with a 40-horsepower motor.

"That's plenty for my boat," I pleaded into the radio, "I'm only a twenty-three-foot sailboat."

To my relief, he agreed to meet me outside the harbor, and I told him to look for a red sail. Just off the harbor entrance he came alongside and shouted, "It's too rough to pass a tow line. Can you make it into the outer entrance?"

I looked ahead at the narrow dredged channel less than 100 feet wide. "I'll try," I shouted back. At the last moment I rolled up the jib, waited until the wind blew the bow off just enough to be aimed up the channel, and gunned the engine. A few hundred yards up the channel it was protected and the seas were quiet. Old Bradley, the pilot, came alongside for my line and took *Tryphena* in tow. I breathed a great sigh of relief. Soon she swung from a mooring in a little basin at the other end of the harbor.

The next morning I began working on the problem of the repair. To my great fortune, I learned that Spanish Wells has one of the few shipyards in the Bahamas, a small place then busy at work on a large fishing boat, and the island had someone who could weld stainless steel. I also called *Tryphena's* builder, Marine Concepts, in Tarpon Springs, Florida. To my even greater fortune, they were building a new Rob Roy 23 and offered to take the rudder and rudderpost off the new boat and send them to me. The quickest repair would have been to have the broken plates welded back on, but I wasn't sure how well this would work, or if I could trust the repair. I decided that I would go with the new rudder and asked them to ship it to me.

I remained in Spanish Wells in this frustrating and unwanted limbo for 10 days, making arrangements to have the rudder shipped and waiting for it to arrive. A fellow cruiser helped me remove the old rudderpost in an exasperating afternoon of hard work and broken tools. Each day I checked and found that the rudder had not arrived. The shipper said it had been delivered, but Customs at the airport on Eleuthera said it had not arrived. I finally insisted on riding to the airport with the local shipping agent from Spanish Wells, and there in the warehouse we found a large box containing my rudder.

That afternoon I managed to bring my boat alongside the shipyard's dock, and hired a diver who pushed the new rudderpost up from under the boat so I could catch it and attach the rudder head. Then I lowered the new rudder, still rough and unpainted, on its retrieving line and he installed the bolt to hold it to the rudderpost. By sunset I had joined friends at Royal Island. I was happy to have *Tryphena* whole again after frustrating delays, but now strong winds held me captive for a very unusual two weeks. Fortunately for me, among the dozen boats in the harbor, two belonged to good friends.

Toward the end of this time my new crew arrived. My friend Otto's son, also named Otto, just to confuse things, flew in from Berlin to Nassau via Miami. Because of the winds I wasn't able to meet him in Nassau as planned, but I managed to send him an email telling him to take the ferry to Spanish Wells. I motored there to meet him, pounding into 35-knot winds and short, steep seas that would hit *Tryphena* like a solid wall and almost stop her.

When at last the winds eased we were one of the first boats to leave Royal Island. We could leave because we were sailing west, dead downwind to Nassau. Most of the other boats were headed north to the Abacos, which were impossible to enter because all of the entrance cuts there were still "in a rage" from the heavy seas and impassable. At first we sailed in the lee of the land, but the farther we got out of its shelter, the greater the wind and seas became, until we were sailing with double-reefed main and reefed genoa poled out, in 25-knot winds and six- to eight-foot seas. I was nervous about my new and untried rudder, of a modified design, but *Tryphena* was in good control though the dory occasionally caught a wave and came surfing past us on its 50-foot painter. By early afternoon we could see the hotels on Paradise Island on the horizon ahead. We used the big Atlantis Resort as a steering target and watched as more buildings and the land slowly came over the horizon. As we came closer to the land the water became more shallow and the seas grew higher, steeper, and closer together, to the point where *Tryphena* was surfing. A mile or two off the beach I crawled forward, attached by safety harness and tether, and took in the pole. We then jibed the genoa and altered course to parallel the beach and go around the island. A Bahamian patrol boat came up astern and hailed us to see if we were all right, having had a report of a sailboat in trouble. We said we were fine and hadn't seen another sailboat all day.

We rounded the end of the island and headed for the jetties at the harbor entrance. Passing close off the end of the nearest jetty we jibed carefully and ducked between the two menacing arms of stone. Within 100 yards the seas went from 10–12 feet to flat calm as we came into the shelter of the jetties. In our exhilaration, we sailed up the harbor, tacking past the cruise ships and anchored yachts to East Bay marina just for the fun of it.

The first leg of our route back to Florida from Nassau was the 35 miles to Chub Cay. Before we left Nassau, I talked to the skipper of a trawler yacht about 40 feet long. He too was headed for Chub Cay, but would be leaving an hour later. "Look for the red sails and wave as you go by," I said. Outside the harbor we found a gentle 10–12-knot breeze from the east that gave us a reach, and considerable leftover swell. We raised full sail, including the mizzen staysail, and were making good time. We had gone 30 miles and had Chub Cay in sight before the trawler yacht caught up with us. I talked to the skipper on the radio and he was amazed that we had made such good speed. "I'd rather be on your boat right now," he said. His top-heavy trawler was rolling heavily in the swells, swinging her crew up on the flying bridge through uncomfortable arcs, while *Tryphena* was steady under her stabilizing press of sail.

We didn't leave Chub Cay until five o'clock the following evening, so we could cross the banks at night and enter the harbor at Bimini in daylight the next day. We had a good breeze and excellent sailing until midnight and then it went light and we motored. In the wee hours an electrical problem put our lights out, but the GPS and compass light worked and I aimed a hand searchlight at the only ship we passed. (The problem turned out to be a corroded fuse.) The entrance channel at Bimini was as tricky as I had read, but no problem in the midday light, and we spent the rest of the day exploring Bimini, with its sport fishing boats and Hemingway memorabilia.

Our crossing of the Gulf Stream was again in a flat calm. Leaving Gun

Cay at first light we were able to reach Miami in daylight since the spring day was longer. It wasn't until the hotels of Key Biscayne were in sight ahead that a breeze filled in and we raised sail to round Cape Florida and cross Biscayne Bay roaring along under full sail. *Tryphena's* American flag, now tattered, flew from the leach of the mizzen, and the Bahamian flag still flew from where the starboard spreader would be — if *Tryphena* had spreaders — following the etiquette of a vessel visiting that country. In addition, we now flew the yellow quarantine flag showing that we had not yet cleared Customs.

We took in sail just off the big Dinner Key Marina and *Tryphena* made a quiet but triumphal return to the United States after three and a half months, 1,000 miles, and 50 islands in the Bahamas, to be quickly swallowed up in a marina slip twice too large for her. My little *Tryphena* had proved to me that a little vessel of less than 23 feet in length and less than 3,000 pounds displacement is fully capable of long-distance cruising. I had gone to all of the same places that the much larger yachts I met had gone, plus a lot of places they could never fit. And I had done it with adequate but less space and comfort, much less cost, often less effort, and often more fun than the bigger boats. I was fully satisfied with my cruise, and proud of my little vessel.

> **Rob Roy 23**
> Length overall: 28' 8"
> Length on deck: 22' 8"
> Length on waterline: 21'
> Beam: 6' 11"
> Draft: 1' 7" / 4' 8"
> Displacement: 2,800 lbs.
> Sail area: 255 sq. ft.

CHAPTER **8**

⛵

A Pocket Cruiser Portfolio

"It would be going too far to pretend that the pleasure of sailing is in directly inverse proportion to the size of the vessel. Yet who, looking back, does not sometimes think this to be broadly true?"
— *John Scott Huges,* Little Ships

T HE FOLLOWING PAGES DEPICT THE BOATS described in this book. In the case of the Marshall 18 and Rhodes 22, sister ships are included because suitable photographs of the original boats were not available at the time of publication. Careful study of the photographs will provide ample food for thought about the potential of a well-designed and thoughtfully equipped pocket cruiser.

The easily managed rig of Charles Stocks' Shoal Waters is evident in this photo as the boat breezes along on the Norfolk Broads. Rope grommets that serve as grab handles are mounted conveniently port and starboard on the bulkhead.

A well-designed and sturdily constructed boom tent that offers good sitting headroom and easy entry/egress creates a second cabin aboard Shoal Waters and maximizes every inch of space.

Cozy and colorful: Shoal Waters' *cabin may be small but all the necessities are neatly arranged and the hull is lined with closed cell foam for insulation. Forward is the boat's sturdy samson post that extends from deck to keel.*

With her gaff cutter rig, Shoal Waters *has a flexible sailplan and it's easy to shorten sail in the face of increasing winds. With a reefed main and reduced headsails, there's not much this pocket yacht need fear.*

The simplicity and charm of a Cape Cod catboat are evident in this Marshall 18. This boat is being easily single-handed in about 12 knots of wind.

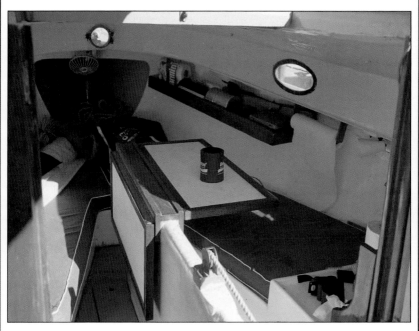

An 18-foot catboat offers a comparatively roomy cabin. This is the space in which Chapter Two author Lance Gunderson lived during a 10-month cruise from Kittery, Maine, to Key West and back.

Here is Sea Dart *after being refinished on the beach in Barbados. Her bilge keels do much to simplify grounding the boat for maintenance.*

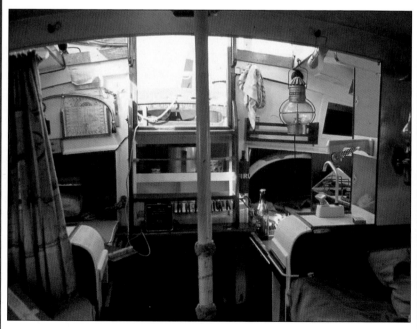

Sea Dart's *cabin is small but fully up to the demands of ocean cruising and life aboard.*

A loose-footed mainsail, flared hull, and a cabin with forward facing, opening ports are just a few of the unique features of the Rhodes 22. Seen here is Windswept, *a sister ship to Chapter Five's* Fretless.

A variety of layout options are available on the Rhodes 22 including an enclosed marine head seen here or the portable version chosen for Fretless *by Mary Lou Troy and her husband Fred and described in Chapter Five.*

Here is the Falmouth Cutter Mariko *chugging along in a glassy calm. The boat is propelled by a two-cylinder Yanmar diesel installed by her owners Mike and Helen Meier.*

Looking aft aboard Mariko: this 22-footer packs a lot of well-planned living space into her sturdy hull.

The Rob Roy 23 Tryphena Chandler *spreads her mizzen staysail to keep things moving in the faint breeze of a Maine summer afternoon.*

Sensibly planned for just two people, the Brewer-designed Rob Roy 23 offers exceptionally practical accommodations that have served owner David Bellows well for almost two decades.

Here is Paul Gartside's beautiful wooden cutter Surprise in all her topsail glory! The 22-footer's easily managed gaff rig provides just the right sail combinations for all conditions and a clever retractable bowsprit shortens the boat and reduces marina charges.

Down below, Surprise offers a cozy, well-lit cabin finished in white paint and varnish. There's a comfortable v-berth and unusually comfortable seating thanks to the configuration of the hull and cabin sides.

CHAPTER 9

⚓

A Designer Goes Small

BY PAUL GARTSIDE

Paul Gartside was brought up in the family boatyard in Cornwall, England. After studying boat design in Southampton, he worked in the family business for almost a decade. In 1983, he emigrated to British Columbia, Canada, where he has spent the last 20 years designing and building boats. He and his wife, Barbara, own a variety of small boats and currently cruise together in the 22-foot cutter Surprise. *Of the boats in this book,* Surprise *is the second gaff-cutter with topsail, a fact that speaks volumes about the virtues of the rig, which may be had by independent-minded sailors willing to look beyond today's production boats.*

O NE MIGHT THINK THAT THE SOLE DETERMINANTS of vessel choice would be geographic location and cruising style and that a simple analysis of the conditions and requirements would yield the obvious choice of vessel. Yet, when I look at the choices I have made in this regard and, especially as I listen to the musings of my clients, I am struck by the fact that the about the last thing we boat owners bring to this question is simple logic. It is much more likely that we will construct a logic to support choices made.

The problem here is that boats are more than a means of transport. They are also expressions of ourselves, our dreams and our fantasies. For many of us boats are symptomatic of a desire to escape the burdensome routine of the everyday, to find the life of romance and adventure we were destined for before it all went terribly wrong. For some people, cars perform the same function but boats have always been the stronger metaphor for me. For one thing, a boat will cut you a lot more slack than a car. It doesn't have to get you to work and back each day. In fact, it can serve much of its purpose simply by sitting half finished in the backyard. I can show you several in my neighborhood that have been doing yeoman service for their owners in just this fashion for many years. Even unfinished, these boats are still representative of dreams.

Small boats are especially appealing because they lie within reach of all of us. You can fantasize all you like about space travel, but it isn't going to happen. Start building a boat and sooner or later, if you keep at it, one weekend at a time, one scrounged fitting after another, one leaking tarp after complaining neighbor, you will eventually find yourself waiting for the boat mover to come and dump you in. If you've gotten it right and if, by happy chance, enough common sense found its way into the mix so that there is a reasonable match between ship and voyage, your boat will transport you to other worlds, both real and imagined.

It is this latter idea that resonates most strongly with me when I am talking with customers and why I enjoy working with the home builders so much despite the frustrations. And there are frustrations! Still, it is the purity of motive that I like. That's what drives the amateur builder and it's what stands in such stark contrast to much of the rest of an industry that is driven by forces I don't fully understand, but am fairly sure should not be encouraged.

I also know this: Voyages of a modest nature are as capable of generating powerful experiences and lasting memories as long ones. I have on my bookshelves the complete works of F. B. Cooke who puttered about the Thames Estuary in England for about 50 years in a variety of small yachts. I don't suppose he ever had a cruise longer than a couple of hundred miles, but the immense pleasure he derived from those weekend escapes — fussing over the gear, making improvements and revisiting familiar anchorages — comes through in everything he wrote. He was my kind of guy.

In my own experience, it is the half dozen or so small boats that I have built and owned myself that stand out as most worthwhile in the sea of projects I have labored over. Without question there is an added depth to the experience if you have built the vessel you command. But regardless, one cannot leave the dock without returning with a cargo of memories, however short the voyage. And every so often will come an episode of such vivid intensity that you will carry it with you to the old folks' home. There are inevitable rewards to small boat cruising.

As to what determines the boats that appeal to us, who can say? Occasionally you meet someone who can change boat type easily, a catboat one minute, a fast runabout the next, but that is unusual and always slightly unsettling, rather like a person who keeps changing their hair color. It is suggestive of inner turmoil or an immaturity of taste. I was reminded of this when I christened my current boat *Surprise* and a friend said, "Where's the surprise? It's exactly what we thought you would build." I am so predictable!

Surprise was built for cruising the coastal waters of British Columbia and Alaska, surely some of the most beautiful small boat country on the planet. Home port is Sidney, on the east side of Vancouver Island, hard against the Canada-U.S. border. To the south and east of us are the waters of Puget Sound and the major population centers of Seattle and Tacoma. To the east is mainland British Columbia and the city of Vancouver, separated from the island by the Strait of Georgia, an inland sea sprinkled liberally with islands through which the international boundary wanders. In summer the climate here is best described as Mediterranean without the wind. It provides some of the most benign boating conditions one can find anywhere.

The ocean proper lies due west beyond the bulk of Vancouver Island. There are two ways to reach it. One goes either south around the tip of the island and out through the Strait of Juan de Fuca, or north to the headwaters of the Strait of Georgia and out through the tangle of islands and channels that separate the top of the island from the mainland. Yachts circumnavigating Vancouver Island in summer will normally go north up the inside and then catch the prevailing north westerlies down the outside, a round trip of about 500 nautical miles.

North of Vancouver Island, the human population thins out quickly. From the top of the island to the Alaskan border lies almost 300 miles of coast with virtually no road access and only small, scattered communities. For boats going up this coast, there are many routes to choose from because from here on the coast is buffered by chains of islands that form a labyrinth of channels and fiords stretching 600 miles north to south.

It is possible to make the run to Alaska almost entirely on the inside in sheltered water, following mist-shrouded channels, occasionally breaking out into open water for a brief taste of the ocean before plunging back into the wet, green maze. For wet it is up here. If the Straits of Georgia are climatically Mediterranean without the wind, this is West Coast of Ireland with a double dose of rain. Prince Rupert, the principal town on the north coast, gets about 100 inches a year. Rain defines the north coast, along with a soft light, dripping forests, slippery docks, and oilskin-clad inhabitants. The rain is also the region's savior in many ways, discouraging overuse by tourists and preserving a sanctuary for the wild life. As someone once said to us: "If rain watching ever catches on, this place is doomed."

Just north of Prince Rupert we run into the Canada-U.S. border again. This is southeast Alaska, known alternately as "the panhandle" or to the locals, simply as "Southeast." While the geography here is a continuation of the British Columbia coast, the scale seems to change as you move up the panhandle. The islands become larger and more mountainous, the channels between them become wide straits, and most noticeably the mountains of the coast range press in close to the sea. The mountains here are snow covered year round and in many places are parent to glaciers, some of which discharge into tidewater. And of course the mountains make rain, lots of it. Up here they measure in feet per year: Juneau and Sitka get about eight, Ketchikan 13.

The sheltered waters reach their northern limit at Glacier Bay amongst retreating glaciers and the summer feeding grounds of humpbacked whales. To the north and west Alaska stretches away in a huge bulge out towards the Aleutians and beyond. To go farther means leaving behind the protection of island breakwaters. Vessels heading west through Icy Strait and Cross Sound find themselves in the open waters of the Gulf of Alaska. While it is entirely possible to push on in a well-found boat with competent crew, the realities of weather to be encountered and time constraints make this the practical limit for summer cruising for most small boats.

To reach this point, a boat leaving Seattle will have covered 1000 miles and 11 degrees of latitude. Almost the whole way is sheltered water, much of it wilderness, or as close to it as we get to true wilderness in our shrinking world. Alternatively one can travel on the outside, past endless log-strewn beaches and surf-bound islets along a coast rich in sea birds and marine mammals. Most likely a cruising boat will have done some of each route, taking the opportunities of favorable winds to sail on the outside, ducking back in as weather threatened.

One moves steadily north, under sail when possible, under power when necessary. If one anchors every night but doesn't linger, if breakfast is taken under way, and if the weather is reasonably cooperative, one might cover the passage in three weeks. If, on the other hand, the crew were disposed to dawdle and savor everything the country had to offer, such a cruise would take a lot longer. In fact, if one were to explore every inlet that cuts back into the mountains and hike the hills and river estuaries or if — as we have so often done — you hang out in the isolated communities enjoying the locals and trying to figure out how a person might make a living up here, then a cruise could easily take half a lifetime.

What kind of a vessel is best to enjoy such a country? Our early explorations of this coast were done by motorboat, and I still think that is the simplest and most effective way to explore the intricacies of the inside waters. At that time we had a 22-foot v-bottom motorboat with a three-cylinder Perkins diesel. It was strictly a displacement boat with a cruising speed of six knots, but it carried enough fuel to give a range of 600 miles. It had a fully enclosed wheelhouse with full headroom and both inside and outside steering. Best of all, the cabin was heated by a Force 10 kerosene stove. That boat taught me a lot about how much more comfortable boating can be and how much less tired the crew becomes if they stay warm and dry and insulated from the elements. Though I am back in sailboat mode at the moment, the lessons learned have not been lost on me. The trips we made in her stand as a benchmark of comfort and efficiency for all our subsequent small boat voyages.

A motor boat has its limitations when it comes to venturing onto the outer coast, however. It is possible, but one does feel terribly vulnerable. A little dirt in the fuel, a clump of weed in the water intake at the wrong time and things can get out of control very quickly. Good ground tackle and a VHF radio go some way to relieving those anxieties, but they can never disappear altogether. A sailboat is so much more relaxed in that respect. There is still plenty to go wrong, but without total reliance on machinery it is easier to deal with problems. Add to that the sailboat's easier motion in open water and the simple pleasure of being driven by the wind, and a small yacht starts to rack up points.

Surprise was built with these thoughts in mind and although I have only sailed her a couple of seasons and still have much to learn about her, she is proving to be a well-mannered little boat and quite capable of making the kind of voyages we ask of her. She is a traditional long keel cutter model, somewhat on the narrow and deep side with plenty of lateral area and the rudder just inboard of a raked transom. My earlier remarks notwithstanding, I will endeavor to make a rational case for the choices made in drawing up her plans.

The size was chosen for affordability both of time and money. If you are going to build yourself a boat, the most important thing is to pick one that you can finish within your lifetime, preferably with a little time in hand to enjoy it. This might seem obvious, on par with that famous Muppet, Miss Piggy, who advised never to put anything into your mouth bigger than your head. But sadly, miscalculations are all too common. In retrospect I might have gone a little larger in size without overextending myself, but better this side of the line than the other. As it was, construction of *Surprise* consumed the spare time of five years.

The choice of model is largely a reflection of personal taste. The keel cutter is a type I have drawn in sizes ranging from 16 to 35 feet, and I believe there is much to recommend such a model on a practical level. If you plan to

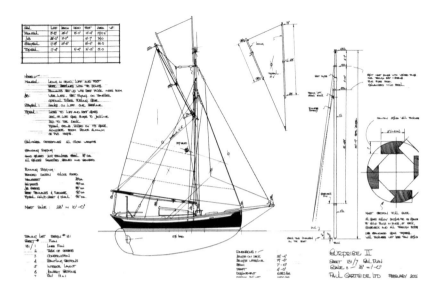

spend any length of time on a small boat, it has to have a livable cabin. This is crucial. Performance is important and aesthetics is important, but if the boat is to be home for weeks at a time, the cabin becomes the heart of the whole enterprise and it must be a comfortable and pleasant place to be. This is the hardest thing to achieve in small boats, but well worth striving for. When it works, there is no better sanctuary from the world.

Probably the most important ingredient here is that there is comfortable seating with sufficient legroom. It is physical discomfort more than actual volume that makes a cabin feel cramped. One beauty of many traditional types is that they have hull depth even in the small sizes. This makes it possible to get the cabin sole low, even though it might be quite narrow. *Surprise* may be heavier on her waterline than ideal for performance, but the trade-off is headroom below without ungainly top hamper. I don't have full headroom, there is just five feet under the hatch, but more important, there is sufficient depth to get comfortable seats port and starboard with room to lean back against the hull side. It is difficult to do that in a shallow fin keel or centerboard model of this size.

In these waters we are not restricted in draft. The only shallow water is to be found in the river estuaries. The nature of the coast elsewhere is rocky shores and deep water. Other cruising grounds will require other solutions. A boat like *Surprise* also results in a "low stress structure," which I consider highly desirable for knocking about a rocky coastline a long way from home. I don't think I am a careless sailor, though I grew up in an area where boats were kept on drying moorings, and running aground was an inevitable part

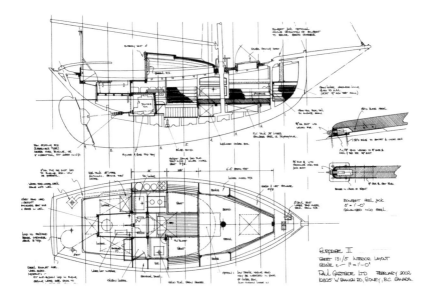

of getting out on the water. Perhaps for that reason I don't share the horror of getting close to shore that many do. In any case, I like poking about a shoreline because that's where so much of the interest lies, and I want a boat that will take a good thump now and then without coming to any harm. A long-keeled boat with the ballast load well distributed and the minimum of built-in stress points has the best chance in these circumstances. (Depending on the configuration, a centerboarder can score high here, too).

A fin-keeled boat is quite different in this respect and I don't know why we don't hear more discussion about this in the press. Perhaps it is more obviously an issue here where running aground means hitting something solid 90 percent of the time, whereas overall more sailing is done in areas where the bottom is more forgiving. I do know that I can walk around the boat yards in Sidney any day of the year and find keel impact repairs underway. One composite repair yard here does a couple of dozen a year, ranging from a simple rebedding of the joint all the way up through repairs to torn laminates on the keel stub and cracked floors and bulkhead tabbing. I see this as a serious weakness in most fin keel production boats and the problem is getting worse as keel sections get thinner and bulbs and wings become fashionable. Sooner or later we are going to have to come up with a better keel attachment method to handle the stress concentrations we are creating. In the meantime I am nervous sailing any boat in which a hard grounding will result in expensive structural damage. It is one thing in a racing boat, but quite out of place in a cruiser.

In terms of performance, *Surprise* has good all-around characteristics.

She loves going to windward and her large lateral area helps her hang on well in rough water. Hull speed is a brick wall that she runs into at about six knots and nothing short of a tidal race will budge her much past it. That of course is the limitation of a short, heavy boat. On the other hand, she has lots of power to get there easily, so while I don't claim to own a fast boat, we rarely disgrace ourselves in company.

It is tempting to think how the same displacement and sail area might be disposed to generate higher performance, and I admit it's a question I do ponder. However, I have been around this loop before in my life and I know how careful one has to be not to focus on a single characteristic if the boat is to be an overall success. Given a fixed displacement, the formula for performance is simple: Maximize waterline length and spread the displacement as thinly over the surface of the water as possible so that it generates the most righting moment. The trouble is, in this size boat we end up sitting in a cabin whose proportions are those of a corridor, with our knees up to our chin. It might be fast, but it won't be comfortable.

The rig is a regular gaff cutter. The mast is hollow spruce; the remainder of the spars are solid. All mast ironwork, gooseneck and gaff saddle, mast bands, and pin rail are welded mild steel, hot dip-galvanized, and painted. The forestay comes to the stem head and the jib is set flying on a traveler that can be hauled out to the sheave in the end of the bowsprit. This means that there is no necessity to go out on the bowsprit – ever. It also means that the sprit can be pulled inboard to save on marina charges. If you can't do that, a bowsprit is a painful thing to own and I can't help feeling one would be better off just buying more waterline length. On *Surprise* I have a jack at the bowsprit heel that tensions the shrouds and bobstay and can be backed off to disconnect the heel from the deck fitting. The spar can then be drawn inboard and the slack shrouds hitched up and belayed.

I like a gaff rig. It suits this particular model and they have to be considered all of a piece, but in general I find I am well disposed to four-sided sails. It is somewhat irrational in terms of performance, I know, so I suppose we have to go back to diaper days for an explanation. Come to think of it, maybe it is the diaper. If Albert Camus was right and we spend our lives trying to recapture the thing that first moves us, perhaps we have found the source of the trouble. Whatever the explanation, it works for me. I like the simplicity of the gear and fact that I can make it all myself. I like the way it sounds and the smell of fresh varnish, and I love watching that big square sail going up. I also get a charge out of fooling with the topsail that is such an intrinsic part of the rig.

If it came to a choice between a topsail and a spinnaker, and we carry both, I will keep the topsail every time. It can create havoc going up and down if the system isn't perfectly worked out and even then there is always potential for comedy. But once up, it looks after itself completely, quite unlike a spinnaker, and it pulls like a mule.

On *Surprise* the topsail is laced to both the luff spar and the jackyard. This is not the simplest way to rig a topsail but I think it gives the best effect. It stands well on the wind and there is no extra weight aloft when it is not set. The luff spar is 11 feet long and effectively adds five feet to the mast height. It goes up just like a burgee with the halyard led to a sheave in the masthead. The sheet from the jackyard leads through a sheave in the end of the gaff, down to a block slung from the gaff saddle and thence to a cleat on the forward end of the boom. Once off the deck, the heel of the luff spar is snapped on to a jackstay that keeps it snug against the mast. When it is all the way up, the downhaul from the tack is tensioned on the pinrail at the foot of the mast and the sail is sheeted home. What could possibly go wrong? When it is not in use the topsail is rolled up around its spars and stows out of harm's way in a pair of aluminum hoops alongside the boom.

The reefing system in the mainsail is simple tie points. There are three reef lines with permanently rigged pennants and a four-part purchase under the boom to haul them down. I have a steel pipe gallows aft that I can get the boom into for reefing. However, unless it is rough, we normally just haul the boom in far enough to work on and use the gallows as handhold. To date I have still not used the third reef, though there have been a couple of times when we probably should have. A removable crutch mounted in the gallows holds the boom and gaff when the sails are stowed.

The jib has a wire luff that allows it to be set flying. I have it set up on a Whykham Martin furling gear, a great convenience that speeds up getting under way while still allowing the bowsprit to be brought inboard. Because the action is not as positive as foil-type furlers, I find the gear can be overpowered in strong winds. More than once, when we have hung on to the jib too long, we have had to bring the whole thing inboard and dump it down the fore hatch for sorting out later. Still I wouldn't be without it.

I also have a reef line in the staysail, though I have yet to use it and rather suspect I never will. The way the boat balances, I find I want to reef the main and hang on to the headsails as long as possible. I could really do with a small jib to be set with the staysail and deep-reefed main. In fact, that's on the list for next season, as are a pair of small sheet winches. Right now the headsail sheets are single-part led directly to cam cleats on the cockpit coaming, which gets a bit much in strong winds. A purchase works well on the staysail sheets but is both a nuisance and a menace on the jib.

An engine is indispensable on this coast. We have gone without in the past, but it is a frustrating business and severely limits the ground that can be covered. So I am an unapologetic engine user. When it comes to cruising I am not one of the world's dawdlers. I like to feel the boat moving and the country slipping by. If I were to go back over the logbooks it would be rare to find us in the same anchorage two nights in a row unless we were in port, and it is only the stress of weather that will cause that. I will sail if the wind allows, motor sail if it starts to get light, and run under power alone if I have to, whatever it takes to keep the boat moving.

The engine in *Surprise* is a Yanmar 2GM diesel, which delivers 18 hp when wound up to 3,600 rpm. I run it mostly at 2,700 rpm, which gives me 5.5 knots while burning about .39 gallons (1.5 liters) of fuel an hour. In the tank I have 23 usable gallons (88 liters), good for about 300 nautical miles. While I am perfectly willing to make use of an engine, I confess I am not exactly simpatico with the beasts. Earlier in my life I was convinced I was a Jonah as far as engines in boats were concerned. Bring me within 10 feet of one and it would act up as if it knew. For a long time this engendered a deep distrust and loathing, which I was quite sure was mutual. My mother was fond of reminding me she once witnessed me kicking a Watermota Shrimp. I don't recall it, but I dare say it is true. I did own one, and as anyone who has shared that fate will agree, if there was ever an engine that needed kicking on a regular basis, it is a Watermota Shrimp. (For the innocents, this was a marinized version of an air-cooled Norton Villiers motorcycle engine that never quite found its sea legs.)

Eventually I came to see that my problems weren't personal. Everyone has trouble with engines in boats and there are very good reasons why. The combination of infrequent use and the damp and salty atmosphere in which they must live is not conducive to reliability, and for gasoline engines, it is deadly. If we treated the engines in our cars this way, they would be just as troublesome.

I was surprised therefore when, at the end of a course in diesel maintenance I took several years ago, the instructor, a highly regarded mechanic, suggested that it makes a difference if we talk nicely to our engines. "My God," I thought, "perhaps it's true after all." I don't believe there has ever been any research on this, but I wouldn't be surprised if there were something to it. I do know there are mechanics who appear to connect with machinery on a different level from the rest of us. My brother is that way. I have yet to see him effect a cure by the laying on of hands, but engines do seem to reveal their troubles to him in a way that to me is miraculous.

So while I know I will always be an outsider in these matters, I do talk to my engine. Not in an arbitrary way, you understand. I talk to it while going through the daily checklist. When cruising I do this every morning (religiously one might say). If we are making an early start, I will do it the night before. I check fluid levels, oil, transmission, and coolant. I shine a flashlight in the water strainer and the bowl of the primary fuel filter. I look in the drip tray for signs of fluid leaks. I check for signs of chafe on belts and hoses. I check the drip of the stuffing box and I wipe any signs of corrosion with an oily rag, all the while uttering words of encouragement. Then I start her up, check the water flow and listen to the familiar rumble with a questioning ear. If all is well, we are off; I can do no more.

In recent years I have had better luck with the engines in my life and I am sure this practice of attentiveness is largely responsible. The soothing words may help too, though I can't help think any engine capable of hearing them must also recognize the shallow self interest from which they spring. That has never stopped human beings from praying though and it is probably better than kicking the brute.

I am also much more careful these days when planning installations to make sure the engine is given the conditions in which it can prosper. They say that clean fuel and good batteries are all you really need to know to keep a diesel happy, and there is much truth to that. Even in a simple boat like ours, it is worth having separate engine and domestic batteries so that the cranking current is always available, and it is worth keeping the fuel topped up to avoid condensation on the tank walls. There are other things I have found that make a difference, too. Access for maintenance is crucial, but always something of a compromise in a small boat. If the engine compartment can be illuminated with the flick of a switch right back to the stuffing box, it makes a big difference even when physical access is limited.

I am also big on getting air to the engine. *Surprise* has a pair of three-inch cowl vents on the aft deck. The port one dumps into a water trap under the deck from which a three-inch PVC pipe leads forward through the galley lockers to the front of the engine box. The cold air entering here forces the hot air up and aft under the cockpit to exit from the starboard vent. Not only does this provide a supply of cool clean combustion air to the engine when it is running, I think it also goes a long way to reducing condensation and corrosion when it is sitting idle.

Modern high-speed diesels need an oil change every 100 hours, which means at least one change during a summer run up the coast. A permanently mounted hand pump plumbed into the sump drain makes this chore so much easier and cleaner. I like to think it also does a more thorough job of removing undesirables than pumping through the dipstick hole.

With an engine comes a supply of free electricity and the temptation to add all manner of electronic gadgetry. If you value your sanity you will resist this – at least up to a point. Salt water and electricity do not do well together and the smaller the boat, the harder it is to keep them apart. All electrical equipment with the exception of the auto helm is mounted inside the cabin. This includes the engine panel, which so often is mounted in the cockpit well where it is sure to be immersed in salt water sooner or later.

I am by no means an advocate of the oil lamps and lead line approach; some electrical equipment is worth having along. But keep in mind that everything you install will break down sooner or later and then it will need troubleshooting and fixing. The law of diminishing returns kicks in early as you bring this stuff aboard, so my advice is to keep it simple, keep it away from the damp, and label all connections clearly.

In *Surprise* I have, in order of importance:

1) Navigation Lights. These are at the masthead in a tricolor fixture. Despite the difficulty of bulb replacement, this the only place they are really visible in a small boat at sea. I don't have the anchor light up there though. The two-story light fixtures seem to me an unnecessary complication and vulnerable to a crack from the topsail spars. The anchor light hangs on the gallows and plugs in to a receptacle in the cockpit.

2) Cabin Lights. I have lots. The draw is small and good illumination makes the cabin feel larger than it is. Placement needs careful thought to give good reading light sitting in the cabin and in the berths.

3) VHF radio with the antenna at the masthead for maximum range.

4) Depth Sounder. Mounted inside the companionway in a housing that hinges out where it can be seen by the helmsman.

5) GPS. The antenna is mounted on the boom gallows. I am still amazed by what this little gadget will do, half of which I still haven't figured out. It is miracle enough to me that it can tell me where I am and give me a magnetic course to where I want to go. Some GPS functions such as backtracking and man overboard location require that the helmsman see the display. This is difficult to arrange in a small sailboat short of mounting the instrument on a board that can be hinged out into the companionway as we have done with the depth sounder. Even then it is terribly vulnerable to salt spray. We have also carried a supposedly waterproof handheld model for use in the cockpit. If you are going to rely on GPS for navigation it is probably a good idea to have a backup, though if it is battery-powered, make sure you have plenty of spares because they don't last long. For the type of coastal cruising we are doing, a GPS is by no means essential equipment, but it takes up little

room and on occasion is a great source of reassurance.

6) Auto Helm. I installed a Raytheon Tiller Pilot 2000. I had previously rigged steering lines to the tiller so that I could sit in the companionway out of the rain when running under power. I also have a chain that stretches across the cockpit and can be clipped into the tiller for a temporary lock. The auto helm is the improved version of those arrangements. It will allow the helmsman to read a book or go below for a cup of tea and a warmup. Of course it also increases the likelihood of hitting a log or running aground by about 500 percent, so it may yet prove a mixed blessing; we'll see. While on the subject of collision avoidance, I have the mast cavity stuffed with crumpled aluminum foil in hopes it will improve our signature on radar. I have yet to do a proper investigation of how we compare with similarly sized boats with wooden masts, but so far nobody has run us down in the fog.

The drawings show the stock plan version of *Surprise* and differ slightly in layout from the original. We have the galley stove on the starboard side aft of the wood heater. The port side seat then extends aft and can be used as a sea berth if needed. The fuel tank is further aft and a wet locker lies between it and the foot of the berth. This is a great little cabin. The hull is finished with semi-gloss white paint throughout to keep it bright. The cabin sides, lockers, and joinery are red cedar all taken from the same cant, and of a deep red hue. To take the wear, the edges are trimmed with mahogany and the finish is a satin varnish.

Upholstery is dark green. On a rainy evening with the wood stove ticking away and a hot toddy in hand, it is the most romantic place in the world, right up there with a gondola on the Grand Canal. For the full effect, of course, one needs the right companion but they, alas, are not so easy to find. A ride in a gondola is one thing, but the privations of small boat cruising call for talent of a rare and special kind. In that respect I consider myself very fortunate.

In *Surprise* we cook with kerosene. The stove is a two-burner model made by Taylor in England. It is the most beautiful stove in all of Christendom, and furthermore, it is reliable. I am particular about the clarity of the fuel I feed it and I believe that helps. Kerosene is not the quickest or easiest fuel to use, propane wins that one hands down, but in our little boat I would hard pressed to find a home for a drained locker and spare tank. I am not of the school that believes kerosene is intrinsically safer than propane. The only time I have had to use a fire extinguisher aboard a boat was to deal with a kerosene stove. The danger lies in the starting alcohol.

Regrettably, *Surprise* has no buil-in icebox. We have debated taking a small cooler along but the space has always been more usefully employed in other ways. Furthermore, the climatic conditions here don't make refrigeration a necessity. We have a deep bilge that is always cool, so cheese, margarine and long-life milk are stowed here wedged between the bottles that occupy the bulk of that space.

We are able to pick up fresh supplies of fruit and vegetables as we go, so there is never any need to carry large quantities. We keep a basic inventory of canned goods, pasta, rice, and dried soups that provide the basis of a repertoire of one-pot suppers. The starting point for these is usually the soup mix of which there is an enormous variety available now. This gets matched to a can of meat or fish and is added to onion and garlic and whatever liquid is at hand. Desserts may be rice pudding or fruit, stewed, canned, or fresh. Lunch underway is usually soup or bread and cheese and fruit. Breakfast is the same on the boat or ashore, the only constant in this world of chaos – porridge laced with golden raisins.

Fresh water is carried in a custom-made welded polyethylene tank of about 23 gallons (90 liters) capacity. I have no sink, so we use a plastic washing-up bowl for the dishes and sponge baths in the cockpit for ourselves.

For heat, I have a miniature wood stove made by Cole in Seattle. It is brick lined and bulkhead mounted. The firebox is just five-inches square, which imparts a distinctly Lilliputian flavor to our firewood expeditions. When cruising these are conducted every three or four days using a collapsible saw and a small hatchet. Wood is easily obtained on this coast, though finding it dry is a practiced art. We also burn bark, which can be picked up in convenient-sized nuggets along the tide lines and burns like coal. For cruising in this area a wood stove is a wonderful way to warm the cabin. It is completely reliable, provides a measure of garbage disposal, and is also rather fun.

Surprise does not have a head and I have never felt the lack of one. Instead we have a bucket that mounts under a fixed seat either in the cabin in a box fitted between the berths, or in the cockpit under the tiller. In practice we only use it in the cockpit, the box in the cabin having been co-opted for firewood storage early on. This is a solution that works for us with the kind of boating we do. We don't cruise in company and avoid heavily used anchorages. We are much more interested in leaving the human race behind when we go off in the boat and are lucky enough to live in an area where that is still possible. I recognize that our toilet arrangement is not the solution for all cases.

There are, however, several good reasons for not installing a head. As the regulations currently stand, we would also be required to fit a holding tank if we wish to enter U.S. waters, which we frequently do. While it is possible to fit a low profile head between the berths in the cabin, the combination of a head and holding tank is physically impossible to squeeze in and on a practical level it is not an arrangement I want to live with in such a confined space. I would sooner fit the head in the cockpit under the tiller and the holding tank in a cockpit locker. But that has no advantage over a bucket, provided certain rules are adhered to.

Aboard *Surprise* the first rule is that the head may not be used for serious business unless the boat is under way in open water. Of course, this should be the rule with any head that is pumped directly overboard, but the bucket system is a good inducement to honesty. It means that if the boat is at anchor and wishes to stay put, it must at minimum, run out to sea for half an hour or so each day, then come back in. If the boat is in port, then shore facilities must be used.

The second rule is that any member of the crew may call for a potty break at any time. The seat is then set up, the bucket primed and the cockpit vacated. If it is raining, the remaining crew retires to the cabin and closes the hatch. If it is fine, they may choose to go forward and keep a lookout ahead. Depending on the conditions it may also be necessary to heave to, although it is pleasant to sit and contemplate with the tiller in the crook of one's neck and the boat slipping along. Among the crew of *Surprise*, a certain competitive attitude has grown up in these matters. I have been present when the maneuver was successfully accomplished during a spinnaker run, a feat of seamanship that calls for talent of a very rare and special kind.

Once the routine is established, this a beautifully simple arrangement. There is never any odor in the boat nor any of the maintenance problems associated with heads and holding tanks. It is a well-known fact that on the scale of reliability, your average marine head lies somewhere between a Watermota Shrimp and a Scud missile. I remember one summer when failure of the head forced me into Campbell River just two days out from home. "I bet you haven't got one of those?" I said to the fellow behind the counter in the local chandlery, offering him a crumpled piece of black rubber the size of a throat lozenge. "Oh sure," he said, "that's a pump seal from a Poop-o-matic XYZ". My relief at scoring the vital part was tempered by the realization that his instant recognition could only have been born from the frequency with which the question had been asked.

While it is true that a good quality head will give better service than one of lower breeding, they all fail sooner or later and in my experience it is the compact models that the owners of small boats fall heir to that are the most troublesome. In England there used to be one called an SL 400 that we installed in a lot of boats. (I use its real name because I am sure they can't still be making it — surely not!). Its chief, and perhaps only virtue was that it offered the lowest profile on the market through an ingenious sideways action of the pump handle. Push in to pump water in, release to empty out. It is 20 years since I have seen one but I know I could take one apart blindfolded now, so practiced at it did I become. It wasn't the reason I emigrated, but I count it as a side benefit that I won't ever see one again.

Good airflow through the cabin is essential if condensation is to be kept at bay in wet weather. In *Surprise*, I have four three-inch cowl vents, two on the aft deck, one on the cabin roof, and one up forward alongside the bowsprit, plus louvers in the top washboard. All but one of the cowl vents work through water traps allowing them to be kept open all the time. The deckhead and the hull sides are places condensation will form if conditions are right with the deckhead being the most troublesome. A wooden boat is at an advantage because of the natural insulating properties of the wood but it is certainly not immune. The thickness of the wood makes a noticeable difference. For instance, our cabin top is a beamless laminate of red cedar an inch thick and rarely attracts moisture, while the underside of the fore deck and hatch, also red cedar but 5/8" thick, will do so on occasion. It is a good argument for a thick cedar deck as opposed to a thin plywood one. In terms of bunks and seats, the hull is lined inside the frames leaving an air gap of 7/8". Bunk boards should be slatted to avoid condensation on the underside of cushions, and the cushions should be turned up regularly to dry.

Not many small boats have the luxury of a dedicated chart space and *Surprise* is no exception. We do, however, have a 27" x 25" chart flat that pulls out from under the cockpit and is supported by a line snapped to an eye in the cabin roof. It is not the easiest spot at which to brace oneself when the boat is jumping as the navigator is quick to remind me, but it has its own light and is much better than nothing at all. A bigger problem turns out to be chart stowage. I have a built-in

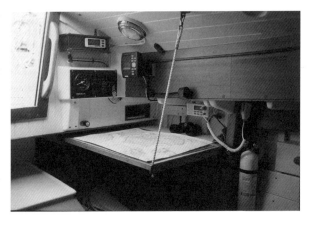

This drop-down chart table is just one of several unique features to be found aboard Surprise.

wooden case that runs back over the fuel tank on the port side that will take a couple of rolls about three-inches in diameter, but that doesn't begin to cover the number we find ourselves lugging around. On long cruises, we may have 80 charts aboard at the start and pick up several more along the way.

When it comes to chart work, I am an overview kind of a person. I favor small scale charts that give the whole picture. I like a chart I can chew away on for a week or so, watching my track as it wanders ant-like across the surface of the planet. They are the most useful for estimating time and distance and for giving an overall feel for the lay of the land and they also ensure there is at least some information on every part of the coast.

The navigator on the other hand feels it desirable to have charts that show all rocks and hazards in graphic detail. I allow there is merit to her position, but that means covering all areas we are likely to go at a scale no smaller than 1:80,000. That's 65 charts right there. Then, to avoid further accusations of recklessness, there should also be large-scale details of entrances and narrows and tidal rapids – another 15 or so. Pretty soon we are using three or four charts a day and they must all be stowed somewhere, preferably where they won't get wet. Clearly it is another of those compromise situations one runs into so often in boats – and marriages.

Ground tackle consists of a 25-pound Danforth and 200 feet of 1/4" high-test chain. I like chain even though it is heavy and its weight is in the wrong place. It selfstows and runs out without fouling, it increases the holding power of the anchor and it won't ever chafe through. I have no anchor winch, but I do have a ratchet on the bow roller that can be engaged to snub the chain. If you suffer from boat-builder's back, it is well worth having. The main advantage of the Danforth is that it stows flat on deck without dismantling. I don't believe it is superior in holding power for its weight, but I have had reasonable luck with it. It doesn't do well in kelp where it has an unfortunate habit of skidding before it can dig in, but I don't think it is alone in that deficiency. For backup I have a 35-pound Fisherman lashed to the side of the boat up forward with its fluke poking up through a hole cut in the bookshelf above. The only time I have had to haul it out is for a stern anchor when we put the boat ashore, but there is great comfort in knowing it is there.

The dinghy poses one of the biggest problems for the small boat cruiser and I confess I don't feel I have cracked it in *Surprise*. There isn't room to stow a rigid dinghy on deck so the simple choices come down to an inflatable, either deflated and lashed on deck, or towed astern, or a rigid dinghy towed astern. I eventually opted for the latter because small inflatables are marginally rowable at best and impossible in any wind.

A towed dinghy is no asset either. It reduces speed, increases fuel consumption, and at sea is a menace both to itself and the ship. To minimize the negative aspects, I built the smallest dinghy I thought I could get away with and built it as cheaply as I could so that it could be abandoned with no great loss. It is a simple v-bottom plywood pram just six feet overall and weighs 60 pounds. It has enough foam flotation under the seats to keep us buoyant in the event of swamping, a hazard that is never far away with two of us aboard.

To keep it from swamping when being towed in rough conditions, I attempted to make it self-bailing. It has a 1 ½" diameter PVC drain pipe through the aft buoyancy tank just above the bottom of the boat and two 3/4" diameter drain holes through the transom in the outboard corners of the aft seat. These are plugged with cedar bungs when the boat is in use. In practice, it turned out that the large bottom drain was entirely superfluous. Any water coming aboard has no difficulty being tossed over the aft seat and out through the seat drains. However the sound of it filling as you step aboard did provide us with a name for the boat — *Little Toot.*

I am still keeping half a weather out for a used inflatable — one would hate to pay for a new one — and am actively pondering other solutions. A boat that comes apart in the middle and stacks is often seen, but the only place I have available for stowage would be the fore deck, which is plenty busy enough already. A canvas and plywood collapsible boat is a possibility that I mean to pursue when time allows. If it could be made to fold flat in two bundles that could be lashed to the lifelines by way of the cockpit and double as lee cloths, it might be worth the fuss of assembly.

While thinking about shelter on deck I should mention that the best $700 I spent on this boat was for the canvas dodger over the hatch and forward end of the cockpit. It was beautifully made for me by Bea's Sail and Canvas here in Sidney, and while it doesn't make getting below any easier, it has done much to reduce suffering and raise morale.

For emergency hull repairs I make sure we have a selection of plywood patches aboard together with a can of fiber gum (a mixture of bitumen and asbestos fiber that stays soft over time and can be used even on wet surfaces) and containers of nails and screws. I also carry beaching legs so that I can get the boat ashore quickly if necessary. These are wooden props shaped to fit the side of the boat. They have 10-inch-square pads to prevent sinking and are bolted in place. They are cumbersome even when disassembled, but they provide such a measure of independence that I am loath to leave home without them. For a keel boat, going aground on a falling tide can be a serious matter. It is no fun spending all day over at 60 degrees unable to make a cup of tea and trying to look nonchalant. If the legs can be deployed quickly, much of the discomfort is removed from that situation. Similarly, if we want to check for damage after grounding, or get at the propeller, we can do it over a tide more or less anywhere without recourse to boatyards and travel lifts.

Clothing selection is important when stowage is limited. The revolution in outdoor wear that has taken place over the last couple of decades makes staying warm and dry a lot easier than it ever used to be. We shop at Mountain Equipment Coop for fleece tops and bottoms and for long underwear. We still take some wool, but the modern garments are so much easier to dry out. For oilskins we use Helly Hansen. We also have a pair of Mustang ocean class jackets aboard that are well worth their cost and the room they take up. Hunkered down in a corner of the cockpit, it is like wearing your own little wheelhouse.

Surprise is built double-planked fore and aft — inner layer 1/4", outer layer 1/2" — using red cedar on oak frames. The planking goes on like carvel planking but the seams are staggered: those on the outer planks fall in the middle of the inner. The inner layer is glued to the frames while the outer layer is glued to the inner and also fastened to the frames with bronze screws. This method has been around for a long time and was popular in high-end construction in Europe (Abeking and Rasmussen in Germany, McGruer in Scotland and in New England, Paul Luke). In the old days, white lead and muslin was used between the skins, later resorcinol glue. Now, epoxy adhesive is used throughout, as in *Surprise*.

The deck, cabin, and cockpit are also fully glued and sheathed in glass cloth so that maintenance is kept to a minimum. All exterior surfaces are painted with the exception of the spars and the tiller.

It is understandably tempting when building a wooden boat to want to show off both the material and the craftsmanship. In my view, the best place to do that is below decks where the sun won't destroy the finish and give entry to fresh water. For the exterior, I use Z Spar enamels. The boat was repainted this year for the first time, so it has gone two seasons. She has been black and white but was changed to gray and white this time. We found the original white deck a little bright in strong sunlight and though a black hull always looks smart to my eye, it does draw the heat and is not kind to the wood. The spars are finished with Z Spar Captain's varnish. The mast and bowsprit get sanded and re-varnished twice a year. The other spars, being under the sail cover, are done once.

In conclusion, I might say that *Surprise* is a very small boat. For myself and my wife, she represents the limit for two people to be comfortable aboard. Yet she continues to do everything we ask of her, and while it is tempting to contemplate larger vessels with more accommodation and greater speed, who is to say the pleasure derived would increase in proportion?

It is clear to me that for exploring this coast a motorsailer, or at least a sailboat with an inside heated steering station would be ideal. But cost and building time follow a cube relationship to length in boats so if, like me, your choice is circumscribed by the desire to build yourself, then great care must be exercised in such deliberations. For instance, if model and proportions stay the same, but hull length increases from 22 feet to 30 feet, we will have approximately 2 1/2-times as much boat. Weight, cost, and building time will all increase by this factor.

Does it make sense then to build a boat rather than buy? The answer lies in an examination of motive. If you are considering building as a means to get a boat and go sailing, the answer is simple: Forget it. The secondhand boat market is awash in the product of four decades of mass production. You can pick up a good used boat for about 30 percent of the material cost of building your own, never mind the years of effort and the upset neighbors. If you are wise in your choice you might get your money back when you come to sell it, perhaps even with a little extra if you do some fixing up.

The only possible justification for building is that you are afflicted with the need to do so. In that case, I am afraid you are a lost soul and are bound for the same institution in which I have spent my entire life. But you know, it's not so bad in here. It smells nice and we have a lot of fun. Everyday there is tangible progress to admire and you would be amazed at the number of visitors we get. Sometimes when I blow the dust off the windows and look out at the world, I am damned if I can tell who's more crazy — them or me. But the best part is, every so often we finish one and then they let us out to go sail it around for a while before we have to go back for more treatment. If that sounds like you, go for it. There are far worse ways of using up your days.

Specifications for *Surprise*
Length on deck: 22' 4"
Length Waterline: 19' 6"
Beam: 7' 10"
Draft: 4' 0"
Displacement: 6,500 lbs.
Ballast: 2,500 lbs.
Sail Area: 337 sq. ft. (not counting topsail)

PHOTO CREDITS

Page 17, photo by Sam Finlay. Page 22 photo by Bob Endicott. Page 23 photo courtesy of Tally Garfield, Marshall Marine. Page 26 photo by Leon Rabidou. Page 27 courtesy of Edey & Duff. Page 28, courtesy of Bridges Point Boatyard. Pages 49, 50, 51, 169 - 170, courtesy of Charles Stock. Pages 94, 172, courtesy of Ron Reil. Pages 20, 61, 171, 173 top, 175 top, photos by Stan Grayson. Page 173 bottom photo by David Walker Photography. Page 175 bottom photo by David Bellows. Pages 24, 174, courtesy of Michael Meier. Pages 176 and 192, courtesy of Paul Gartside.